"Dr. Farmer teaches us that hope is communal and institutional. She challenges us to practice compassionate mobility in prisons, theological schools, churches, and communities to activate restorative hope as theological and educational practice."

— RACHELLE GREEN
assistant professor of practical theology and education,
Fordham University

"*Restorative Hope* theorizes hope and tells the story of hope in action. It is one of the best examples of the integration of experiential knowledge and scholarly insight I have come across in the literature on mass incarceration. Farmer engages deeply with literature about hope, the carceral continuum, and conditions inside prisons. She provides a conceptual apparatus for thinking about hope while sustaining engagement with her interlocutors—women entangled in the carceral continuum whose insights form the core of the book. This book thus gives hope life well beyond its colloquial existence as a cliché or empty promise, ultimately arguing that it is both radical as a force for change and practical in the sense that it must be practiced. This book is essential reading for anyone wishing to understand the carceral continuum. Farmer's book shows that understanding is best cultivated by learning from those who have made meaning from and in spite of its impacts on their lives."

— RENÉE J. HEBERLE
University of Toledo

"Read the preface of this wonderfully written and carefully researched book by my former colleague and you will be hooked. As you read further, you will see hope come and spread its wings in some of our most desolate social spaces—prisons. A compelling practical theology and pedagogy of restorative hope."

— MIROSLAV VOLF
Henry B. Wright Professor of Systematic Theology, and
founding director of the Yale Center for Faith & Culture,
Yale Divinity School

Restorative Hope

Creating Pathways of Connection in Women's Prisons

Sarah F. Farmer

WILLIAM B. EERDMANS PUBLISHING COMPANY
GRAND RAPIDS, MICHIGAN

Wm. B. Eerdmans Publishing Co.
4035 Park East Court SE, Grand Rapids, Michigan 49546
www.eerdmans.com

Book design by Leah Luyk

Printed in the United States of America

30 29 28 27 26 25 24   1 2 3 4 5 6 7

ISBN 978-0-8028-8268-4

Library of Congress Cataloging-in-Publication Data

A catalog record for this book is available from the Library of Congress.

Unless otherwise noted, Scripture quotations are from the New International Version of the Bible.

This book is dedicated to all those in my family who have passed during this time of writing: Frances Poole, Bobbie Poole, Barbara Fuller, Janet Johnson, Nicole Bacon, Quentin Johnson, Sariah Deligar, Brother Deligar, and Shunous Wright. And this book is dedicated especially to my mother, Roslyn Renee Poole. Though she is gone, her inheritance of faith continues to give me hope.

And to my husband, Ronnie Farmer, and my four children, Elisha, Micah, Acacia, and Isaiah Farmer.

CONTENTS

PREFACE

I first went to prison to visit my brother. Undergoing pat downs, standing in a long line, walking through a metal detector, relinquishing valued items such as jewelry and cell phones—these actions marked my
entrance into the prison. Amid emotional greetings and excited conversation with my brother, I could also feel my body tense, aware of
the guards nearby walking back and forth to ensure our compliance.
Surveillance monitored my movements within the carceral space. When
I left, I felt as if our conversation had been cut off midflight. A breath
escaped me as I moved outside, a breath of relief—that I could move
freely again, unsurveilled.

My ability to move in and out of the prison stuck with me. I get to
leave. It's a privilege that I never want to take for granted.

I am a Black American woman who grew up in a community where
going to prison rather than to college was the rite of passage. Yet not
until I matriculated into my doctoral studies was I able to connect what
I saw in my neighborhood with theories and concepts. No theory or concept, however, takes the place of lived realities witnessed on a daily basis.
My matriculation into school became a vehicle for me to move away from
witnessing the harsh reality of young boys and girls being recruited into
the carceral system. Yet what I saw in my community lingered like a bit-
ter taste in my mouth, creating in me a desire to understand more deeply
what I had witnessed. I wondered: Is there a name for the stuckness that
seems to plague so many people from my community?

Despite my efforts to move away from carcerality, I soon found myself
right back in proximity to it. This time, it was through my academic studies. Sitting in an educational studies course with Maisha T. Winn, I felt as if
I were being reintroduced to parts of my life using a different framework
of understanding. I wasn't just hearing stories about young kids—others

who were disproportionately surveilled, punished, and placed on the pipeline to prison—I was mapping some of my own personal experiences with police officers in the school and with suspensions and expulsions. Not that I was ever suspended or expelled. Nor was I ever placed in a juvenile detention center. But these experiences were so close to me growing up that I recognized that they could have happened to me. And so our mom completely spent herself trying to move my brother and me away from carcerality. For our mom, moving away from carcerality had implications for our future: moving away offered hope. Hope had wings. Hope could transport us away from experiences that might entrap possibility.

Ironically, it was precisely possibility that moved me toward prison rather than away from it. Possibility invested my life with ways to create spaces—especially educational spaces—that resurrect and foster instead of kill hope. Creating such educational spaces pushed me to see prison, hope, and people in new ways.

On my first stint of teaching in a prison, my colleague and I took a group of students in with us every week to explore the prison industrial complex. The class consisted of students on the inside (those who were currently incarcerated) and on the outside (those who came from the university). One particular week we noticed that three of the women inside had dropped our course. We decided to inquire why. "You are talking too much about race in this course," one said. "Just remember, you and your students get to leave when the class is over. Me, I have to stay here. If I say anything in this class and it gets misinterpreted and makes its way onto the block, it could be bad. [For me,] it's a matter of life and death." When she reminded me how high the stakes were for her, for all of them incarcerated within a space that restricted how far they could run, I recognized something new about myself: I could move to and from this space, and they could not. No matter how badly I wanted to relate to the women, I got to leave. That simple fact of movement, of being able to leave, afforded me a privilege I could not deny.

While hope as mobility has been a key theme throughout my entire life, until I went to the prison I never saw how central the concept (and action!) of *movement* is to hope. This book emerges from my yearning to explore the depths of hope and hope's possibility for those who are marginalized by institutions, society, communities, and the church. It is written from a place of confusion regarding America's captivity to retributive justice, which keeps more and more bodies confined behind bars, their movements restricted.

Mass incarceration, the school-to-prison pipeline, and police brutality are never just distant theories for me. They evoke particular names and faces. These names and faces are my community of accountability to, with, and for whom I write. These names and faces are the community of concern that helped birth this passion I have of building hope with men, women, boys, and girls who are susceptible to incarceration.

My faith elicits concern and then seeks understanding about how bodies behind bars navigate confinement, especially when it is so easy for their hope to be confined. My intention is not to sanitize hope by emphasizing the touchy-feely; rather, I seek to expand our understanding of the nature of hope by recognizing how it is able to come alive in spaces that seem so dead.

In this book, I examine the narratives of formerly incarcerated women. Few books have been written about their experiences. Even fewer foreground their voices. I intend to do just that: create a space in which we can learn from those who have been incarcerated. They are, as a returning citizen named Rochelle tells us, *"naked people"*—not in the sense that their exposure to confinement should bring shame but in the sense that they have lessons to teach us. The names of all interviewees have been changed to protect their privacy.

The Scope of the Book

I write this book not for incarcerated populations as a "how to" manual, nor for theologians as a "why this matters" text; rather, I write for those who are interested in expanding their definition of hope by exploring what nurtures and sustains hope in dehumanizing contexts while also discovering ways to create learning communities that contribute to hope-filled lives.

To this end, I seek to mine instances of God's intervention in human experience; thus, I find my home within the discipline of practical theology. Yet I am also keenly aware of the book's interdisciplinary nature, and so I consider its ideas to be relevant to discussions about hope and transformative teaching practices, especially in relation to marginalized social groups. Further, with a distinct focus on mobility, in this book I will

- explore how formerly incarcerated women define and employ hope in their lives during and after their incarceration;

- identify specific practices within the prison that build hope and promote agency in the lives of incarcerated populations; and
- construct a pedagogy of hope that promotes holistic transformation in the lives of women on the carceral continuum.

I draw on my own ten years of experience teaching in prison. That teaching has to do mainly with theological education and is particularly rooted in my teaching and co-directorship of a Certificate in Theological Studies Program at a prison in the south.

In 2010, I taught my first course at a state prison for women in Georgia. This course, entitled Lyrics on Lockdown: The Moral Responsibility of Education, Not Incarceration, helped shape my dissertation topic and questions. Following this course, I taught two other courses—Exploring Spirituality and Identity through the Arts (in 2012) and Perspectives on Hope (in 2014). These two courses gave me concrete understanding of hope and art in the prison context.

Besides this, being co-director of the Certificate in Theological Studies Program at a prison also provided me with indirect insights and ways to understand hope with populations in confinement.

Overall, these experiences shaped this research. In my research design section, however, I focus primarily on my experience teaching the Exploring Spirituality and Identity through the Arts course in 2012. Many of the examples I use I draw directly from this course. Further, several of those who participated in the research study as interviewees had earlier been students in this course.

My qualitative research focuses on understanding the concept of hope from the perspective and life experience of those who have been incarcerated. To complete this research, I interviewed ten formerly incarcerated women in Georgia. Nine of the participants are African American, while one is Caucasian. Although race is truly a driving force in my conception of restorative hope, it is important to note that women who are not Black also experience some of the same challenges. The prison itself is marginalizing. Exploring the distinctions and similarities between race-related conceptions of and engagement with hope is less important to this research project than naming these challenges. Moreover, while this study could have been expanded to include participants from elsewhere, I limited it to the state of Georgia.

One fundamental challenge in writing this book lies in naming the multiple and co-occurring challenges that women on the carceral continuum face. By naming these physical, theological, psychological, social, or maternal challenges, I risk reinscribing the stereotype that incarcerated women in prison are poor, uneducated, and from "bad" homes. This is not the case. Women in prison come from a variety of socioeconomic and religious backgrounds. My small sample, in fact, consisted of women who do not conform to these stereotypes.

For example, many of the women I interviewed matriculated through the Certificate of Theological Studies Program. This means they had to meet particular criteria: all the women had to have a GED and no disciplinary reports six months before entering the program. Some of them had education far beyond their GED, with both college and professional degrees. Their level of education varied along with their demographic background. Some came from poor financial beginnings, while others came from two-parent homes that enjoyed all the benefits of easy access to social and financial capital. In the larger prison context, however, there is no guarantee that women graduated from high school or earned their GEDs. Neither would I be able to make assumptions about their infractions. These two criteria alone preclude the type of woman I interviewed. If I had had the opportunity to recruit women from a different sample pool, my data might have included a more representative and diverse range of experiences. Thus, important to my research is understanding that the women I worked with may or may not fit perfectly into any one category. Moreover, since I have an ethical responsibility to limit and censor what I share, some details in what follows may be lacking simply out of respect for and to protect these women students' privacy and anonymity. All names have been changed for privacy. Further, while the carceral continuum encompasses before, during, and after incarceration, I focus in this book on during and after incarceration. Focusing on what leads to incarceration is outside the scope of this book, although overlap exists in what leads persons to incarceration initially and how they end up back in prison. Challenges obtaining Institutional Review Boards clearance limited my ability to interview women during their incarcerations.

Nevertheless, inviting formerly incarcerated women to use the lens of hope to reflect on their incarceration and lives post incarceration simultaneously proved fruitful, enriching this idea that movement is central to hope. Part of my exploration of hope is trying to understand how hope functions along the continuum. To clarify my discussion of hope, I turn now to an outline of the book.

Outline of the Book

I seek to understand the challenges to and possibilities for experiencing hope in prison spaces. Further, I intend to enrich dialogue between and across diverse fields that take interest in carcerality, bringing practical theology to bear on those conversations. I examine mobility, specifically carceral mobility, through the analytic lens of hope. By mapping the diverse ways in which women on the carceral continuum navigate the system, I essentially argue that hope functions as a form of mobility, enabling women to move within and beyond the prison space. In each chapter I explore women's movement in prison spaces and the implications of their movement in these spaces for identity, power, faith, relationships, and society. Each chapter offers thick description, reflection, and connection to mobility. Each movement in the chapters moves us toward an enriched understanding of hope.

What is hope? Hope is anything but passive. The introduction describes why activity, movement, becomes such a critical aspect of understanding what hope is and how hope functions in the lives of women on the carceral continuum.

What happens when hoping seems more dangerous than living? *"It's just too difficult to hope,"* a student said. *"Hope is like a roller coaster for me. With my parole hearing coming up and the recent medical news I received, I just cannot afford to hope."* Chapter 1 shows through the women's stories the necessity for hope in prison contexts. In particular, I explore how physical, psychological, social, and maternal challenges place hope in crisis for women along the carceral continuum, thus creating a dire need for hope.

Chapter 2 explores resilience. Resilience inside and outside of prison is marked by creativity, strength, determination, and the will to survive. In this chapter I identify the ways in which women both in and after prison demonstrate and mobilize resilience in order to survive with limited resources, oppressive contexts, and collateral consequences. What becomes evident is that women must rely on something beyond themselves in order to hope in the face of despair-inducing circumstances.

What if the only means for you to connect with another person were through a small vent in the wall? Chapter 3 explores the great lengths incarcerated women go to in order to form meaningful relationships in a place that systematically and deliberately erects barriers to meaningful connections. In this chapter I affirm the human need for connection that all people experience, and I show the creative ways women seek out or mobilize connection within the prison. Hope happens as women find fulfillment in meaningful relationships.

What does it mean for women to embrace a valued identity during and after incarceration? Chapter 4 examines the numerous ways in which society constructs the "criminal" identity by assigning incarcerated persons a status that conceives of them as less than human. To counter this carceral identity construction, I draw attention to the various ways in which women on the carceral continuum construct alternate identities. Women who discover a valued identity experience a sense of restorative hope.

Chapter 5 examines specific ways that theological education in prison provides an alternative and transgressive space for women to build the resilience, identity, and connection that move them toward hope. I share specific narratives of what takes place in the theology classroom that makes the space a resilience-building, identity-reclaiming, connection-forming site of restorative hope.

Is it possible for hope to be nurtured, maintained, and restored amid dehumanizing circumstances? The narratives in each chapter answer this question with a resounding yes, creating a path to recommendations of how to care for women who find themselves navigating the carceral continuum.

My ambition in this book is to develop a practical theology and pedagogy of restorative hope, and I assert that the role of good theology and good pedagogy is to transform self, others, and the world. Ultimately, I intend to bridge hope-talk across and within disciplines in order to emphasize the multidimensional nature of hope. I focus on the intersection of space and the narrative of embodied beings in order to challenge the idea that hope is simply a disembodied theory. Instead, I privilege the voices of women on the carceral continuum to highlight the ways in which hope is grounded in lived realities—even daunting realities.

Throughout this book, I mine their lessons in hopes of learning from them. I've reflected on the ways these lessons might implicate change in other areas of our lives, such as teaching. I've allowed myself to rethink hope from the perspective of those whose hope has been confined. I invite you to join me on that journey of thinking how to reconceive hope.

ACKNOWLEDGMENTS

This book is the product of all the support I have received from the various communities, organizations, and people that have graciously walked with me on this journey. I am deeply appreciative of your support.

First, my dissertation committee—Emmanuel Lartey, Elizabeth Bounds, John Snarey, and Anne E. Streaty Wimberly—has been excited about my research and committed to my growth as a scholar and teacher.

Elizabeth Bounds's commitment to prison education reminds me to stay connected to the things that give me life.

Mary Elizabeth Moore, Theodore Brelsford, Jennifer Knight, and Carol Lakey Hess sparked the flames of my passion for religious education during my Master of Divinity program. They started me on a trajectory that has consumed my thoughts—to provide transformative pedagogy to the church and world.

To the many prestigious programs that provided me financial and networking support: Berea College, the Black Women in Ministerial Leadership Program, Laney Graduate School's Grant Writing Program, Religious Practices and Practical Theology Program, Community Building and Social Change Program. I am both humbled and encouraged by their support throughout the years. Specifically, the Forum for Theological Exploration provided me with a networked community of scholars of color who helped motivate me throughout this process. Thank you!

The Certificate in Theological Studies Program introduced me to the "inside" and the power of prison education and community even behind bars. To the community of sisters who find themselves at some point along the incarceration continuum: your tenacity to hope in spite of everything inspires me. To those women who so graciously responded with honesty to my inquiries, to those women who trusted me to teach them in a classroom space where I could refine my pedagogical skills and insights, I am deeply grateful. To the community of sisters who allowed me to be their student in the classroom, during interviews, and in everyday conversations: I am deeply grateful for your tenacity, courage, and strength to hope despite confinement.

To Ulrike Guthrie, you have helped me accept my own voice as a scholar.

To Lynne Westfield, you exemplify womanist values not just in your scholarship but also in your leadership, pushing me to grow in my own confidence and leadership.

Also, to my encouraging husband, Ronnie Farmer, who never ceases to believe in me. For the many times you have held down the house and children when I needed to write, I am grateful.

To Elisha Farmer and Micah Farmer, thank you for your patience. Thank you for the joy and laughter you have brought into my life. Thank you for reminding me that my life is grounded in something more than what my hands can touch.

There are many unnamed persons who have walked with me and cheered me on through this process. Please know that all your support has mattered and contributed to this moment in my life.

Introduction

My interviews with each formerly incarcerated woman began with this simple question: If hope were an image, what would that image be?

"Hope is a tree," said one woman. "*A tree recovers when the seasons change.*"

"*Hope is my dream of being an evangelist and helping young women conquer their obstacles,*" said another.

"*Hope is that I can help somebody.*"

"*Hope is a clear sky. It is like looking at a blank piece of paper.*"

"*Hope is a tree. The roots of a tree are strong. It has many branches and leaves and life. And it's strong. And it has endurance. And it also serves . . . provides shade.*"

"*Hope is working, community, giving back.*"

"*Hope is flowers in bloom; sunflowers that turn to the sun seeking energy from the sun. These are expressions of praise.*"

"*Hope is Jesus Christ, the cross.*"

"*Hope is the cross, and reentry is new life, resurrection.*"

"*Hope is the sky. It's immense, beautiful, open space. It's free out there.*"

"*Hope is a smile.*"

"*Hope is light.*"[1]

Hope gropes for possibility, moves through seasons, and moves toward others. For incarcerated and formerly incarcerated women, hope

---

1. These images come from the interviews I've had with women shortly after their release. Their voices are woven throughout the pages of this book. These are pseudonyms used: Eden, interviewed April 17, 2014; Indigo, interviewed March 21, 2014; London, interviewed April 9, 2014; Laura, interviewed February 25, 2014; Myeshia, interviewed August 7, 2015; Nona, interviewed January 30, 2015; Rochelle, interviewed July 21, 2014; Sherry, interviewed January 3, 2015; Toya, interviewed September 15, 2014; and Yvette, interviewed July 30, 2015.

is a lifeline, moving persons through, around, and against experiences that are meant to entrap them. For the purposes of this research, I move in two "times"—the time inside of prison and the time of return. Whether inside the prison or outside the prison, the women's incarceration impacts how they experience life and thus engage hope.

Prison as Immobilizing

"Prison is time-out," London says in response to my question about her experience in prison.[2] She relates it to when parents tell their children that they must sit in a chair in the corner as a punishment and not participate in activities. For her, the prison represents a chair in which she sits, outside of society. A time-out is immobilizing, limiting the ability to live. Yet "doing time," as many call it, does not stop time from moving on. Rather, it restricts individuals' capacity to engage meaningfully as time moves on outside of prison. As London notes, many find the experience of prison to be immobilizing. It is a type of corporeal immobility that leaves some people feeling exiled—moved away and completely barred from society. Others experience prison as a sojourn, a temporary place in which one must reside to pay for one's crime. Yet whether prison is actually temporary is tested upon release.

For often one moves out of the physical prison space only to realize one still carries prison within oneself. The label "formerly incarcerated" seems to define some women's existence in the eyes of others. And sometimes, the most heinous voice is one's own, as those recently released internalize how others label them. Formerly incarcerated folks' reality has been colored so much by their prison experience that they cannot always see clearly anymore. Others may experience their lives as lost, lives constantly seeking fulfillment, wholeness, and an internal anchoring. All these experiences of incarceration beckon one to consider hope as an embodied phenomenon, which is grounded in the existential experience of people's lived realities.

The women whose voices you hear in this book characterize prison as immobilizing. Immobilization also shows up as a theme in contemporary scholarly prison discourse. And no wonder: prison is designed to immobilize. Incarcerated populations face a multitude of immobili-

---

2. London, interview with the author, April 9, 2014. London is a pseudonym.

ties: a sentence that restrains movement and removes legal rights, and a physical structure that isolates incarcerated persons from one another and from their families and home communities.[3] These immobilities can create a sense of hopelessness.

Incarcerated persons are isolated from the world and restricted in where they can go. They experience major loss of civil and political rights, and they are incapacitated from freely engaging those outside the prison walls. This incapacitation also takes place inside prison through solitary confinement and other restrictions. In other words, immobilization is not only about the physical, social, and political restraints that embodied beings experience in prison; it is also about the psychological, emotional, and spiritual restraints they experience—and that those waiting for them experience on the outside.

While I highlight immobility, I want to hold in tension the difference between immobility and mobility within carceral spaces. For example, women can be swiftly moved within the prison or among prisons, disrupting any semblance of stability. This movement is coerced. Coerced mobility and ongoing instability actually perpetuate a sense of powerlessness or lack of control. Such powerlessness threatens hope.

What mobilities scholars help us undo is the dichotomy between inside and outside the prison by highlighting the "activity imperative," which also takes place in the prison. For them, inside prison represents immobility and outside prison represents mobility.[4] For example, in describing a "good prisoner," mobilities scholars Christophe Mincke and Anne Lemonne write:

> The *activity* imperative applies to all the actors in a prison world in perpetual movement. In this sense, the period of incarceration is no longer a time lost, one of inaction, merely waiting to be released. It is a time that must be put to use to develop the activities (training, compensating, work and so on) that are laid out in the detention plan. The activity, however, must not be just busywork, suggested by someone else and limited to repeating instructions already set by experts. The *activation* imperative means that the actor must be proactive, capable of taking initiatives. He is also the only one who can determine the

3. Christophe Mincke and Anne Lemonne, "Prison and (Im)Mobility: What about Foucault?," *Mobilities* 9, no. 4 (2014): 531–32.
4. Mincke and Lemonne, "Prison and (Im)Mobility," 537.

most suitable action in his precise situation. In this way, assistance in prison moves from the paradigm of supervision to that of services offered. It is not enough, however, to be active yet sitting in a corner all alone.[5]

In this sense, it is possible to be both active and inactive, mobile and immobile in prison. What makes the difference in the example above is the incarcerated person taking initiative during their incarceration through participation and activity in programs that contribute to their own well-being. My framing of mobility in the prison holds mobility and immobility in tension. For even in spaces that are immobilizing, movement can still exist. And even in spaces where movement should prevail, immobility still exists. For example, release represents a place of freedom; yet even "outside," there are so many obstacles that immobilize women, such as the inability to get housing or employment. The tension between mobility and immobility exists, then, both inside and outside the prison, complicating any clear dichotomy that one might seek to create.

Through the following stories of these women, I suggest that hope in many ways represents mobility and mobility, hope. Hope drives the agency of individuals to breathe, scream, protest, and survive in dehumanizing circumstances, demonstrating a type of mobility that embraces "power within" and "power to" even when one lacks "power over" within the prison and society.[6]

Prison is a constant threat to immobilize hope. Hope dies when there seems to be no reason to live. Hopelessness incapacitates life in a way that nothing else does. It causes an internal catastrophe or rupture that steals the breath from one's very being. For many people, hopelessness has led to more than a figurative death: literal deaths in the form of completed suicides, overdoses, and murder. I ask throughout the book, *Where is hope when one feels lost, abandoned, dehumanized, and thrown away? In what ways does hope mobilize one from immobility within carceral spaces? How might one nurture and sustain hope in these contexts?* The women I interviewed give us many unexpected clues.

---

5. Mincke and Lemonne, "Prison and (Im)Mobility," 537–38. Italics in the original.

6. Valerie Miller et al., *Concepts for Revisioning Power for Justice, Equality and Peace*, Making Change Happen: Power, no. 3 (Washington, DC: Just Associates, 2006), 7–8. https://justassociates.org/wp-content/uploads/2020/08/mch3_2011_final_0.pdf.

The Carceral Continuum

Powerlessness can be mapped along the carceral continuum, drawing clear connections between hope and movement, between hopelessness and immobility. The *carceral continuum* refers to the movement throughout life that keeps imprisonment as a permanent fixture in the backdrop of some lives. Even when one is out of prison, the possibility of prison is constantly close, whether in one's imagination, one's history, or one's lineage. Proximity to carcerality can breed hopelessness. The continuum represents the range of entry points that exposes and entangles people with the criminal justice system. Prior to incarceration, it includes policing, courts, poverty, the school-to-prison pipeline, and untreated forms of abuse.[7] All these circumstances facilitate entry into the criminal justice system. Further, while women released from prison have lower recidivism rates than men, those who do recidivate usually do so because of drug or property offenses. Probation and parole violations, such as not paying a parole fee, also become an unfortunately easy way to reenter prison.

The continuum further includes both the intentional and unintentional ways in which persons seek to survive in a racist, classist, sexist society, which complicates the path for those who already face diverse forms of trauma, making them more likely to be sucked into the pipeline to prison.

Here, I use the notion of the carceral continuum to illustrate connections between the ways in which persons navigate life during and after incarceration and the ways in which they talk about the function of hope.

To connect the continuum and one's mobility to carcerality, I borrow from Tim Cresswell's three-part framework, which defines place as *descriptive, social constructionist*, and *phenomenological*.[8] At the center of the concept of carceral continuum is place. The most natural way to understand place is through a *descriptive* lens, through which one engages in an analysis of what is unique about a set of places.[9] Because

---

7. Erica Meiners, *Right to Be Hostile: Schools, Prisons, and the Making of Public Enemies* (New York: Routledge, 2007); Erica Meiners and Maisha Winn, *Education and Incarceration* (New York: Routledge, 2011).

8. Tim Cresswell, *Place: An Introduction*, 2nd ed. (Malden, MA: Wiley Blackwell, 2015), 56.

9. Cresswell, *Place*, 56.

I focus in this book on prison as a place, it assumes that exploring the prison teaches us something about the world. The descriptive lens allows us to see how place creates an experience for those who inhabit it. It allows us to explore how one is affected by incarceration as well as how one affects the prison environment. My research explores the function of prison, the mundane experiences within prison, and the community that emerges because of being in prison, aware that these descriptive elements have a direct effect on one's sense of hope or hopelessness.

But to describe prison as "place" may create the illusion that prison is fixed. While I do identify prison as a location on the carceral continuum that might just happen to reside in a building that is fixed, I am also expanding my understanding of prison by using the term *carceral space* (which I use interchangeably with *prison*). Carceral spaces exist within and beyond the prison. Prison's impact on families, children, generational cycles, and communities requires us to talk about prison more broadly—as one carceral space alongside many other forms of carcerality. As carceral mobilities scholars Kimberley Peters and Jennifer Turner indicate, "Place is mobile, only at a different pace. . . . [With] sites of incarceration, here the 'inside' appears less mobile than the outside. The 'outside' appears more mobile than the inside. . . . [But] carceral spaces reach into, beyond, spill over, muddy, and blur any socially and materially constructed boundaries."[10] The concept of *carceral continuum*, then, accounts for the messiness of place and the boundaries used to construct place.

A *social constructionist* lens, the second way of understanding the continuum, looks not only at those who are currently incarcerated but also at those who are at risk of incarceration. Those at risk of incarceration, while they may never have committed a crime, are those automatically placed in proximity to incarceration because of their race, class, experiences of trauma, mental health, or other psychosocial aspects of their lives that make them more likely to end up in prison. These same people are more likely to end up *back* in prison through what seems like a revolving door. Sociologist Loïc Wacquant, in his discussions on the "penal management of poverty," has best articulated the social con-

10. Kimberley Peters and Jennifer Turner, "Carceral Mobilities: A Manifesto for Mobilities, an Agenda for Carceral Studies," in *Carceral Mobilities: Interrogating Movement in Incarceration*, ed. Jennifer Turner and Kimberley Peters (New York: Routledge, 2017), 2.

structionist impulse behind the carceral continuum in relationship to poverty.[11] He calls attention to the intimate link between the ghetto and prison. Rather than simply a place in which a person is put, the social constructionist lens views prison as an instance "of wider processes of the construction of place in general under conditions of capitalism, patriarchy, heterosexism, postcolonialism, and a host of other structural conditions."[12]

Persons' relationships to prison, then, are affected by these wider social processes that complicate their ability to navigate the very circumstances that are likely to place them in prison.

At the same time, I examine the ways in which incarcerated and formerly incarcerated women use overt and subversive strategies to resist the social constructions that place certain bodies at risk for incarceration and recidivism. Thinking of the carceral continuum as such a social construction enables me to examine the way in which identities are (im)mobilized along the continuum.

The final way of understanding carceral continuum is through a *phenomenological* lens—thus through the notion that place is essential to one's existence.[13] Such a perspective assumes that being human requires place or the human being as one who is in place. This phenomenological understanding of place is not a physical location or a social construction; rather, it refers to how one exists within the world. Seeing carcerality through this lens allows me to examine the ways in which one exists in prison spaces and in light of the carceral continuum. It raises the question, What does it mean to be human on the carceral continuum?

Theologizing Mobility as a Language of Hope

Hope embodies the human capacity to resist, wait, run, fight, push, pull, and even stand firm. In other words, hope embodies movement. It is impossible to flourish without hope. Yet restoring hope is not just

11. Loïc Wacquant, *Punishing the Poor: The Neoliberal Government of Social Insecurity* (Durham: Duke University Press, 2009), xix–xxiii, 11–13, 48, 281–86; Loïc Wacquant, *Prisons of Poverty* (Minneapolis: University of Minnesota Press, 2009), 19.

12. Cresswell, *Place*, 56.

13. Cresswell, *Place*, 56.

a matter of resuscitating one's breath: it requires resuscitating one's capacity to be and become in a world that is ever changing. My description of hope as movement is centered on a thorough investigation of what it means to navigate the chaos that is part of life. This book is grounded in the insights of those who know firsthand what it means to be immobilized yet gain the courage to move toward, against, around, under, and over for the sake of sheer survival. This book claims that hope centers on movement; and that movement can be seen along the carceral continuum.

The words and lived realities of formerly incarcerated women who know what it means to struggle in order to establish, nurture, and sustain hope inform my "turn" to mobilities. The language I use throughout attests to movement. It is a language of becoming, of evolving, of possibility. I highlight the absolute necessity of hope for life, that humans must struggle for hope if they desire to live. My focus on the way hope functions in women's lives as they navigate the carceral continuum places me in conversation with carceral mobilities scholars. Throughout this book, I argue that hope sits at the intersection of diverse forms of mobilities, becoming the driving force one uses to move toward an expected outcome even in difficult circumstances. Further, because hope is present within the women in the prison, I reevaluate the prison itself for its various forms of mobility and immobility.

Throughout this text, I examine the ways in which hope moves persons toward a future with hope, the ways in which movement propels persons to hope. In particular, I examine how movement is a key marker for incarcerated women's experience of hope. While my discussion on ways hope can be sustained and nurtured is generalizable beyond prison contexts, women's relationship to carcerality and prison spaces plays a key role in how I think about mobility and immobility. Likewise, incarcerated women's mobility or immobility plays a critical role in the way *they* assess how life is going. When women perceive that their lives are not going well, this quickly disrupts hope, and this in turn often inhibits movement in other areas of their lives—physical, emotional, and spiritual.

On the other hand, hope is more complicated than this. A life that is going well is not the only factor that determines hope. For women whose lives are seemingly not going well still muster up the ability to hope. *That* is what is so compelling to me: the question of *what hope looks like as it moves through and against chaos.*

The Mobilities Paradigm

To explore these questions, I use the mobilities paradigm. The mobilities paradigm within social critical theory sheds light on movement—blocked, potential, halted, or actual—to demonstrate how movement shapes social and material realities. Sociologists Mimi Sheller and John Urry in a 2006 article introduced a "new mobilities paradigm," and in so doing challenged the field of social science.[14] We might all agree that there is no life without movement, either actual or potential. Yet the slippery nature of mobilities research—what constitutes movement/mobility, what it means, and how it's done—is apparent whenever scholars try to define it. As Cresswell points out, "mobility as progress, as freedom, as opportunity, and as modernity, sit side by side with mobility as shiftlessness, as deviance, as resistance."[15] In other words, what scholars describe as mobility can appear contradictory and is open to further exploration.

One important distinction to be made is the difference between mobilities and movement. Mobility equals movement plus meaning plus power.[16] Mobility, as an interpretive framework, understands even the simple movement of walking from location A to B as a way of being in the world. We walk differently according to how we feel or how we experience the world. For example, someone in love may walk completely differently from someone who is burdened down and sad.[17] Meaning, then, is inherent in the understanding of mobility.

In other words, mobility is distinguished from movement because of how one ascribes meaning to it. This way of using mobility is critical for how I frame hope throughout the book. Mobility assumes a type of agency that moves one from being stuck or feeling powerless; this movement takes place even in the infrastructures of institutions such as prison and along the entire carceral continuum. The mobilities paradigm is concerned with "the inter-related movements of people, objects[,] information and ideas, and the different scales and infrastruc-

---

14. Mimi Sheller and John Urry, "The New Mobilities Paradigm," *Environment and Planning A: Economy and Space* 38, no. 2 (2006): 207-22.

15. Tim Cresswell, *On the Move: Mobility in the Modern Western World* (New York: Routledge, 2006), 1-2.

16. Cresswell, *On the Move*, 2-3.

17. Mincke and Lemonne, "Prison and (Im)Mobility," 537-38.

tures through which such movements occur."[18] In this book, carceral spaces serve as an infrastructure through which movement occurs (or doesn't). Using the mobilities lens enables us to see the distinct ways in which the presence of human beings in prison actually destabilizes notions that the prison is a fixed entity. For the women I interviewed made it clear that they do in fact daily find ways of becoming—of moving on with their lives—within the prison. On the other hand, that mobilities lens also helps us to recognize the way in which carceral spaces exist on a continuum outside of the physical location of a prison.

Mobilities inquiry offers scholars interested in carcerality a framework for examining and enriching our understanding of how power operates within the prison environment, both to mobilize and to immobilize incarcerated persons at the same time.[19] Staying in this place of tension, between mobility and immobility, becomes a critical opportunity for exploration as we think about carceral spaces. Even more exciting, new questions emerge about the types of things that make incarcerated bodies mobile, mobilize, and be mobilized. For me, hope does this—enables incarcerated women to be mobile, to mobilize, and to be mobilized, through their laying hold of a sense of agency in a situation that seems otherwise immobilizing.

My framing highlights the mobilizing influence of hope, which functions as a subject and a verb: hope can both demonstrate mobility and mobilize it in the face of immobility. More recently scholars have focused mobility discourse on issues related to detention and carcerality. Some of these have focused more prominently on immigrant detention while other texts are focused more broadly on prison.[20] I expand the conversation about prison by focusing it on the ways hope enables women to move within the carceral space. For the purposes of this research, my focus emphasizes *the mobilizing power of hope* while simultaneously exploring how hope is mobilized, inviting women into a movement that embodies agency, survival, and resistance. I contend that even though prison can be immobilizing, hope can be a powerful mobilizing

---

18. Javier Caletrío, *Mobilities Paradigm*, Forum Vies Mobiles, September 2, 2016, http://en.forumviesmobiles.org/marks/mobilities-paradigm-3293. Accessed October 11, 2017, at https://www.researchgate.net/publication/308388524_Mobilities_Paradigm.

19. Peters and Turner, "Carceral Mobilities," 3.

20. Jenna M. Loyd, Matt Mitchelson, and Andrew Burridge, *Beyond Walls and Cages: Prisons, Borders, and Global Crisis* (Athens: University of Georgia Press, 2012), 13.

force that counters that immobilization, and I ultimately shed light not only on how women move but also on the ways hope itself moves in prison spaces.

As a practical theologian who teaches in the area of religious education, I suggest that it offers us new ways of thinking about theology and pedagogy in carceral spaces as well as in more traditional educational settings (which may also suffer from carcerality). The mobilities paradigm expands how we might understand the purpose of theology and theological education. The question with which I wrestle in later chapters is whether or not theology and theological education *should* be mobilizing. And if it should, then toward what should it be mobilizing people? At the same time, I wonder about the ways in which theological education is immobilizing. What I discover is that both mobility and immobility can take place within theological education.

What distinguishes my work from other mobilities research is my integration of theology as a way of analyzing movement and what movement means for people. Few mobilities scholars have written on issues related to theology or spirituality.[21] And yet I suggest that incorporating theology into mobilities research enhances the way we think about mobilities.[22]

Mobilizing Theology as a Language of Movement

Diverse theologies support and inform my understanding of hope as mobility. Womanist scholars such as Jacquelyn Grant, Delores S. Wil-

21. One of the few studies I found is by Maximiliano Korstanje, which characterizes one of the principal gods in Norse mythology, Odin/Wodan, as a mobile God who wanders to other regions in order to learn about other customs. The writer argues that this mobile deity shaped the establishment of the Grand Tour in medieval times. Korstanje, "Examining the Norse Mythology and the Archetype of Odin: The Inception of Grand-Tour," *Tourism: An International Interdisciplinary Journal* 60, no. 4 (2012): 369–84.

22. While this is beyond the scope of my project, interesting studies could be done on religious communities that have moved outside the church and are forming communities online or in parks or pubs. Studies could be done on televangelism and its impact on religiosity in America. Further explorations might include whether (im)mobility makes one more or less human; mobility and the body; mobility and worship; the relationship between mobility and disability; and the relationship between mobility, sin, and salvation.

liams, Monica A. Coleman, Emilie M. Townes, Karen Baker-Fletcher, and Rosetta E. Ross have written of hope as embodied, manifesting in the mundane art of surviving oppressive contexts.[23] Black and Latin American liberation theologians such as James H. Cone, Major J. Jones, Gustavo Gutiérrez, and Rubem A. Alves have challenged us to think about hope as political, as a reality that is in the here and now, beckoning the very structures toward equality and justice among those most marginalized.[24] Among White European scholars, German theologian and onetime prisoner of war Jürgen Moltmann's theology of hope is an advent-based eschatological understanding of hope centered on forward movement: hope moves us toward active participation in the fulfillment of God's promise for a better world.[25] Moltmann is interested not in a static present but in God's promised future that breaks into the present to bring about the hope of the future.

The mobilities paradigm calls attention to this dynamic process taking place between future and current events. God's inbreaking presence has material consequences that show up in the world, whether that re-

23. This is an incomplete list of scholars who have contributed to womanist thought: Jacquelyn Grant, *White Women's Christ and Black Women's Jesus: Feminist Christology and Womanist Response*, American Academy of Religion, Academy Series (Atlanta: Scholars Press, 1989); Delores S. Williams, *Sisters in the Wilderness: The Challenge of Womanist God-Talk* (Maryknoll, NY: Orbis, 1993), 108-13; Monica A. Coleman, *Making a Way out of No Way: A Womanist Theology*, Innovations (Minneapolis: Fortress, 2008), 33-37; Emilie M. Townes, *Womanist Justice, Womanist Hope* (Atlanta: Scholars Press, 1993), 17-19; Karen Baker-Fletcher, *Dancing with God: The Trinity from a Womanist Perspective* (St. Louis: Chalice, 2006), 128; Rosetta E. Ross, *Witnessing and Testifying: Black Women, Religion, and Civil Rights* (Minneapolis: Fortress, 2003), 14-15; and A. Elaine Brown Crawford, *Hope in the Holler: A Womanist Theology* (Louisville: Westminster John Knox, 2002), 1.

24. This list names only a few scholars who represent these perspectives. There are countless other scholars who are not named but also contributed to Black, Latin American, and Womanist liberation theology. James H. Cone, *A Black Theology of Liberation*, 2nd ed. (Maryknoll, NY: Orbis, 1986), 87; Cone, *God of the Oppressed*, rev. ed. (Maryknoll, NY: Orbis, 1997), 117; Major J. Jones, *Black Awareness: A Theology of Hope* (Nashville: Abingdon, 1971), 16; Gustavo Gutiérrez, *A Theology of Liberation: History, Politics, and Salvation*, rev. ed., trans. Caridad Inda and John Eagleson (Maryknoll, NY: Orbis, 1988), 3-12; and Rubem A. Alves, *A Theology of Human Hope* (Washington, DC: Corpus Books, 1969), 11.

25. Jürgen Moltmann, *Theology of Hope: On the Ground and the Implications of Christian Eschatology* (London: SCM, 1967), 8-9; Moltmann, *Experiences of God* (Philadelphia: Fortress, 1980), 28-32.

sults in transformed personhood, transformed politics, or transformed systems. Using the mobilities paradigm helps us think of the ways in which the embodied political, sociological, and theological nature of hope intersects in a dynamic and active process.

I therefore describe hope as theological and God as one who intervenes in situations that are hopeless. Further, I propose that movement also shapes theological realities, which are interdependent on social and material realities. Putting the mobilities paradigm in conversation with hope pushes me to move my analytic gaze back and forth across space, time, and the material realities of people and places. It challenges me to reckon with the immobilizing forces that threaten hope while at the same time to explore hope as a prevailing force that enables people to reconstitute themselves, in spite of circumstances. In other words, exploring hope through a mobilities paradigm allows me to explore how one *moves toward* hope and how hope itself invokes movement. I do not assume that hope guarantees everyone's flourishing. Instead, I propose, hope is *on the move* toward flourishing. But women's flourishing comes at a cost as they move against the hardships that seek to restrict movement.

CHAPTER 1

Hope in Crisis

Exploring Challenges along the Carceral Continuum

Women on the carceral continuum—those incarcerated, those formerly incarcerated, and those susceptible to incarceration—face challenges that make hope difficult. What might those challenges be? What physical, psychological, social, maternal, and faith challenges do women, with a particular focus on Black women, on the carceral continuum encounter that make it difficult for them to hope? In this chapter I identify and explore those challenges. They are often so complex and all-encompassing that it becomes particularly difficult for such women to maintain hope.

Chronic and infectious disease, reproductive health challenges, substance abuse, sexual victimization, poverty, unemployment, housing insecurity, maternal incarceration, shame and stigma, grief, trauma, diminished faith: in this chapter I unveil those multiple and complex hardships. One chapter alone cannot capture the magnitude of hardships women face; yet naming at least a few examples gives some idea of what these women encounter. Besides, naming these hardships helps to expose injustice while also eliciting empathy, care, anger, and a desire for change.

Yet to describe only the challenges that women face would be short-sighted and partial. Women also experience moments of triumph, joy, and hope along the carceral continuum. Programs that inspire, friendships that transform, and prison classrooms that create space are also part of the narrative that must be told. In this book I attempt to share both sides of the story. While I focus in this chapter on hardships that women face, in subsequent chapters I explore the ways in which hope coexists with the challenges and ultimately becomes a way by which women move forward.

Physical Health as a Crisis of Hope on the Carceral Continuum

That poor health would have a direct impact on feelings of happiness, and thus any sense of hope, seems understandable. And while the American College of Obstetricians and Gynecologists proposes that incarcerated women receive the same standard of care as nonincarcerated women, specifically when being treated for infectious diseases and mental illness, the reality within prisons is far from that goal.[1] These disparities reflect the larger disparities that Black women face throughout the US population. Challenges to sustaining hope emerge when women on the carceral continuum do not receive adequate care for chronic diseases, infectious diseases, substance abuse, and physical and sexual violence, because they have few or no other options to access better care.[2] I consider each of these in turn.

Chronic Diseases

In research done in 2009, 40 percent of the total prison population reported a chronic medical issue, which is a much higher rate than among other Americans of similar age.[3] Research shows that being overweight is the leading chronic medical condition in prison, followed by hypertension, arthritis, asthma, obesity (as a specific category of being overweight), and hepatitis. These conditions are significantly more prevalent and more severe in women than they are in men.[4] Inadequate medical

1. Committee on Health Care for Underserved Women, "Reproductive Health Care for Incarcerated Women and Adolescent Females," in *Committee Opinion no. 535, Obstetrics and Gynecology* 120, no. 2, pt. 1 (2012): 425–29.

2. There are other concerns that emerge in the prison context, such as hospice care. Here, however, I aspire to introduce the topic only, rather than provide an exhaustive account of all the physical barriers to hope that exist for women on the carceral continuum.

3. David Cecere, "Inmates Suffer from Chronic Illness, Poor Access to Health Care," *Harvard Gazette*, January 15, 2009, http://news.harvard.edu/gazette /story/2009/01/inmates-suffer-from-chronic-illness-poor-access-to-health-care/.

4. Ingrid A. Binswanger, "Chronic Medical Diseases among Jail and Prison Inmates," Society of Correctional Physicians, http://societyofcorrectionalphysicians .org/corrdocs/corrdocs-archives/winter-2010/chronic-medical-diseases-among -jail-and-prison-inmates; and Ingrid A. Binswanger, Patrick M. Krueger, and John F.

treatment prior to incarceration, poor nutrition during incarceration, and limited access to health care after incarceration can make it difficult both to manage chronic illness and to feel hopeful about physical health at every point on the carceral continuum.

Infectious Diseases

Many of the behaviors that lead to a woman's incarceration are high-risk behaviors. Incarcerated women tend to have higher rates of STDs, vaginal infections, and abnormal Pap smears. Those who are at high risk for incarceration are usually in the same population as those at risk for HIV infection.[5] Not only is there a high incidence of women entering prison with HIV/AIDS, once in custody women become infected with and transmit HIV/AIDS at a high rate.[6] Oftentimes the correctional setting is where incarcerated women are first diagnosed and provided treatment for HIV. Ultimately, not having adequate care during incarceration and after incarceration, particularly for persons with chronic and terminal diseases, can lead to a crisis of hope, and hence to apathy and depression.

Reproductive Health

Reproductive health highlights a distinct gendered aspect of physical (ill) health among women in prison. Statistics show that between 6 and 10 percent of incarcerated women are pregnant.[7] Repro-

Steiner, "Prevalence of Chronic Medical Conditions among Jail and Prison Inmates in the USA Compared with the General Population," *Journal of Epidemiology and Community Health* 63, no. 11 (2009): 912–19.

5. Nina Harawa and Adaora Adimora, "Incarceration, African Americans, and HIV: Advancing a Research Agenda," *Journal of the National Medical Association* 100, no. 1 (2008): 57–62.

6. Laura M. Maruschak, *HIV in Prison, 2020—Statistical Tables*, Bureau of Justice Statistics (Washington, DC: US Department of Justice, 2022), 1–2, 4–5; Anne S. De Groot, "Alarming Statistics about Incarcerated Women," *HEPP News* 3, no. 4 (2000), www.hivcorrections.org.; HIV Education Prison Project, "Infectious Diseases in Corrections Report (IDCR)," *HEPP News* 3, no. 4 (2000), http://digitalcommons.uri.edu/idcr/14.

7. Jennifer G. Clarke et al., "Reproductive Health Care and Family Planning Needs

ductive health care refers, among other things, to prenatal and postnatal care, and to access to contraception and abortion services.[8] Such health care takes seriously the needs of women before, during, and after pregnancy. The same factors that put women at risk for infectious sexually transmitted diseases put women at risk for unplanned pregnancies, factors including lack of condom use, use of substances, and multiple sexual partners.[9]

Women's criminality often drives the physical treatment of incarcerated pregnant women. More specific issues deserve to be addressed, issues such as what type of shackling laws exist in women's prisons, and how they are applied to pregnant and postpartum women, and what resources are available for women suffering from postpartum depression, particularly when mothers are forcibly separated from their newborn children.[10] Those issues ought to be considered in tandem with how the criminal justice system treats a woman, as well as how a woman feels emotionally about issues related to giving birth and maternal incarceration. Not having a space in which to talk about these concerns can contribute to a crisis of hope.

Substance Abuse

Many women on the carceral continuum, though not all, wrestle with abuse of substances. Studies indicate that 59 percent of all women sentenced to federal prison are serving time for drug offenses.[11] Many women that enter prison have a history of drug dependence, connecting the increase in women's incarceration rates directly to the implemen-

among Incarcerated Women," *American Journal of Public Health* 96, no. 5 (2006): 834–39.

8. Committee on Health Care for Underserved Women, "Reproductive Health Care for Incarcerated Women and Adolescent Females."

9. Clarke et al., "Reproductive Health Care," 834–39.

10. Shackling here refers specifically to the practice of restraining women during active labor and childbirth. This may include confining a woman's legs to opposite sides of the bed during childbirth, which can increase the chances of physical harm to the woman, as well as giving her few options about the position(s) in which she prefers or indeed needs to labor. States have different laws concerning shackling, but it is still a common and widespread practice.

11. E. Ann Carson, *Prisoners in 2019*, Bureau of Justice Statistics (Washington, DC: US Department of Justice, October 2020), 22.

tation of harsher sentences for drug users. The number of women convicted of drug offenses is rising disproportionately to men, increasing from 12 percent in 1986 to 26 percent in 2019.[12] Even when treatment is offered inside, the stress caused by separation from families, violence from other inmates, and loss of identity can counteract substance abuse treatments given in prison and cause women to relapse.[13] Continued substance abuse then becomes a means to self-medicate or cope with trauma or stressors in life, particularly for women who are low income and already face multiple challenges.

Interwoven with the actual abuse of substances is the trauma that predates substance use, the trauma that follows substance use, and the stigma associated with being part of a marginalized group.[14] As Mindy Thompson Fullilove and her colleagues identify so clearly, the labels of "crack whore and skeezer" are only superficial terms that hide, and through such hiding often distort, the complex pattern of childhood sexual and physical abuse that often underlies past drug use, and now also continued use and the sexual favors done to attain drugs. Such labels tend to persist and take form as public and private rebuke of such women's failure to be "good" mothers.[15]

For poor women of color, the "crack whore" stigma was typically applied and was reinforced by what Renny Golden calls a theatrics of punishment, whereby Black and Latina women became a spectacle, punished for not upholding "maternal integrity and family values."[16] In the late 1980s and early 1990s, the "social condemnation" of the pregnant crackhead led to accusations and blaming, in turn leading to women who struggled with substance abuse being condemned and subsequently incarcerated in order to protect their fetus and children who

12. The Sentencing Project, *Incarcerated Women and Girls* (Washington, DC: Sentencing Project, 2021), 4, https://www.sentencingproject.org/fact-sheet /incarcerated-women-and-girls/.

13. Center for Substance Abuse Treatment, *Substance Abuse Treatment for Adults in the Criminal Justice System*, Treatment Improvement Protocol (TIP) Series (Rockville, MD: Substance Abuse and Mental Health Services Administration, 2005), 30–41.

14. Mindy Thompson Fullilove, E. Anne Lown, and Robert E. Fullilove, "Crack 'Hos and Skeezers: Traumatic Experiences of Women Crack Users," *Journal of Sex Research* 29, no. 2 (1992): 275.

15. Fullilove, Lown, and Fullilove, "Crack 'Hos and Skeezers," 276.

16. Renny Golden, *War on the Family: Mothers in Prison and the Families They Leave Behind* (New York: Routledge, 2005), 45–46.

would likely be affected by their addiction.[17] Incarceration, rather than other methods, became a core means by which to deal with the disease of addiction.

Addiction, however, is more complicated. It cannot be resolved simply by incarcerating a person. Substance abuse is often a symptom of underlying mental or interpersonal issues. One research study indicates that women who abuse substances were also more likely than others to express needs for mental health care, family support, education, job training, and housing once released from jail. Researchers concluded that even if prisons provide substance abuse services, if their other critical needs are not met, women may still return to drugs.[18] Not having alternative options available simply perpetuates the hopelessness and despair of women on the carceral continuum.

Physical and Sexual Victimization

The effect of physical and sexual victimization of women on the carceral continuum is a core obstacle to sustaining women's hope. In one study, 70 percent of incarcerated women reported serious sexual assaults. These sexual assaults often took place multiple times by multiple abusers.[19] Even those women able to flee situations of domestic and sexual violence subsequently often become homeless, and face job loss, poverty, and loss of health insurance and health care, which leads to poor health, both mental and physical.[20] If then they commit a crime, perhaps simply to survive, and land in prison, conditions there have their own horrors. Sexual abuse by inmates and by guards occurs frequently, which puts women at risk of revictimization even during their incarceration.[21] Even upon release, women still struggle with

---

17. Golden, *War on the Family*, 46.

18. Sonia A. Alemagno, "Women in Jail: Is Substance Abuse Treatment Enough?," *American Journal of Public Health* 91, no. 5 (2001): 798.

19. Cathy McDaniels-Wilson and Joanne Belknap, "The Extensive Sexual Violation and Sexual Abuse Histories of Incarcerated Women," *Violence Against Women* 14, no. 10 (2008): 1120.

20. Alexandra Cawthorne, *The Straight Facts on Women in Poverty* (Washington, DC: Center for American Progress, 2008), 2.

21. Quinn Owen, "Former Female Inmates Speak about Widespread Sexual Abuse by Prison Staff," ABC News Network, December 13, 2022, https://abcnews

the effect of the initial abuse if they did not receive adequate support in prison.

Social Crises of Hope on the Carceral Continuum

Women also face multiple social barriers. Because social support helps counteract the despair that can emerge when women feel stuck, it is critical that we explore the ways in which housing, poverty, and unemployment can lead to a form of social death that snuffs out life in women. Identifying these challenges illustrates even more the transformative nature of hope, whereby women survive despite the challenges and take hold of a life in which they can flourish.

Housing

Many returning citizens expect to live with their family upon reentry; yet their families are not always prepared to receive them. When relatives or friends are unable to open their homes to them, returning citizens face other complications to housing, including discrimination and limited affordable housing and federal subsidy options.[22] Not only is obtaining housing important for women on the carceral continuum but where they live is important. Space and place matter for such women. Researchers emphasize the need for returning women not only to do different things but to be in a different place in order to desist from criminal involvement. For example, in *Criminal Careers in Transition: The Social Context of Desistance from Crime*, researchers explored the space, time, and activities of those who left crime behind. What they discovered is that the space one inhabits can become a key contributing factor in providing opportunities for criminal activities, opportunities that prompt people to reoffend.[23]

.go.com/Politics/senate-report-documents-widespread-sexual-abuse-female -inmates/story?id=95157791.

22. Council of State Governments, *What Works in Reentry Clearinghouse* (National Reentry Resource Center: Justice Center, updated 2013), http:// whatworks.csgjusticecenter.org/focus_areas/housing.

23. Stephen Farrall et al., *Criminal Careers in Transition: The Social Context of Desistance from Crime*, Clarendon Studies in Criminology (Oxford: Oxford University Press, 2014), 159–63.

Unfortunately, many returning citizens have no choice but to return to the same community upon release. These communities are fraught with the "same old, same old." This is of particular concern when recently released mothers receive children back into their homes yet are forced to return to underserved or drug-infested neighborhoods—the very same neighborhoods that in various ways prompted their incarceration. When women are reintroduced into places and communities with a concentration of illegal activities, they are more likely to reengage in illegal acts. Not only are they at risk of reoffending, but the future life options of their children also face serious risks. They are released without society or the criminal justice system making much of an effort to reroute the pipeline to prison. For women to reroute the pipeline to prison is a "herculean task."[24] The risks they face coupled with the risks their children face can be debilitating for mothers who actually do seek alternative possibilities for their lives. In other words, feeling restrained to spaces and places that serve as constant reminders of a person's offense can function as a mental trap and make it difficult to escape.[25] To be clear, physically moving elsewhere assumes women have options outside of where they currently live, which may not be the case. As women seek to survive from day to day, the mental prison of being physically confined to a particular neighborhood context may also hold hope captive.

Oftentimes, housing represents a challenge for Black women on the carceral continuum before and after incarceration, mainly due to high rates of poverty. One report indicates that African American women, particularly those from disadvantaged neighborhoods, are evicted at higher rates than men. Some reasons have to do with their typically low wages, but others center on gender.[26] Eviction has its own stigma and makes it difficult to secure safe and affordable housing, particularly for Black women from poor neighborhoods.

24. Golden, *War on the Family*, 44.
25. Farrall et al., *Criminal Careers in Transition*, 180–84.
26. Matthew Desmond, *Poor Black Women Are Evicted at Alarming Rates, Setting Off a Chain of Hardship* (Chicago: MacArthur Foundation, 2014), 2.

Poverty and Unemployment

There is also an economic burden in motherhood. The Center for American Progress indicates that eight in ten guardians of children are women, and mothers who raise their children are twice as likely to be poor as fathers raising children. In other words, women are more likely to absorb the economic costs associated with raising children and pregnancy. To complicate this dynamic between men and women still further, unexpected pregnancies may curtail educational and employment opportunities for women, but not necessarily for men.[27] Even when women are experiencing significant poverty, the burden typically rests on them to survive and be strong, and to raise their children.

Poverty and unemployment are challenges Black women faced before prison; these same challenges are waiting for them when they return home. Black women, particularly low-income Black women, face barriers to employment. A report by the National Partnership for Women and Families indicated that inadequate education, childcare, and transportation are the three most common hindrances to a woman's employment.[28] Some sources say that the wage gap is not due to inadequate education and training but to discrimination, particularly when women have the same qualifications as their male counterparts, yet are still paid less.[29]

In *A Woman's Nation Pushes Back from the Brink*, Maria Shriver and the Center for American Progress examine the financial insecurity that accompanies single motherhood.[30] They find that more than one hundred million people in the United States live on or over the brink of poverty; of these, 70 percent are women and the children who depend on them.[31] In other words, one in three women are living in poverty or on the brink of poverty. These statistics on poverty, employment, and single motherhood demonstrate that real social factors exist that threaten women's hope and may push them on the path toward prison.

27. Cawthorne, *Straight Facts on Women in Poverty*, 2.

28. National Partnership for Women and Families, *America's Women and the Wage Gap* (Washington, DC: National Partnership for Women and Families, September 2014).

29. Cawthorne, *Straight Facts on Women in Poverty*, 2.

30. Maria Shriver, "Powerful and Powerless," in *The Shriver Report: A Woman's Nation Pushes Back from the Brink*, ed. Olivia Morgan and Karen Skelton (New York: Palgrave Macmillan, 2014), 11–43.

31. Shriver, "Powerful and Powerless," 11.

Pathway-to-crime theorists identify the feminization of poverty as an entry point to crime, meaning, for example, that impoverished women with access to few social services commit crimes such as fraud, counterfeiting, forgery, and embezzlement of funds in order to survive.[32] Black and Latino women, for example, are twice as likely as White women to be living in poverty.[33] These statistics on the impact of poverty on Black women in general mirror the statistics on Black women prior to incarceration and on the carceral continuum. Returning women citizens struggle to find jobs that pay them a living wage, making it difficult for them and for their children, if they have any. Further, statistics show that two out of five women in jail or prison failed to obtain their high school diploma or GED, meaning they lack the most basic requirements to gain employment.[34] No wonder that women who remain in poverty once released are more likely to be recruited into a cycle of criminal involvement due to economic deprivation.

What makes poverty and inadequate employment opportunities worse for women who have been released is the stigma that accompanies them on every job interview. Research shows that stigma does affect who does and does not get hired. When persons are perceived as untrustworthy or as lacking people skills (which are commonly held perceptions of formerly incarcerated persons), they are limited in the kinds of jobs for which they're likely to be hired, as well as the kinds of jobs that companies offer them.[35] Such limits are a kind of social death.

Manifestations of Social Death

The pipeline to prison looks different for women than men. For men, the path to prison often involves violent offenses or involvement in the sale of drugs. For women, whether or not they take the path to

32. Joanne Belknap, *The Invisible Woman: Gender, Crime, and Justice*, Wadsworth Contemporary Issues in Crime and Justice Series, 2nd ed. (Belmont, CA: Wadsworth, 2001).

33. Cawthorne, *Straight Facts on Women in Poverty*, 1.

34. Caroline W. Harlow, *Education and Correctional Populations*, Bureau of Justice Statistics (Washington, DC: US Department of Justice, 2003).

35. Rachelle Giguere and Lauren Dundes, "Help Wanted: A Survey of Employer Concerns about Hiring Ex-Convicts," *Criminal Justice Policy Review* 13, no. 4 (2002): 396–408.

prison often hinges on their ability—despite race and class—to obtain adequate care and professional support in order to cope with the complex trauma they face in their lives. If women do not receive this care, they are more likely to view life as hopeless and use coping mechanisms that sometimes prove harmful and criminal. In short, women tend to internalize their stress by engaging in behaviors that harm themselves and dislocate them from communities of care. Research demonstrates that for Black women such "structural dislocation" is the result of a variety of other marginalities but also a key indicator of criminal involvement.[36] Rather than providing Black women on the carceral continuum access to social services that could potentially enable them to live a hopeful future, social systems do little to support women during the transitions and challenges they experience in life. In many ways, the system of entrapment in cycles of poverty makes women's prisons "the social program of last resort."[37] Those prisons also are also places of social death, and oftentimes the death of hope. They needn't be so.

When police officers arrest women, the women don't stop being human. They still feel love, pain, and joy. They are still mothers, sisters, and wives. Their criminal acts cannot take away their souls. Nevertheless, their entry into incarceration does often subject them to social death. According to Orlando Patterson in *Slavery and Social Death: A Comparative Study*, the social death that emerged from slavery refers to "the permanent, violent domination of natally alienated and generally dishonored persons."[38] Through practices of alienation and exclusion from society, incarcerated populations become dead to society. Incarcerated women even go through a ritual-like process of dying socially, which makes it almost impossible to reintegrate into society once they are released.[39] From the arrest to the humiliation in the court to the assigning of a number, women lose themselves behind their prison garb. Like an underground caste system, the color of their prison garb identifies them as new intakes versus inmates who have been there

36. Regina A. Arnold, "Processes of Victimization and Criminalization of Black Women," *Social Justice* 17, no. 3 (1990): 160–63.

37. George J. Church, "The View from Behind Bars," *Time*, November 8, 1990, 20.

38. Orlando Patterson, *Slavery and Social Death: A Comparative Study* (Cambridge, MA: Harvard University Press, 1982), 13.

39. Shadd Maruna, "Reentry as a Rite of Passage," *Punishment & Society* 13, no. 1 (2011): 11–12.

for a while. Many no longer see them as humans, but as their Department of Corrections numbers; from here on out, the prison typically identifies them by these numbers rather than by their names. Insubordinate women have a greater chance of experiencing punishment from the guards, some of which comes in the form of degrading language, threats, and even violence—other forms of social death. The correctional officer's response reinforces who holds power and who does not hold power.

While social death is not physical, it has both psychological and physiological manifestations. Psychological characteristics include the rejection that women feel from society, even after serving time. Furthermore, their deaths are institutionalized by the policies that make it nearly impossible to obtain adequate services. Hope provides a critical resource to overcome social death; yet social death can also be a leading cause of hopelessness and despair. In the face of social death, the crisis of establishing a social identity that is both valued and nurtured in the larger society can be a major hurdle to experiencing hope.

And yet, women on the carceral continuum see hope as capable of helping them overcome such hurdles. Women's hope, even—maybe particularly—amid life's crises, can still endure. As Indigo, a returning citizen, notes,

> Hope and life are very intertwined. Hope is the desire to keep on living, to move—to be in a thriving mood in life, and you can't have life, an effective life without hope. When you're in survival mode you want to thrive. That's why you hustle and do all the things you need to do to survive, so that you can move into thriving, and what propels that desire for survival or thriving is hope. As long as there's hope, you're thinking of a future that has benefits, that looks good, that you can meet the challenges of life.[40]

Hope is connected to housing, poverty, and unemployment. Nor is it disconnected from the physical and psychological challenges women face. Rather, hope allows women to continue hustling, this time so that they can survive, and then thrive.

---

40. Indigo, interview with the author, March 21, 2014.

Maternal Incarceration and the Crisis of Hope
on the Carceral Continuum

Of all these challenges, maternal incarceration is perhaps one of the most daunting. Yet for us on the outside to try to understand these challenges helps us empathize so that we can provide support for women during and after incarceration. Maternal incarceration refers to women who are mothers, particularly those who were the primary caregivers of their children before they were incarcerated. It can also refer to women who enter the criminal justice system pregnant and give birth to their children while incarcerated. Over half of women in US prisons are mothers, and 80 percent of women in jails are mothers.[41] Maternal incarceration leaves children and their caregivers to sort out the broken pieces of the lives the mothers have left behind. For the mothers themselves, it is their maternal separation, Black maternal stigma, maternal shame and guilt, and maternal reintegration that challenge any sense of hope.

Maternal Separation

Maternal separation has profound negative effects on the children, some of which may last longer for the child than for the incarcerated mother. Many researchers liken the separation from a child during incarceration to that of death or divorce.[42] Statistics show that over 64 percent of incarcerated mothers report that they lived with their children a month prior to incarceration, which means the child will have to find another home, either with a relative or in the foster care system.[43] Complications around who cares for their children while they are in prison contribute

41. Laura M. Maruschak, Jennifer Bronson, and Mariel Alper, *Parents in Prison and Their Minor Children: Survey of Prison Inmates, 2016*, Bureau of Justice Statistics (Washington, DC: US Department of Justice, 2021), 1–5; and Julie Poehlmann, "New Study Shows Children of Incarcerated Mothers Experience Multiple Challenges," *Family Matters: A Family Impact Seminar Newsletter for Wisconsin Policymakers* 3, no. 2 (2003): 1.

42. Alison Cunningham and Linda Baker, *Waiting for Mommy: Giving a Voice to the Hidden Victims of Imprisonment* (London, ON: Centre for Children and Families in the Justice System, 2003), 10.

43. Sentencing Project, *Incarcerated Women*, 3.

to emotional stress and maternal shame during the mother's incarceration. Mothers no longer have control of the decisions that alternative caregivers make for their children. Studies also show that caregivers of the children of incarcerated parents may not always have sufficient income to meet basic needs, which explains why these children are at greater risk of poverty and its attendant harms.[44] While studies show that maintaining a parental connection is critical for children of incarcerated parents, visitation and phone calls can become too costly and impede maintaining these familial bonds.[45] This failed support often limits the future trajectory of the children whose mothers are on the carceral continuum, making it easy for the children likewise to enter the pipeline to prison and to reinforce the cycle of incarceration within the family.

Black Maternal Stigma

Not only are Black women left to face the structural and emotional challenges of maternal incarceration; they must also face the Black maternal stigma that stems from the historic representation of Black mothers, both during and since slavery. The Mammy character that has historically been depicted in media is a desexualized, heavy-set, unattractive, and often overly sacrificial Black woman who is loyal to her master.[46] She knows her place in society and yields to it. The Mammy image intersects with that of Black maternity in two distinct ways. First, as Sybil DelGaudio points out, Mammy signifies "surrogate maternalism" that is asexual, domesticated, and in service of raising White children.[47] She is the aunt who comes to the rescue, the one whom everyone loves.[48]

44. Jessica Meyerson, Christa Otteson, and Krysten Lynn Ryba, *Childhood Disrupted: Understanding the Features and Effects of Maternal Incarceration* (St. Paul: Wilder Research, 2010), 25.

45. Stacey M. Bouchet, *Children and Families with Incarcerated Parents: Exploring Development in the Field for Opportunities for Growth* (Baltimore, MD: Annie E. Casey Foundation, 2008), 5.

46. Nargis Fontaine, "From Mammy to Madea, and Examination of the Behaviors of Tyler Perry's Madea Character in Relation to the Mammy, Jezebel, and Sapphire Stereotypes" (master's thesis, Georgia State University, 2011), 12–13.

47. Sybil DelGaudio, "The Mammy in Hollywood Film: I'd Walk a Million Miles — for One of Her Smiles," *Jump Cut: A Review of Contemporary Media* 28 (1983): 23.

48. K. Sue Jewell, *From Mammy to Miss America and Beyond: Cultural Images and the Shaping of U.S. Social Policy* (New York: Routledge, 1993), 95.

Other depictions of the Black matriarch recognize her as the failed Mammy, the Black mother who is absent from the home, emasculates Black men, and is overly aggressive.[49] In *Black Feminist Thought: Knowledge, Consciousness, and the Politics of Empowerment*, Patricia Hill Collins articulates the quandary of Black maternal stigma, which happens to be perpetuated by Black males. In one sense, Black mothers are glorified in media and throughout Black literature for their resilience, strength, and sacrificial nature. At the same time, in order to maintain that respectable image, Black mothers must continue to sacrifice at the expense of themselves.[50] Mothers who do not sacrifice according to the strong Black female image are perceived as "selfish," or worse yet, as "bad mothers." These demoralizing socially constructed images contribute to Black maternal stigma; its controlling power affects Black incarcerated mothers, confirming and solidifying the guilt and shame they already feel for being incarcerated. Furthermore, the controlling image captivates the imagination of society; Black maternal incarceration reinscribes the old myths around Black motherhood.

Furthermore, Black women are constantly measured against the social narrative that identifies "good mothers" as married, educated, and middle-class. This idealized notion, for Black mothers who also face multiple forms of marginality endemic to poverty, creates an internal crisis that easily affects how such mothers view themselves.[51] Instead of the idealized image, poor Black mothers are depicted as welfare queens or women who take advantage of the system rather than work to earn money. Such women are lazy, passive, and demoralizing to their children. This myth has also been used to justify shaming Black mothers for having children or, if they already have children, for collecting social benefits such as food stamps. The visibility of poor Black women becomes representative of what's wrong with America, justifies harsher policies, and shifts the focus away from the structural, systemic factors that actually support discrimination and produce the poverty and powerlessness that Black women experience.[52] Their inability to fit into the social norms of White, middle-class motherhood creates perceptions

49. Jewell, *From Mammy to Miss America*, 95.

50. Patricia Hill Collins, *Black Feminist Thought: Knowledge, Consciousness, and the Politics of Empowerment*, Perspectives on Gender (New York: Routledge, 1991), 174.

51. Kathleen J. Ferraro and Angela M. Moe, "Mothering, Crime, and Incarceration," *Journal of Contemporary Ethnography* 32, no. 1 (2003): 14.

52. Collins, *Black Feminist Thought*, 36–37.

that Black mothers are inadequate; furthermore, the reality that poor, marginalized mothers are more likely to engage in criminal behavior means that their maternal rights are under constant surveillance.[53] The term "throwaway moms" describes how incarcerated mothers are treated as disposable in society.[54] Collins argues that these images serve two distinct purposes: to subordinate Black women and to mask the social relations that affect all women.[55]

Acknowledging the role of such narratives, both self-constructed and socially constructed, is therefore critical to understandings of hope. When women compare themselves to unrealistic narratives that demean rather than empower them, they grasp for hope against insurmountable odds. On the other hand, if women construct narratives about themselves that supersede these images, these narratives can function as a coping tool that enables them to resolve their crisis of hope.

Maternal Shame and Guilt

The stigma associated with this maternal imaging is nothing compared to the internal trauma women experience when they have no control over the issues that directly affect their children. The negative effects of maternal incarceration and separation on their children create maternal shame and guilt. Often referring to them as "hidden victims," some researchers identify the children of incarcerated parents as the most vulnerable of all children.[56] For shame and stigma about their parent's incarceration makes maternal incarceration distinct from other parental losses.[57] In fact, trauma is often recycled and multiplied, with children having trouble learning healthy attachment to others, and instead becoming depressed and anxious. For children, being moved to a foster home—and often many—typically only ex-

53. Suzanne Allen, Chris Flaherty, and Gretchen Ely, "Throwaway Moms: Maternal Incarceration and the Criminalization of Female Poverty," *Journal of Women and Social Work* 25, no. 2 (2012): 162.

54. Allen, Flaherty, and Ely, "Throwaway Moms," 162.

55. Collins, *Black Feminist Thought*, 72.

56. Alison Cunningham and Linda Baker, *Invisible Victims: The Children of Women in Prison* (London, ON: Centre for Children and Families in the Justice System, 2004), 1.

57. Julie Smyth, "Dual Punishment: Incarcerated Mothers and Their Children," *Columbia Social Work Review* 3 (2012): 36–37.

acerbates this trauma-related stress.[58] Children may also begin to act out at school or at home because they do not know how to cope with economic and social challenges as well as with the stigma of their parent's incarceration. The pain, shame, and guilt that children experience because of their parent's mistakes threatens hope. On the other hand, for the incarcerated mother, motherhood itself can be the vehicle to new perceptions of the self. Some women, whose crimes were motivated by a desire to provide for or defend their children, wear the status of mother instead of criminal to redefine their perception of self.[59] Finding a purpose and identity in being mothers, even while in prison, often enables women to avoid social death and to hold on to hope during their time in prison.

Maternal Reintegration

Maternal reintegration can be just as hard as maternal separation. Not only are mothers usually more economically and socially disadvantaged than fathers, but they face more parenting challenges when they return home.[60] Women experience fears associated with creating a safe and secure environment for their children. After all, it is not a given that mothers can always welcome their children home. Mothers may not always have a stable home to return to. Furthermore, children may remain in limbo until parents reach the milestones necessary to provide a stable environment conducive to raising children, milestones such as holding a job, earning money, and specifically earning enough to provide for one's children as well as oneself.[61] In particular, women who have struggled with substance abuse must have additional support to assist with their sobriety, particularly if they are returning to the same communities in which they lived prior to their incarceration. Such additional support is never guaranteed and often lacking.

58. Smyth, "Dual Punishment," 35-38.
59. Angela M. Moe and Kathleen J. Ferraro, "Criminalized Mothers: The Value and Devaluation of Parenthood from Behind Bars," *Sociology Faculty Publications* Paper 7 (2006): 5-10.
60. Bouchet, "Children and Families with Incarcerated Parents," 17.
61. Meyerson, Otteson, and Ryba, *Childhood Disrupted*, 25.

Psychological and Emotional Hope among Women in Crisis on the Carceral Continuum

Women on the carceral continuum experience a range of psychological and emotional traumas. But for many of these women, such trauma began long before they were ever incarcerated, and the trauma itself is or contributes to what led them to prison. In what follows, I explore mental health, emotional trauma, grief and mourning, and incarceration itself as a few of the challenges that such women face on a daily basis, challenges that make hope difficult to sustain.

Mental Health Conditions

According to the Federal Bureau of Prison Statistics, roughly 73 percent of females in state prisons and 61 percent in federal prisons had mental health problems; these rates were much higher than those of male inmates.[62] Approximately half of women on probation or parole experience mental illness; furthermore, women on probation and parole are twice as likely to experience mental illness as other women.[63] Some studies even argue that because of the deinstitutionalization of mentally ill patients from the 1950s onward, there are now more mentally ill men and women behind bars than in hospitals. There were good intentions behind this deinstitutionalization of mentally ill patients—namely, to treat mentally ill individuals rather than punish them. However, failure to sustain funding of community mental health programs led to the release of many individuals who were subsequently not adequately treated for their conditions.[64]

With the massive increase in incarceration rates and the disproportionate number of mentally ill people who are incarcerated, it appears

62. In the research, it is unclear whether women had mental health illness prior to incarceration or if they developed that during and as a result of their incarceration. See Doris J. James and Lauren E. Glaze, *Mental Health Problems of Prison and Jail Inmates*, Bureau of Justice Statistics (Washington, DC: US Department of Justice, 2006), 4.

63. Substance Abuse and Mental Health Services Administration, *Half of Women on Probation or Parole Experience Mental Illness* (Rockville, MD: Center for Behavioral Health Statistics and Quality, 2012).

64. E. Fuller Torrey et al., *More Mentally Ill Persons Are in Jails and Prisons Than Hospitals: A Survey of the States* (Arlington, VA: Treatment Advocacy Center, May 2010), 2.

that America has continued to punish rather than treat those who struggle with mental illness. Unfortunately, prison was never designed to be a mental health hospital, nor have most officers and other staff been trained how to work with people suffering from mental illnesses. To compound the problem, women who may or may not have received treatment for their conditions while in prison often leave with no options or plans for psychiatric aftercare. Understandably, those who suffer from mental illness are more likely to return to prison than those who do not.[65]

How is it that women who struggle with mental illness may actually leave prison in a worse condition than they came in? Among the many reasons is solitary confinement. Research unsurprisingly shows that being in solitary confinement typically worsens or causes mental illness in individuals.[66] Some studies go so far as to describe solitary confinement as "a form of living death."[67] Negative effects include suicidal thoughts, hallucinations, and irrepressible anger.[68] Lisa Guenther notes that solitary confinement is a type of violence that goes beyond racial and gender violence: it is violence against human being itself. Since relationality is critical to humanness, the experience of solitary confinement threatens loss of self.[69]

And yet for Black women, mental health issues are very much both gendered and raced. Black people with mental illness are more likely to be incarcerated than people of other races, particularly those who suffer from psychoses like schizophrenia and bipolar disorder.[70] Similar to treatment of Blacks, those in prison with a mental illness were more likely to be punished for violating the rules than those without a mental illness.[71] Such persons are also more likely to be abused or raped in jail than other women or men.[72]

65. Torrey et al., *More Mentally Ill Persons*, 9.

66. Craig Haney, "Mental Health Issues in Long-Term Solitary and 'Supermax' Confinement," *Crime & Delinquency* 49, no. 1 (2003): 130–31.

67. Lisa Guenther, *Solitary Confinement: Social Death and Its Afterlives* (Minneapolis: University of Minnesota Press, 2013), xii.

68. Haney, "Mental Health Issues," 133.

69. Guenther, *Solitary Confinement*, xiii.

70. William B. Hawthorne et al., "Incarceration among Adults Who Are in the Public Mental Health System: Rates, Risk Factors, and Short-Term Outcomes," *Psychiatric Services* 63, no. 1 (2012): 26–32, https://doi.org/10.1176/appi.ps.201000505.

71. James and Glaze, *Mental Health Problems*, 10.

72. E. Fuller Torrey et al., *The Treatment of Persons with Mental Illness in Prisons and Jails: A State Survey* (Arlington, VA: Treatment Advocacy Center, April 2014), 5.

Such maltreatment does not end upon release from prison. The stigma of having been incarcerated presents great difficulties for returning citizens, not least because people in general associate both prison and mental illness with danger. To be perceived as a mentally ill, recently released prisoner compounds the harm done to a person, and certainly thwarts any budding hope associated with release, and can even destroy it altogether. To face the stigma of incarceration at the very same time as the stigma of mental illness creates additional obstacles for Black women, whether still inside or upon release.[73]

What does the mental illness of women on the carceral continuum have to do with hope? Research supports the claim that hope is critical to recovery and management of mental health conditions.[74] The difficulty of sustaining hope in the midst of great challenges is compounded when dealing with multiple co-occurring issues that exacerbate mental health conditions. Statistics show, for example, that those who have a mental illness are more likely to have experienced some form of sexual abuse and are more likely to use or have used drugs.[75] In other words, it is not just managing mental health conditions that makes sustaining hope difficult; it is managing all the challenges simultaneously that threatens hope.

Emotional Trauma from Abuse

Some scholars report that as many as 90 percent of incarcerated women have experienced some form of victimization.[76] Coping with the impact of that abuse prompts many women's entry into crime.[77] This pattern of "gender entrapment" is particularly prevalent among poor Black women

73. Jason Schnittker, "The Psychological Dimensions and the Social Consequences of Incarceration," *Annals of the American Academy of Political and Social Science* 651, no. 1 (2014): 134.

74. Yvonne Darlington and Robert Bland, "Strategies for Encouraging and Maintaining Hope among People Living with Serious Mental Illness," *Australian Social Work* 52, no. 3 (1999): 18.

75. James and Glaze, *Mental Health Problems*, 5.

76. Angela Browne, Brenda Miller, and Eugene Maguin, "Prevalence and Severity of Lifetime Physical and Sexual Victimization among Incarcerated Women," *International Journal of Law and Psychiatry* 22, nos. 3–4 (1999): 301–22.

77. Meda Chesney-Lind and Lisa Pasko, *The Female Offender: Girls, Women, and Crime*, 3rd ed. (Thousand Oaks, CA: SAGE, 2012), 1–9.

who come from poor neighborhoods.[78] Beth Richie identifies Black poor women as "the most stigmatized, the least protected, and therefore in the greatest danger" in the larger context of the antiviolence movement.[79] After these experiences of trauma, women are more easily immersed in a cycle of revictimization. If trauma is not adequately dealt with, women continue during and after prison to exhibit symptoms and behaviors common among abuse victims. Symptoms include internal behaviors that make women feel unworthy and prompt them to withdraw from life, or external behaviors that include aggression and unhealthy patterns in interpersonal relationships.[80] Trauma theorists describe trauma as an organizing experience that has a profound impact on a person's identity and how she views life.[81] The view of herself is further complicated by the view that others have of people who have experienced sexual abuse.

Building on the common stereotypes associated with Black women, another image emerges in the media—that of the woman as liar. Grounded in Greek mythology, this image echoes the curse placed by Apollo on Cassandra, a Greek prophetess, because of his failed attempts to seduce her.[82] Because of his curse, the town no longer heeded her warnings against pending doom. The "Cassandra curse" refers to the way patriarchal societies dismiss and ignore the concerns of women, particularly around issues of sexual violence against women.[83] The liar image plays over and over again when women and girls report sexual miscon-

---

78. *Gender entrapment* refers to the circumstances that nudge women to commit crimes in a hyperpunitive system that overlooks both the conditions of extreme poverty and of abuse that victimize and lead women on a pathway to crime. See Beth Richie, *Arrested Justice: Black Women, Violence, and America's Prison Nation* (New York: New York University Press, 2012), 18.

79. Beth Richie, *Compelled to Crime: The Gender Entrapment of Battered Black Women* (New York: Routledge, 1996), 1–15.

80. Dana D. DeHart, "Pathways to Prison: Impact of Victimization in the Lives of Incarcerated Women" (Columbia, SC: Center for Child and Family Studies, 2004), 43–44.

81. Roger D. Fallot and Maxine Harris, *Creating Cultures of Trauma-Informed Care (CCTIC): A Self-Assessment and Planning Protocol* (Washington, DC: Community Connections, April 2009).

82. Marilyn Yarbrough with Crystal Bennett, "Cassandra and the 'Sistahs': The Peculiar Treatment of African American Women in the Myth of Women as Liars," *Journal of Gender, Race & Justice* (Spring 2000): 627–32.

83. Yarbrough with Bennett, "Cassandra and the 'Sistahs,'" 627–32.

duct, sex workers report rape, and allegedly promiscuous women seek help—but because of sexual violence. Being considered untrustworthy as a result of victimization and then incarceration is a double stigma with which women on the carceral continuum must wrestle. Restoring one's identity, then, becomes a critical component of restoring hope.

Incarceration as Trauma

Mapping the experiences of trauma that many women face before, during, and after incarceration does not take away the fact that incarceration, itself, is a traumatic experience. While many incarcerated and formerly incarcerated people attest to experiences that have helped point their lives in positive directions during incarceration, other stories, even by those same people, report the ways in which prison can be a life-draining, hope-stealing experience. In the words of Mika'il DeVeaux, "The experience of being locked in a cage has a psychological effect upon everyone made to endure it. No one leaves unscarred."[84] He talks about how traumatic it was for him to observe some of the bloody fights that took place while in prison: "I remain haunted by the memories and images of violence—violence I experienced, violence I witnessed, and violence that I heard or learned about. I can still see the murders I witnessed. I still see the image of a person being hit at the base of his skull with a baseball bat on a warm, sunny afternoon during recreation hours. The entire scene plays like a silent movie."[85] Such physical violence and victimization experienced and observed by those in prison is all too common. These memories, if not processed in therapy, continue to haunt men and women upon release from prison.

Returning citizens experience real trauma before and during their incarceration. Not dealing with this trauma during incarceration stifles the possibility for a hopeful life direction. Paying serious attention to the trauma that incarcerated people experience is not just about justice; it is about public safety. When trauma is not adequately processed, these unresolved emotions can easily manifest in seeking unproductive coping mechanisms or even returning to previous criminal acts. Since statistics

84. Mika'il DeVeaux, "The Trauma of the Incarceration Experience," *Harvard Civil Rights-Civil Liberties Law Review* 48, no. 1 (2013): 257.
85. DeVeaux, "Trauma of the Incarceration Experience," 257.

show that at least 95 percent of incarcerated people return to the community, it is not surprising that a concern emerges for public safety and re-engagement in cycles of crime.[86] Disrupting trauma during incarceration is therefore just as important as meeting the social needs of returning citizens through employment and housing services following release.

Grief, Mourning, and Transition

Within prison, transition is constant. Women are moved from facility to facility or released from prison. More permanent transitions, like the deaths of loved ones, happen while women are behind bars. Executions may be scheduled or suicides attempted. Or even more commonly, women witness peers being diagnosed with a severe sickness, and then dying. Often, incarcerated persons in the dying process are treated with little or no dignity by correctional officers and staff.[87] Prisons do not hold funerals, nor can women go to funerals to mourn the loss of loved ones. This lack of sufficient spaces to mourn contributes to a sense of hopelessness. This is further complicated by a stigma that strong Black women don't cry; those who do cry perceive themselves as weak or fear that others will perceive them as weak. In prison, the image of weakness is avoided at all costs for fear that other women will take advantage of one's weakness or grief. Holding in this grief can exacerbate depression and other forms of mental illness, rather than heal it.

One phenomenological study that sought to understand the effect of incarceration on grief and loss discovered that incarcerated women experience impediments in four dimensions during their grieving process: temporality, spatiality, corporeality, and relationality.[88] *Temporality* refers to the inability to grieve until the loss feels real or one is no longer in shock. *Spatiality* refers to the lack of privacy that exists within prison, limiting the places available for women to feel safe and vulnerable enough

86. Timothy Hughes and Doris James Wilson, *Reentry Trends in the United States: Inmates Returning to the Community After Serving Time in Prison* (Washington, DC: US Department of Justice, 2004), 2.

87. Vernetta D. Young and Rebecca Reviere, *Women Behind Bars: Gender and Race in US Prisons* (Boulder, CO: Lynne Rienner, 2006), 139–52.

88. Holly M. Harner, Patricia M. Hentz, and Maria Carmela Evangelista, "Grief Interrupted: The Experience of Loss among Incarcerated Women," *Qualitative Health Research* 21, no. 4 (2011): 454–64.

to grieve. *Corporeality* represents the tendency for incarcerated women to bury their emotions rather than express them for fear of vulnerability or being treated as a suicide risk. This emotional blockage impedes the grieving process and can contribute to a sense of hopelessness or despair as women try to make sense of their loss. The term *relationality* emphasizes that while women are not alone, they still feel lonely.[89] This relational bankruptcy compounds a sense of isolation and creates an illusion that no one understands or is available to help. Experiencing all four of these during what should be the grieving process threatens hope, so it bolsters the need to understand what hope means and does for incarcerated women. The process of grieving, for incarcerated women, is intensified by lack of social support and feelings of powerlessness and guilt. This heightened level of grief contributes to a tendency for incarcerated women to experience unresolved emotions that plague them not only during their incarceration but also upon their release from prison.

Faith and Spirituality and the Crisis of Hope on the Carceral Continuum

When one's existence is challenged, existential questions emerge about hope, life, meaning, purpose, and God. The belief in a transcendent being or the ability to see in a transcendental way lies at the core of hope. The comorbidities of physical, social, maternal, and emotional trauma throw fuel on the fire, and questions surrounding faith can also become traumatic along with the other traumas. It is not only the questions that women ask that complicate a crisis of hope; it is also the moral stigma and trauma that threaten to make women on the carceral continuum suffer through an existential trauma of demoralization.

An Existential Crisis of Meaning: Suffering on the Carceral Continuum

The experience of suffering and its existential questions place survival and the quality of life at the forefront of being.[90] Questions of theodicy

---

89. Harner, Hentz, and Evangelista, "Grief Interrupted," 458–61.
90. Delores S. Williams, *Sisters in the Wilderness: The Challenge of Womanist God-Talk* (Maryknoll, NY: Orbis, 1993), 20.

center on how one makes sense of evil in the world in the presence of an allegedly Omnipotent All-Knowing God.[91] Not making sense of these very questions is perhaps what sets many women on their pathway toward incarceration. The physical, social, psychological, and maternal challenges press against the soul, prompting profound questions around one's faith and spirituality to emerge. The first one held captive to these questions is God. The words resemble those of Jesus on the cross, "My God, my God, why have you forsaken me?" (Matt. 27:46). (Other questions such as Why me? or What is the purpose of this? place hope on trial.) Some women may think God does not see them or that they deserve to suffer. Others may be so familiar with abandonment and rejection in their interpersonal relationships that the comorbidities of trauma simply serve as a reminder of their unworthiness before God.

The second one held captive by the existential questions of life is the self. More than likely, the self gets hit the hardest. Internalized labels that have been ascribed to a woman's character coupled with her own feelings of guilt and shame about her past mistakes leave many a woman in the pit of despair. In my own observations, it seems that to receive God's forgiveness is just as hard as forgiving oneself. When women are faced with the image of an unaccepting or unforgiving God and this image is simultaneously reinforced by those within the faith community, it is much easier to internalize the shame and guilt rather than overcome it and forgive the self.

Demoralizing Labels: Sin, Evil, and Punishment

Incarcerated women often experience isolation from their children, family, spouses, and God. To complicate an existential trauma of meaning and purpose still further, there is no institution that highlights the fact that criminals deserve punishment more than the church. Society functions as if those who transgress social mores are considered guilty until proven innocent. Indeed, the church often fails to acknowledge that we are all criminals, that is, sinful beings. Beyond that, the stigma associated with being a criminal continues to condemn women to an inferior moral status, from which they have to work their way back to

---

91. Kaia Stern, *Voices from American Prisons: Faith, Education, and Healing* (New York: Taylor & Francis, 2014), 63.

respectability and virtue in the eyes of others. This works-based moral ladder can also be internal, whereby women condemn themselves to moral death and never experience freedom from guilt and shame. Perhaps this is what T. Richard Snyder means by "ontological superiority," that is, when some are seen as nonpersons and in need of grace while others are seen as having obtained grace, perhaps even being bearers of grace.[92]

Furthermore, theologies have historically relegated women to a particular status. In the past, women were "helpmates" or "mothers." Their productivity as a woman, in this sense, was always in relationship to a man. While the conversation has shifted over the years, the practices within the church, especially the Black church, have not necessarily shifted. These theologies become dangerous when they support women's wearing a humanity that is devalued or restricted.

A crisis of hope, however, does not always cause people to run from God; some people run to God. Research suggests that religion may offer coping strategies that sustain rather than destroy hope, and this I explore in chapter 4.[93] Theologies of hope can counter restrictive theologies by opening the path for women to be who they are outside of the traditional socially ascribed role. Furthermore, theologies of hope value women for their humanity rather than simply their productivity.

Theologies that restore hope are therefore needed to serve as a bridge between those who have been thrown away or thrown into exile and those who have been restored by God's grace. These theologies revive the gospel message of love and grace to understand all people as valued beings. Furthermore, theologies of hope remind the church of its role to act in the world in a way that brings justice to those experiencing these multiple and co-occurring challenges. They call the church to present a message that is sufficiently comprehensive and broad to wrestle with the many dimensions of life that jeopardize hope.

The litany of challenges can leave readers so overwhelmed that it is hard to imagine ways to nurture or sustain hope. My assumption is

92. T. Richard Snyder, *The Protestant Ethic and the Spirit of Punishment* (Grand Rapids: Eerdmans, 2001), 43.

93. Shadd Maruna, Louise Wilson, and Kathryn Curran, "Why God Is Often Found Behind Bars: Prison Conversions and the Crisis of Self-Narrative," *Research in Human Development* 3, nos. 2–3 (2006): 161–84.

that those on the carceral continuum, who have faced and continue to face these challenges, offer insights about hope's ability to propel one forward even when faced with these challenges.

Laura, a returning citizen, knows such challenges all too well, and after two years in the Theology Program she talks about how the need to know all the answers to complex challenges in the world dissipated. She attributes this surrender to hope. She says:

> Hope and God are almost the same for me maybe. So I don't understand everything, but I'm so happy I don't. And I'm so okay with the fact that I don't, and I don't have this incredible drive to figure it all out, and that comes with the whole empowering feeling you get from a certain type of surrender for me.[94]

Women like Laura search for hope in the midst of the complex hardships they face; hope does not always remove their hardships, but sometimes it brings them insight that drives them to move forward. Laura continues, saying:

> Because I had so many questions, and I wanted to know this, and something just kind of finally happened and took place in me, and I enjoyed listening to everybody, but I just didn't have those same burning desires to ask questions, which for me, is not a bad thing. I think it's a great thing, because it wasn't like a give up, like "Oh, this is crappy. You can't tell me the answer, forget it, you know . . ." [laughs].[95]

For Laura, and for several of the women I interviewed, hope functions as a type of knowing. This knowing doesn't require knowing all the facts; rather, it requires knowing God, and knowing that God has a future beyond what they are currently experiencing:

> Just knowing that God loves me, that I am an heir to his kingdom, that nothing but infinite goodness is planned for me, and it's mine for the taking, and this comes along also with my belief that there's more than just these years on Earth. It's really strongly connected to that, so I just know—I don't know the answers as to why people suffer.

94. Laura, interview with the author, February 25, 2014. Laura is a pseudonym.
95. Laura, interview with the author, February 25, 2014.

> *I don't know the answers as to why did there have to be a Holocaust for someone to learn a lesson about something. Like I don't know those answers. I don't know the answer to why kids get raped. Like I don't know that. I can't put God in that. I can't arrange that. I don't know that, but I'm confident in knowing that in the great scheme of things, it's all where we need to be, and it's all going to get us closer to being with God. I know that. It's kind of like, I don't know how when you cut a light on how the electricity gets to the—I don't know all that, but I just know it's going to happen.*[96]

She doesn't claim to understand the "why" or the "how," but she does claim to know that God is somehow in the mix of working things out. As Laura suggests, something about hope mitigates the challenges a woman and her child might face.

Conclusion

Challenges manifest in all forms for women on the carceral continuum and create crises of hope for women who are trying to survive. While these challenges are not an excuse for women to be hopeless, they do remind us that complex trauma can make it difficult for one to sustain hope. The challenges that women face are often urgent and require immediate care: How can a woman have hope for an intangible future when her fingers are cut almost through and are hanging off, bleeding right in front of her face? While this is a somewhat dramatic analogy, many women on the carceral continuum do in a sense have parts of their selves hanging off. They bleed because of wounds caused by traumatic events they have faced, both emotionally and physically. These events take place before, during, and after incarceration. Without tending to these wounds, it is difficult for women to be and become healthy individuals in all facets of their lives. But when a person feels cared for and taken care of in multiple areas of her life, she is more likely to experience and sustain hope, even when in crisis. Not having these needs met tends to create a context in which women feel emotional stress that makes it difficult to be motivated or enact agency.

96. Laura, interview with the author, February 25, 2014.

It is clear why women on the carceral continuum fight to maintain hope. Nevertheless, while taking seriously all the challenges along this continuum, I explore in this book how these women are able to still hope. In the next three chapters, their voices will help us make sense of ways they nurture and sustain hope.

CHAPTER 2

Building Resilience

The Quest to Survive

I am sitting in a comfortable black leather chair in London's office in downtown Atlanta where she has secured what many would deem a prestigious job. London, who had been released from prison ten years prior to this interview, looks at me and smiles. Ready to engage, she invites me to begin the interview. I tell her, as I tell the other women, that I will be asking questions relating to her incarceration and release. She nods and invites me to continue. I want to know how she was able to overcome the hopelessness that seemed to pervade the prison, return to society, and secure such a prestigious job. She has already beaten the odds. In ten years, she has not recidivated. What does London know about hoping against the odds? What lessons has she learned that might give insight into her success? With a confident expression on her face and a glint in her eye, London looks at me and says, *"I had to be a person that exceeded all bounds."*[1]

To exceed all bounds is no easy feat. It means to be resilient, to surpass expectations, especially those placed upon someone because of his or her circumstance. As the introduction suggests, for women on the carceral continuum, "exceeding bounds" refers to the multiplicity of ways in which women navigate life during and after incarceration.[2] In prison, resilience manifests as an uncanny capacity to resist the effects of confinement, to push against them. Nelson Mandela, who experienced lengthy incarceration, shared this perspective on resilience: "Do

1. London, interview with the author, April 9, 2014.
2. By the term *carceral continuum,* I am referring to the movement throughout life that keeps carcerality as a permanent fixture or constant possibility in the backdrop of lives of those who have been incarcerated and who are most susceptible to (re)incarceration.

not judge me by my successes, judge me by how many times I fell down and got back up again."[3]

In this chapter I describe how women on the carceral continuum attempt to exceed all bounds and surpass expectations through resilience. More specifically, it explores three ways of *being* resilient: dogged resilience, creative resilience, and embodied resilience. In the face of circumstances that make vulnerable the women who are or have been incarcerated, resilience demonstrates a movement toward life that both nurtures and sustains hope.

Dogged Resilience

Eden is the type of person who does not pull punches. She tells it like it is. After twenty-seven years in prison, she exudes confidence about who she is and what she can offer society. Eden is actively engaged in educating people on the impact of incarceration as well as in helping other returning citizens transition back into society.

"Eden," I ask, "how does hope function in your life?"

"Hope urges me to engage because I am a contributing factor . . . but sometimes, I feel like I'm running up against brick walls."[4] The specific term Eden uses to describe how hope functions in her life is *perseverance*. *"Something inside me tells me to carry on,"* she says. Hope thrives when someone has a will to live, to push against the brick walls that block women's attempts to flourish during and after incarceration. The hope that women in prison exhibit requires the capacity to face obstacles that seem immovable. Hope, in a sense, functions as resilience.

Resilience is active resistance against death, an internal refusal to allow oneself to surrender to disappointment and defeat. "To carry on," as Eden says, requires what I refer to as dogged resilience. *Dogged* denotes a stubborn persistence or determination. Such resilience is "the capacity to rebound from adversity, strengthened and more resourceful. It is an active process of endurance, self-righting, and growth in response to crisis and challenge," writes psychiatrist Froma Walsh.[5] Dogged resil-

3. Nelson Mandela, in *Mandela*, directed by Angus Gibson and Jo Menell (SUA: Clinica Estetico, Island Pictures, 1996).

4. Eden, interview with the author, April 17, 2014. Eden is a pseudonym.

5. Froma Walsh, *Strengthening Family Resilience*, 2nd ed. (New York: Guilford

ience sustains and nurtures hope for women on the carceral continuum. It empowers and equips them with the emotional fortitude to practice hope. Resilience, in other words, becomes an indicator of hope.

Myeshia's story embodies just such dogged resilience. Following Myeshia's release from an eight-year prison term, a friend offered her a place to stay.[6] Not long after Myeshia moved in, her friend realized that Myeshia was not the same person. Being in prison had changed her. Because Myeshia now refused to sell drugs and engage in other criminal activities, her friend pulled a gun on her. To avoid a fight and ending up back in prison, Myeshia left the house and did not return. Homeless again, she called one of her former chaplains who offered some encouragement. Rather than going to a homeless shelter or to the house of another friend (which could have gotten her in trouble), she stayed in the stockroom of a friend's boutique. Living in this stockroom provided just enough shelter to keep her safe and allowed her to avoid trouble. It also gave her the space to land a job at a local restaurant—but she made very little money there. She already knew it would be a challenge to find a job with a felony on her record. Compounding the challenges of finding employment and housing, she still faced $2,000 in ticket fines she had accrued before her incarceration. She began to save her money to get her license and purchase a vehicle, which she would need to travel to work. No work means no food and no housing. When Myeshia finally had about $600 saved, a wealthy man gave her $1,400 so that she could pay off the fines and get her license. Getting her license felt like such an accomplishment for Myeshia. But that exhilaration was short-lived. She ended up being fired from her job because her boss discovered she has a felony on her record. This pattern of working for a little while and then getting fired because of her record continues.

Myeshia encountered a local ministry in the community that provides her with housing and pays for utilities and other bills. In our conversations, Myeshia also mentions church people who simply put money in her hand. These sporadic gifts make a difference. Slowly but surely, she gets back on her feet. As she's getting back on her feet, a close

Press, 2006), 4. Froma Walsh derives this understanding in her research on strength-based approaches to family resilience.

6. Myeshia, interview with the author, August 7, 2015. To respect the identification and personhood of Myeshia, I am intentionally leaving out details about who she is, what she looks like, and why she was incarcerated.

friend helps her budget. Before prison, Myeshia never had to manage money. With the limited financial resources she currently has, budgeting becomes a critical skill for survival.

Dogged Resilience against the Impasses of Life

Myeshia's claim to possess greater strength after prison manifests her resilience, for she demonstrates precisely "the capacity to rebound from adversity strengthened and more resourceful."[7] As psychologists emphasize, those who demonstrate resilience do bounce back, but they are indeed not the same people.[8] The circumstances they have encountered have changed them. In the face of adversity, their personhood is transformed. The resources and strength Myeshia gained in prison became critical resources for the impasses she encountered after prison.[9] The endurance manifested through dogged resilience is active and persistent, requiring internal capacities and providing resources for the future. For example, by resisting the pressures to be defeated (and commit suicide) in prison, Myeshia has built up her capacity to defeat the unemployment and housing obstacles she faced after prison. And by fighting against unemployment and housing obstacles upon release, she has increased her capacity to overcome future obstacles. In other words, resilience is never simply about refusing to be stopped by a single obstacle in the moment; rather, resilience in the current moment always builds the capacity to resist in the future. Each "no" that Myeshia said to the pressure to attempt suicide or to get into a fight in prison strengthened her resolve for the future. The more she flexed that "no" muscle, the more she developed the habit, the stronger she became.

But she also rooted her dogged resilience in her belief that conquering prison meant she could conquer anything. Spaces within the prison gave her contexts in which she could enhance her sense of a positive

---

7. Walsh, *Strengthening Family Resilience*, 4.

8. Older scholarship describes resilience as simply bouncing back with no indication that a person's fundamental nature had been shaped by the adversity they experienced. Newer scholarship, however, takes into account the impact of adversity on one's personhood. Resilience, then, is more than one simply bouncing back from adversity but includes a person bouncing back from adversity with greater strength and capacity to face future adversity. Walsh, *Strengthening Family Resilience*, 4.

9. Walsh, *Strengthening Family Resilience*, 6–9.

identity, and this contributed to both her self-image and her agency. She talked powerfully about her own strength. Pointing back to her prison experience, she said:

> *I just experienced so much that nothing can penetrate. I feel like [because] I made it through [everything] that there's nothing that I can't conquer and go through. . . . Honestly, I feel like I became a better person because I got to know myself. The good and the bad. I probably would have never gotten to know myself and know who I was and what I was capable of doing and what I was capable of going through if it hadn't been for prison. It's a dark place but there's optimism in there. Nothing else can [keep] me down. Because, if I can find peace and joy in a place like that, nothing in life can just bring me down to where I feel like I don't want to live or I don't want to make it. Because that [feeling] is like the worst thing. I think it's worse than death.[10]*

Feelings of helplessness and hopelessness, according to Myeshia, are worse than death. She survived these feelings in prison. She knows how to push back against them now. Because of her survival of prison, Myeshia views her life in light of what she can do, rather than what she cannot. This can-do attitude informs her doggedness.

Internal fortitude is critical in doggedness. Women who have internal fortitude seem more capable of resilience, even when the odds against them are high. Their doggedness pushes them forward, and if it cannot move them forward, it also enables them to stand face-to-face with the impasse, refusing to be forced backward. That is a reminder not to confuse immovability with immobility. In this instance, to remain immovable in the face of the impasse is mobility. Dogged resilience is a stance against death-dealing circumstances, a stance rooted in having done all one can do. That moment of immovability is a moment in time, yet it also transcends the constraints of time, for it brings with it all the resources of previous successes and attempts at perseverance, ultimately creating a greater chance for mobility.

In short, immovability is not a passive waiting, but an active drawing upon one's internal store of affirmations, one's memories of past victories, and divine activity. The above narratives tell of women who stand because they refuse to surrender. Their groundedness or ability

10. Myeshia, interview with the author, August 7, 2015.

to remain makes their forward movement possible. Sometimes, mobility is not about actual movement but about potential movement, about the anticipation created by standing in the face of tough times for a season. Resilience is never passive, even if it means appearing to stand with one's feet glued to the ground. Resilience is the capacity to withstand and counter the very feelings Myeshia described as being "worse than death."

Myeshia must be resilient against a system that says that what she gets is what she deserves, even though she has already served her time. From unstable housing to financial insecurity to real physical danger, Myeshia faces tough circumstances. How can she stand firm and face defeating circumstances without herself being defeated? The answer is hope.

Hope as Dogged Resilience

Myeshia's account of transitioning from prison is weighted with hardship. But it is also threaded with hope. Myeshia exemplifies hope through her dogged resilience. The threat of loss or injury is imminent in Myeshia's story. Yet in Myeshia's persistent pursuit of basic needs and employment she demonstrates dogged resilience. Myeshia did not stop pursuing the bare essentials. Even when unemployment threatened her livelihood, Myeshia moved toward survival. Even when her friend attempted to lure her back onto an illegal path, Myeshia moved forward toward survival. Even thin threads of hope are enough to inspire movement. Such thin threads of hope are no luxury, but essential for survival. Hope adopts dogged resilience as an existential stance against defeat. Hope seeks an end: possibility. Hope manifests as an unwavering commitment to move forward. The nature of hope is forward-moving. Resilience is a practice of hope in that it is a forward thrust toward the job, house, car, and future that incarcerated and formerly incarcerated women seek.

Myeshia is not alone in her depiction of hope. When women described to me the way hope functioned in their lives, it often felt as if they were describing dogged resilience. Yvette names this driving force *determination*. It was determination that enabled her to buy a house despite the many obstacles that face returning citizens. After describing her own experience with having to resist the many barriers upon release, she states, *"There's nothing I believed this far that hasn't happened. The energy I put out in my belief is the energy I received in return."*[11] Hope for Yvette is a stick-with-it-ness that moves in sync with positive beliefs about self and God. She understands her story of getting out of prison and of being able to get a job, house, and car as being because she had set her priorities when she was first incarcerated. She did not allow others to set priorities for her. Yet even though she can name her successes, the road has not been easy. Determination, she says, forces her to press on toward her goals rather than pursue things that might distract her. In Yvette's words: *"Everything they said I wouldn't do, because I believe in it, I made it happen."*[12] Rather than hinder her, others' words fuel her determination. She shares how she began saving money for a house even while she was in transitional housing. And she notes that her long sentence did not deter her: *"I looked twenty years beyond in the beginning."*[13] She looked ahead and set priorities, deciding what was most important to her. Having a realizable goal became an incentive for dogged resilience, which in turn enabled her to press toward a livable future.

Resilience for a Herculean Task

Of course, Myeshia's story is not the only type of narrative there is about women's reintegration into society, but it provides a snapshot of the many challenges they face, even after they have served their time. Because of their criminal records, formerly incarcerated women often have difficulty finding a job. When they finally do find jobs, very seldom do they pay enough to cover living expenses, not to mention the fees related to parole and to discharging previous tickets or other fines. Housing often presents a challenge for women, especially Black women, both before and after incarceration, mainly due to their high rates of poverty. Many who return from prison expect to live with their families upon reentry, but families are not always prepared to receive them. If relatives or friends are unable or unwilling to open their homes to such women, the women may face other complications

11. Yvette, interview with the author, July 30, 2015. Yvette is a pseudonym.
12. Yvette, interview with the author, July 30, 2015.
13. Yvette, interview with the author, July 30, 2015.

with housing, including discrimination and limited affordable housing and federal subsidy options.[14]

Where women live when they return to society matters. Those who return to where they lived before incarceration are typically at greater risk of recidivism. Being in spaces and places (and with people) that constantly remind one of one's offense can function as a mental trap, and it can be difficult to escape that cycle without physically moving elsewhere.[15] A familiar place can invite familiar behavior and interactions that might prove detrimental to personal and spiritual growth. A new start can instead mobilize women, helping them toward their goals and relieving them of the pressure to conform to old behavior. Yet often women have no choice upon their release but to become part of their former communities again.[16]

Challenges are multiple, complex, and persistent, and encompass issues such as housing, employment, and child custody. They are also systemic, and so they tend to increase hopelessness in newly returning citizens.[17] Upon leaving prison, some women find they are totally unprepared for the challenges they must face, which makes them feel helpless. Escaping from the "pipeline to prison" is a "herculean task" for these women.[18] Without the help of society, the criminal justice system, and individuals, incarceration can be a revolving door, with women returning to prison multiple times because they cannot surmount the challenges of being on the outside, especially as former felons.

14. Council of State Governments, *What Works in Reentry Clearinghouse* (National Reentry Resource Center: Justice Center, updated 2013), http://whatworks.csgjusticecenter.org/focus_areas/housing.

15. Stephen Farrall et al., *Criminal Careers in Transition: The Social Context of Desistance from Crime*, Clarendon Studies in Criminology (Oxford: Oxford University Press, 2014), 180–84.

16. Space and place matter for women on the carceral continuum. Researchers emphasize the need not only to do different things but also to be in a different place in order to continue to desist from criminal involvement. Researchers explored the space, time, and activities of those who left crime behind. What they discovered is that the space one inhabits can provide opportunities for criminal activities, which lead people to reoffend. Farrall et al., *Criminal Careers in Transition*, 159–63.

17. Advocates recognize that terms such as *ex-convict* or *ex-felon* can reify stereotypes about formerly incarcerated persons, making it difficult for them to reintegrate into society.

18. Renny Golden, *War on the Family: Mothers in Prison and the Families They Leave Behind* (New York: Routledge, 2005), 44.

When concrete circumstances threaten to crush women's being, they need dogged resilience. Many times during my work with incarcerated women I saw instances of this dogged resilience that refused to be thwarted by an obstacle or setback. Myeshia's account of reintegration is a startling depiction of how the carceral continuum works. The boundary between incarceration and post incarceration is blurred precisely because of the difficulty women face in moving away from incarceration upon release.

Myeshia's incarceration is in the past, but it continues to shape her present. On one hand, for example, threats to mobility are compounded by her being labeled a felon. On the other hand, however, her experience of overcoming within the prison empowers her internal will to live outside of the prison. The memory of her prison narrative undergirds her conviction that she will refuse to be contained by the bars she still encounters. Myeshia's and Yvette's spirits were not held down in prison and will not be held down after prison. Both women describe an internal determination directly related to the ability to overcome their incarceration experience both during and after the experience itself. The source of this internal fortitude, say the women, emerges from a combination of faith in God, in self, and in their future. The testing of their faith—that is, practicing hope through resilience—then builds more faith.

Friction Makes Things Happen

The difficulties women often encounter upon release contribute to what mobilities scholar Tim Cresswell has described as "friction"—a sociocultural phenomenon involving experiences of resistance, blockage, and slowdown.[19] The idea of friction, Cresswell suggests, draws attention to how the flow of people, ideas, or things is decelerated.[20] Friction can be political, used as a tool to slow down those with less power.[21] An exercise of power is manifest in the management of friction, which is increased

19. Tim Cresswell, "Friction," in *The Routledge Handbook of Mobilities*, ed. Peter Adey, David Bissell, Kevin Hannam, Peter Merriman, and Mimi Sheller (New York: Routledge, 2014), 108.
20. Cresswell, "Friction," 108.
21. Cresswell, "Friction," 110.

for some and erased for others.[22] Race, gender, and carceral status can all determine the extent of the friction one encounters.

Friction threatens mobility, but friction does not necessarily destroy mobility and indeed can enable it. As Cresswell points out,

> Mobility is often impossible without friction. Friction makes things happen. In some contexts, friction takes the form of quite literal blockages and coagulations that prevent the mobility of undesirables. At other times, friction produces a fog of chance and turbulence that make the logistical desire for smoothness a vain dream. There is no necessary politics to friction—it can be a force of domination, a tactic of resistance, or neither.[23]

Within a sociocultural framework, mobility-inducing friction can be identified when people, ideas, and objects rub against each other. Cresswell describes the relationship between friction and mobility as producing heat. When two objects rub against each other, they produce energy in the form of heat. The presence of that heat can highlight the power differentials that create friction for some but not for others. Context and detail shape that friction and heat, as those with power seek to exercise that power against those who lack it.[24]

Friction has two effects: it both inhibits and enables.[25] Similarly, a person can move toward or away from carcerality. The "heat" that is produced by being blocked in can take the form of mobility. Incarcerated women do not typically experience friction as good, but they do find it to be revelatory, for it not only exposes the systems that keep them chained to carcerality, it also creates a sense of urgency that can force them to *choose* mobility. In other words, what counts most with friction is how one responds to it. Friction can lead to resilience, and resilience to hope.

In Myeshia's case, friction was manifest in the hurdles she faced in securing employment and housing, and in other family circumstances. Even when formerly incarcerated women are out of prison, the blockages that they experienced during their incarceration exert a pull that

22. Cresswell, "Friction," 110–11.
23. Cresswell, "Friction," 114.
24. Cresswell, "Friction," 110–13.
25. Cresswell, "Friction," 108.

draws them back to carcerality and prison spaces. Human suffering and tragedy create obstacles for incarcerated and formerly incarcerated women. But policies and systems of power make trying to leave incarceration behind feel like a losing battle.

The collateral consequences of incarceration are friction that can generate an orientation toward life and lead to quality of life. Women will go to great lengths to stay out of trouble and maintain their freedom: recall that Myeshia lived in a boutique stock room until she was able to find another living situation. Formerly incarcerated women know that being in particular places around particular people can halt movement and prevent them from becoming who they hope to be. Orienting toward life ensures that these women move in a life-giving direction. The movement toward flourishing sustains hope and affirms that life is possible.

Dogged resilience is propelled by friction. For Myeshia, unemployment made life more difficult, but not impossible. Instead, it elicited in her the internal resources needed to enact hope. To borrow from systematic theologian Antonio D. Sison, "Human suffering produces the very oil that enkindles the lamp of resistance, which then militates against the experience of suffering."[26] Human suffering as a producer of oil is the perfect analogy of the way mobility works against the very circumstances that seek to make one immobile. When one begins to move against human suffering, one finds a hope or a strength in being that counters the paralyzing beliefs that threaten to make one immobile. Mobility against human suffering reasserts a belief in the possible. Impasses are not impossibilities. What once seemed to be an impassible roadblock can become a challenge to be overcome. The ability to see a challenge rather than a roadblock engenders dogged resilience—a willingness and capacity to endure and press on.

Resilience does not justify the impasses that women on the carceral continuum encounter in life. Yet the need for resilience does engender an awareness of one's agency to press against the impasse. Resilience represents a force against the hopelessness and despair that might accompany the impasses women face. Human suffering exists, but doggedness can make women impervious to its debilitating impact. Women do not have to surrender to inertia or stasis. Dogged resilience grounds

26. Antonio D. Sison, *World Cinema, Theology, and the Human: Humanity in Deep Focus* (New York: Routledge, 2012), 83.

a person in the force of determination, ultimately moving one from im-mobility to immovability. Women draw from the reservoir of the human spirit to push back so they are not crushed beneath the weight of the impasse. Resilience mobilizes against the impasse, restoring hope in one's own strength and in the strength of God. Dogged resilience rein-forces the resolve that quitting is not an option. Thus, Myeshia relied on her faith in God to strengthen her when times became challenging both during and after her incarceration. Faith in God seemed to stabi-lize incarcerated women in the midst of navigating a very chaotic and pressure-filled continuum of carcerality.

Creative Resilience

In the prison context, women are made more aware of what they cannot do than what they can do. A strict schedule regiments their activities. Officers strictly monitor every interaction, including reading through the mail women receive. Food can be eaten only at specific times, and there are very limited options. In other words, the list of "dos" and "don'ts" around what, when, and how they can interact, eat, and play is extensive. But if women are able to look beyond these constraints, they will see possibility. When women in prison engage their imaginations, they are able to see possibilities beyond the limitations placed on them. I call this *creative resilience*. Such resilience enables them to *see* beyond where they are, and then *do* more than they and others expect of them, even with fewer resources.

In this chapter, women's movements toward hope are often focused on creative resilience. Driven by imagination, creative resilience takes the shape of adapting one's actions, behaviors, thoughts, and ways of relating. Women across the carceral continuum demonstrate how such creative resilience emerges from their ability to adapt their vision, and as a result their sense of their own agency, to see possibility in difficult circumstances. Behind prison walls, the ordinary can become an expression of creative resilience. One example is sourcing, creating, and making a meal.

Reenvisioning the Table

In prison, ordinary acts of cooking, sharing, and eating become imagina-tive acts of creative resilience. The women I interviewed described prison food as unsatisfying—neither tasty nor nutritious. For example, Indigo said, *"The food is so bad, you buy snacks."*[27] Dissatisfaction around food invites reenvisioning. I was surprised to learn that food preparation was viewed as a form of art. London's response was matter of fact: *"Cooking was definitely an art form, because you'd be amazed at what a pack of Ramen noodles could become."*[28] Indigo's response was similar: *"Yes. I think cooking and trying to make a meal as homely as possible was a form of art."*[29] Laura describes how an activity that could be considered a mundane chore outside the prison draws on women's creativity in these conditions: *"You decide you want to make fried rice, chicken fried rice. How do you make that in prison with a bag of oriental rice and noodles and bell peppers?—a bell pepper and onions that you bought on the black market and you have to plan it, and it gets your juices flowing. You want to make sure you don't get caught, and you're using your ID as your knife to cut up the onion, and that was pretty creative."*[30] A commonplace prison item—an ID card—is used to make a flavorless dish, dull on the senses, into a satisfying, flavorful experience. Desires for different tastes and food textures spark imaginations, challenging the women to re-create, repurpose, and reenvision prison food.

How incarcerated women get, prepare, distribute, and consume food are acts of creative resilience.[31] Take food preparation. Regular items in cells take on new meaning within the prison. For example, items are repurposed to heat, cut, and season food: the aforementioned ID card serves as a knife, a hairdryer as an oven. As Amy Smoyer discovered in her research on resistance in a women's prison, "Cell cooking was an activity of re-invention and re-purposing that allowed inmates to resist institutional power by assigning new meanings to prison food and commissary items."[32]

When cooking in prison, women might employ what Delores Williams calls "the art of cunning"—a combination of skill and imagination, intellectual knowledge and lived knowledge that Black women use to ensure the survival of the community as well as themselves.[33] This

27. Indigo, interview with the author, March 21, 2014.
28. London, interview with the author, April 9, 2014.
29. Indigo, interview with the author, March 21, 2014.
30. Laura, interview with the author, February 25, 2014. Laura is a pseudonym.
31. Amy B. Smoyer, "Making Fatty Girl Cakes: Food and Resistance in a Women's Prison," *Prison Journal* 96, no. 2 (2016): 192.
32. Smoyer, "Making Fatty Girl Cakes," 202.
33. Delores S. Williams, *Sisters in the Wilderness: The Challenge of Womanist God-Talk* (Maryknoll, NY: Orbis, 2013), 209.

cunning helps them to navigate a system that is not designed to generate hope, connection, or community. Some may view cunning as a form of deceit. But for women who are incarcerated, cunning is a survival strategy to care for self and others in the prison. In the case of cooking, women create spaces where hope and connection can thrive. Like Pharaoh's daughter who saved Moses from drowning by Pharaoh's henchmen, incarcerated women employ the art of cunning to rescue women from the sea of isolation.

Creating a new and tasty dish is a task that requires strategy, foresight, creativity, and collaboration. Laura tells me about this process of food preparation. She says:

> *Yeah, because on the weekends people really took it serious. . . . You all go to the store once a week and you get with your friends and you kind of talk about what do you all want to try to make this weekend? So it was almost like an art thing, because everybody would get the needed ingredients, and it was a very social, uplifting thing for the group to come up and make this, whatever it was, thing, dish. So yeah, that was actually a very therapeutic art-style practice.* [34]

While cooking created personalized meals, the *experience of cooking* created community. Oodles and noodles were no longer simply a quick snack; they became a homely meal that invited women to see themselves as a community. Dishes were not just imagined but also created, through what Smoyer describes as "collective, mundane acts of resistance that were performed by and for the inmate community."[35] Women ultimately resisted the institution through hoarding, stealing, and smuggling food, defying the rules of what, when, where, and with whom they could eat.[36]

---

34. Laura, interview with the author, February 25, 2014.

35. Smoyer, "Making Fatty Girl Cakes," 206.

36. Smoyer, "Making Fatty Girl Cakes," 194. Studies of foodways in prisons across the globe confirm the ways incarcerated people use food in collective and individual acts of resistance against the institution. See Rebecca Godderis, "Dining In: The Symbolic Power of Food in Prison," *Howard Journal of Criminal Justice* 45, no. 3 (2006): 255-67; Thomas Ugelvik, "The Hidden Food: Mealtime Resistance and Identity Work in a Norwegian Prison," *Punishment & Society* 13, no. 1 (2011): 47-63; and Gill Valentine and Beth Longstaff, "Doing Porridge: Food and Social Relations in a Male Prison," *Journal of Material Culture* 3, no. 2 (1998): 131-52.

Even though rules prohibited sharing, it was not uncommon for women to share food with other women who lacked the resources to buy food. It did not matter that they were breaking rules; what mattered was their ability to share with someone who did not have the same resources as they did or to share with someone they valued. According to Smoyer's study, women identified themselves as "good" when they shared their food with others, enabling them to build a positive identity, to demonstrate goodness, even generosity, and to feel connected.[37] Such food practices build women's positive identity, which ultimately helps nurture and sustain hope. Women's ability to construct a positive identity is related not only to their agency in determining what they do and don't do with food, but also to how food practices can become a means they use to view themselves differently in the prison context. Smoyer suggests that correctional policies should be changed to promote women's desire to use food to build positive identities, since there is a proven correlation between feeling positive about oneself and one's ability to desist from crime after prison.[38]

Food practices are relational. Concealed from the view of correctional officers, women break bread to create a gathering space that in the prison context is a sacred space.[39] Women share, extend, and offer themselves as they participate in gathering together. The space is made sacred by women enjoying food and each other's company. Food practices function as rituals. Women do not simply make food: they create it, after careful discussion, with carefully selected ingredients, and for a group of women who are invested in the experience of sharing a meal together. Women approach the table hungry not just for physical food but also for the emotional and spiritual connection that takes place when people share a meal together. The reenvisioning of prison food becomes a site of

37. In a study on foodways, Amy Smoyer interviewed formerly incarcerated women to learn about their food practices while they were incarcerated. She discovered that the women used their food practices to construct a positive identity for themselves while in prison. Smoyer, "Good and Healthy: Foodways and Construction of Identity in a Women's Prison," *Howard Journal of Criminal Justice* 53, no. 5 (2014): 530-37.

38. Smoyer, "Good and Healthy," 537-38.

39. Nancy Lynne Westfield examines the womanist practice of hospitality that has been embedded in the tradition of Black women for centuries. Westfield, *Dear Sisters: A Womanist Practice of Hospitality* (Cleveland: Pilgrim Press, 2001), 39-42, 78-94.

mediated relationships between women. Shared meals are about more than what one receives naturally into one's body through eating: they are about the "uplifting." What Laura said about food demonstrates that the soul receives something as well. Incarcerated women create a table to fulfill their deep longing to be in relationship with one another. The table is a transgressive space at which women are willing to take great risks to be present. The gathering of the women at the table to meet physical and nonphysical needs counters isolation and underscores the human desire for connection.

The table becomes sacramental in prison when food practices lead women to share, connect, and carve out space at the table like this, shifting the very notion of who is invited to the table. For some, the table becomes a means to mediate God's grace to those who participate in the fellowship that emerges from the table. Womanist theologian and religious educator Lynne Westfield talks about hospitality as a means of grace because of how it creates a context where empathy and compassion can take place.[40] Similar to Jennifer Ayres, I see the prison table as a disruption of power and a site of contestation, mutuality, hospitality, humanization, and solidarity.[41] In prison, this is especially the case because the very act of preparing the table can be risky business for incarcerated women. Yet women take on the risk because food becomes a means to gather, a reward in itself. And gathering becomes a means to celebrate laughter, connection, and enjoyment. Ayres recalls a biblical image from Psalm 23 that seems to resonate with what is taking place at the prison: "You prepare a table before me in the presence of my enemies."[42] Perhaps this text is an indication that God not only sits at the table to commune with incarcerated women but is directly involved in their resistance efforts to prepare the table. In other words, God functions as both host and guest within the prison.

While women's desires to love, taste, and feel are often restricted in prison, their engagement with food can empower them by showing them they are capable of fulfilling a physical need. Stealing bell peppers and onions was a concealed act of resistance against food policies; it was

40. Westfield, *Dear Sisters*, 41.

41. Jennifer R. Ayres describes the social, moral, and economic implications of tables. I draw on these descriptions of round, kitchen, and welcome tables to describe the powerful implications at work in the prison table. Ayres, *Good Food: Grounded Practical Theology* (Waco, TX: Baylor University Press, 2013), 56.

42. Ayres, *Good Food*, 10.

also an act of satiation. Creative resilience ultimately moves women toward fulfilled physical and relational desires, helping nurture and sustain a sense of hope in prison.

Adorning Place

Prison can seem a hopeless place. Yet by transforming the external space, women make that potentially hopeless place endurable. Their creative acts are performed in particular during holidays, when the prison may give women a little more leeway to use materials such as construction paper that would typically be considered contraband. Lacking traditional art materials such as glue and markers, women repurpose materials to re-create the space they occupy. Indigo shared some examples when I asked her where she had seen art in the prison:

> What blew my mind was the creative uses of what is there, like floor wax. Decorating our doors for Christmas became a huge art expression, and I saw things I couldn't believe. Someone had a scene from Happy Feet on their door with a train, a 3D train swirling down the door. They made paper boxes. I don't know where they got the supplies from. Another person took the inside of Dorito bags, chip bags, that is, foil, cleaned it up, and laminated the whole door with that foil and put a bow. So that was silver, and it looked like they trimmed the pieces just right so it didn't look like the inside of a Dorito bag. I never would have thought [of] that.[43]

Decorating the doors represented a deliberate intention to make the physical location more aesthetically appealing, and an expression of their individuality. Women removed the dullness from the space by replacing it with dynamic images.

Creative resilience finds hope in the mundane but is experienced through deep emotion, in the nourishing of the self and the embracing of enjoyment. Cooking and decorating doors become imaginative acts that engage the whole person. As these examples of the embellishment of food and prison doors demonstrate, creative resilience is expressed in concrete changes that are achieved when women use the resources at hand to transform their experience of the space they inhabit and, in

43. Indigo, interview with the author, March 21, 2014.

turn, their feelings about that space. Women achieve change by seeing differently, which allows them to think, feel, and act differently. Agency emerges from a woman's encounter with her imagination. Ultimately, their creativity derives from and enhances their agency, and this moves them toward hopeful spaces, attitudes, and selves.

As evident in the case of art making, imagination is a core factor in women's ability to be resilient in prison. The example of art highlights that those who live within the prison space are constantly moving back and forth between the real and imagined, the objective and subjective, and the social and psychological. In his discussion of the ways in which persons escape carceral regimes by reverting inward, James Gacek claims, "The use of imagination by [incarcerated women] is crucial when adapting to carceral spaces, as instances of imagination provide [incarcerated women] the capacity to emotionally adjust to incarceration, while simultaneously reviving and recalibrating the inner self."[44] These movements of the imagination can contribute to resilience, enabling the resilient person to combat feelings of hopelessness. One example is the way women turn Doritos bags inside out so that the silvery foil sheets become Christmas door wrappings. What would typically be discarded becomes a way to bring the holiday spirit into the prison. These artistic creations engender something new in the prison space. Not only does art bring delight to the artist, art in the prison is an invitation for others within that setting to open their imaginations and to delight in beauty and in the artist's creativity.

Art inspires hope within the artists themselves, but the art also becomes a tool for place-making, for re-creating prison environments into something more homely. The ability to use one's imagination to effect change in the physical environment mobilizes hope. Women participate in producing social life in the prison through a mobility that involves place-making. Monika Büscher and John Urry describe this form of mobility as physical movement; physical movement includes the "(re)configuration of people, objects, and spaces as part of dwelling and place-making."[45] Place-making tools serve as symbols of hope. The

---

44. James Gacek, "'Doing Time' Differently: Imaginative Mobilities to/from Inmates' Inner/Outer Spaces," in *Carceral Mobilities: Interrogating Movement in Incarceration*, ed. Jennifer Turner and Kimberley Peters (New York: Routledge, 2017), 79.

45. Monika B. Büscher and John Urry, "Mobile Methods and the Empirical," *European Journal of Social Theory* 12, no. 1 (2009): 101.

sheer creativity that exists within prison destabilizes notions that the prison or prison environment is fixed. Women's activity in the prison draws attention to the flexibility of carceral space, underscoring in turn the nature of creative resilience. The fixed walls and doors of a prison are intended to keep people in or out, not to encourage engagement. Yet while prison itself is spatially fixed, women constantly make and remake the prison through their artistic creativity. The idea that a deliberately immobilizing place like prison can in fact be mobilized through a little subterfuge and creativity is hopeful.

Likewise, though the aesthetics of the prison space encourage "sensual (dis)engagement," art transforms space and mobilizes the senses.[46] By looking at works of art that are aesthetically appealing, one can easily be moved from boredom to sensual engagement. The art that women create in prison appeals to the senses but also to the emotions, enabling one to experience positive emotions even when one is in a situation that would not seem to warrant them.

Creative Pathways

Creative resilience depends on the emergence of inventive insight that allows the individual to forge new pathways of being in relationship to the circumstance. As I heard in the women's accounts, creative resilience became an essential skill women used to navigate and press against hopelessness. When women's focus centered on the negative circumstances of the moment, hope felt low, especially when these circumstances seemed unchangeable. Even in moments of hopelessness, creative resilience enabled women to overcome the barriers of circumstance mentally and emotionally by using the resources at hand to create new pathways of possibility. Some neuropsychologists might say that creative resilience is a form of mental flexibility, the ability to shift one's own thinking or actions to engage the changing demands of a situation.[47] One might have learned to see the world in one particular way, but imagination encouraged new patterns of seeing, often resulting in changes in perception, cogni-

46. Gacek, "'Doing Time' Differently," 76.
47. Chris Loftis, "Mental Flexibility," in *Encyclopedia of Clinical Neuropsychology*, ed. Jeffrey Kreutzer, John DeLuca, and Bruce Caplan (New York: Springer, 2010), 1572.

tion, and behavior. Those who *see clearly* can use their ability to *think creatively* to determine alternate routes to their goals. The circumstance does not change, but the way a person decides to see—or to frame—her situation and subsequently respond to the circumstance is what changes it.

Creative resilience can involve moving one's vision away from situations, attitudes, and dispositions that stagnate hope. When one sees the world differently, one is more likely to think differently about the world. And seeing is done through imagination. Imagination enables perceptions to shift, ultimately restoring and sustaining vision in grim circumstances. Driven by the ability to maneuver the material and immaterial resources at one's disposal, creative resilience uses the mind's eye so that what seems ordinary becomes a tool to create a more hopeful orientation toward life. Creative resilience does not depend on being given new resources or new circumstances; instead, creative resilience relies on one's ability to imagine different possibilities. As the biblical scholar Walter Brueggemann notes in his exploration of the postmodern imagination, imagination is "the human capacity to picture, portray, receive, and practice the world in ways other than it appears to be at first glance when seen through a dominant, habitual, unexamined lens."[48] This reordering can lead to a new experience in the world. Unlike external remedies to "fix" women, imagination invites women to reorder the world through concrete proposals to act and to be differently in that world.

Creative resilience enables women to see and use the resources in front of them to transform their feelings about their circumstances, and this becomes a valuable way of enacting agency. As so many examples illustrate, in creative resilience the circumstance is no longer blinding. As Paulo Freire stresses, limit situations can be transformed as women begin to engage in the world in a creative and improvisational way.[49] Women learn to transform their feelings and responses to circumstances even when they cannot immediately change the circumstances. Such a mental transformation is particularly necessary when it comes to embodied resilience, as we see next.

48. Walter Brueggemann, *Texts under Negotiation: The Bible and Postmodern Imagination* (Minneapolis: Fortress, 1993), 13.
49. Paulo Freire, *Pedagogy of the Oppressed*, trans. Myra Bergman Ramos, 30th anniversary ed. (New York: Continuum, 2000), 49.

Embodied Resilience

Nona's vivid description of a strip search puts the body front and center in our conversation on resilience. *"One of the worst things about being incarcerated is having to take off all of your clothes in front of somebody and . . . to pull your butt apart, bend over and cough for them to examine all of you and leave you there just to put back on a uniform that has a number on it."*[50] As we will see in chapter 4 on identity, the stripping of a body has severe emotional and spiritual consequences. Here, too—indeed here in particular—resilience is needed.

How the body moves and who controls its movement are existential realities with which women must grapple daily in prison. Once in prison, a woman is no longer entitled to free movement. Her body is contained, restricted, and uniformed within prison walls. Incarcerated bodies become regimented under a system that decides where the body goes, what the body wears, who interacts with the body, when the body needs to be in certain places, and what the body produces. Yet bodies are not simply physical realities; bodies carry the experiences of the world that surrounds them. One's body mediates one's relationship with the world and others. One way to locate hope in the lives of incarcerated women is to pay close attention to how their physical bodies navigate the prison space. The stories I heard show that incarcerated women's bodies embody hope through their resilience in the face of carceral restriction.

In this section I explore the ways women manifest hope in the resilience practices they employ to attest to their worth as embodied beings in the criminal justice system.

Asserting the Self: Embodying Resilience

In a system in which women are strip-searched and told where to go, what to do, and how to look every minute of the day, restoring a sense of agency is a creative act, a performance of self. Incarcerated women tend creatively to the need to be seen as unique, distinct from their peers in the prison. Women use their very bodies as ways to proclaim the value and significance of their lives. A woman's body performs

50. Nona, interview with the author, January 30, 2015.

doggedness as it seeks to assert itself against the prison norms. This "dogged strength," a power that comes from knowing one's self-worth, resists the negative prison image that seeks to damage one's concept of self and lead to internal immobilization.[51] Revaluing and reprioritizing oneself through embodied practices of assertion and care represents what I call *embodied resilience*.

Embodied resilience manifests in the ways that incarcerated women perform their identities through embodied ways of moving in the prison. Such embodied practices of resilience might involve concrete changes in physical appearance, which women undertake despite the strict restrictions on how the incarcerated are supposed to dress. Women will reconfigure their hair, nails, and even body parts to ensure their self stays alive in the prison. For example, Indigo recounted how women use magazines to embellish their toenails:

> Toenail polish. We didn't have access to that, but we were allowed to have clear toe nail polish, and they would take pictures out of magazines and cut them—We would keep blades. We're given razors to shave with. There was a time where you could break it down, take the razor piece out and cut things up or do whatever you want with it, so we used it to sharpen pencils, we used it to cut wrists, whatever [laughs], but they would take pictures out, like a Coco Chanel logo, the interlocking Cs, cut it out of a magazine, put it on the big toe and use the clear nail polish and floor wax as a sheer veneer over it and walk around with Coco Chanel toenails. That's art.[52]

Those outside prison might take for granted (magazine-derived) toenail art. But for those within the prison, their adorned toenails display a differentiated, unique self, a resistance to being seen simply as a number. In this case, the toenail designs become a way for a woman to

---

51. Josiah Young describes this dogged strength as "the black person's will to be more than the white world's negative image." W. E. B. Du Bois displays it as a wonder and a pain. He emphasizes that this dogged strength is rooted in a double-consciousness or spiritual striving where he (and Black people) must measure themselves against a racist world that sees Blackness as the problem. Within this self-consciousness, Young explores dogged strength, which resides in Du Bois's ability to resist the hatred that would damage one's spirit. Josiah U. Young, *Dogged Strength within the Veil: Africana Spirituality and the Mysterious Love of God* (Harrisburg, PA: Trinity Press International, 2003), 41.

52. Indigo, interview with the author, March 21, 2014.

perform and ultimately assert her unique identity. Embellished bodies are a statement of women's resistance of, and moving away from, prison uniformity. So, too, are healthy and fit bodies.

Caring for the Self: The Art of Becoming Whole

How does a woman care for her body in a place where her body is so easily objectified and so readily picked over? Eden's response is exercise!

> *Hope . . . to me? Every day I jogged in the prison because I didn't want to take medicine. A lot of times people will [at]tribute everything to your mental status and it's not always that. When you try to look at too many bad situations at one time, it will become overwhelming, so I would jog and use that as my medication. And in that, there was always a good stretch of a feeling, and that would be my hope. And in my mind, I seen my family and what I could do to contribute to making that situation better.*[53]

In a punitive system that believes that incarcerated persons do not deserve leisure and physical activities, the choice to exercise is an act of defiance. When women choose their bodies, they simultaneously choose their health.

Eden discusses the significance of exercise in the prison setting by relating it to a nontraditional form of art: "*I saw art in exercising. I saw people lifting weights. I saw people not missing—They call it exercise, but people really started using that hour of exercise . . . and me, I started running, and I'm still a runner. Twenty years later, I'm still a runner.*"[54] Viewing exercise as art speaks to the unique way in which exercise has the power to strengthen and mold physical bodies, alongside invoking emotional energy that transforms Eden's experience in prison. Although exercise was mandatory, it also became a way of showing up for herself. Twenty years later, the practices of self-nurture developed in the prison continue to contribute to Eden's regimen of self-care.

Eden's experience mirrors that of many incarcerated individuals who identify the benefits of exercise. These benefits are holistic—social, physical, and psychological—and become a coping mechanism to re-

53. Eden, interview with the author, April 17, 2014.
54. Eden, interview with the author, April 17, 2014.

lease emotions that might be counterproductive in a carceral context. Some of the psychological benefits incarcerated women experience are immediate. As a strategy for coping with incarceration, a direct correlation exists between increased exercise and decreased hopelessness.[55] The same chemicals released when one smokes marijuana (tetrahydrocannabinol or THC) or uses opiates (endorphins) are released during exercise, causing the brain to send neural signals that reduce pain and anxiety while also creating a sense of well-being.[56] Exercise also boosts serotonin activity, which increases motivation and willpower.[57] Each move feeds into a cycle of increased serotonin, a cycle of increased willpower and motivation. Of course exercise strengthens one's muscles; it also strengthens one's brain so that it becomes more resistant to depression.[58] The same movement strengthens one's physical self and one's affective self. In other words, exercise in the prison context is mobility, helping both to nurture and to sustain hope.

Exercise is generative and a form of self-care. That it contributes to the body's emotional and physical sustainability is critical for incarcerated women, in particular because many already suffer from chronic diseases such as diabetes, hypertension, and high cholesterol when they enter prison. With limited food options and limited opportunities for physical movement, prison can work against a person's health. Exercise, however, is a movement toward health, and participation in exercise signifies agency within a system that controls bodies.

There are also social benefits to exercise in prison that embody hope. Exercise enhances the public and personal image of incarcerated persons while at the same time serving as a form of self-preservation.[59] This is particularly true in cases in which incarcerated men and women need physical and emotional strength to defend themselves physically.

55. Andrew Cashin, Emily Potter, and Tony Butler, "The Relationship between Exercise and Hopelessness in Prison," *Journal of Psychiatric and Mental Health Nursing* 15, no. 1 (2008): 66–71; and Bobby J. Buckaloo, Kevin S. Krug, and Koury B. Nelson, "Exercise and the Low-Security Inmate," *Prison Journal* 89, no. 3 (2009): 328–43.

56. Alex Korb and Daniel J. Siegel, *The Upward Spiral: Using Neuroscience to Reverse the Course of Depression, One Small Change at a Time* (Oakland, CA: New Harbinger Publications, 2015), 86–87.

57. Korb and Siegel, *Upward Spiral*, 83.

58. Korb and Siegel, *Upward Spiral*, 81.

59. Yvonne Jewekes, "Men Behind Bars: 'Doing' Masculinity as an Adaptation to Imprisonment," *Men and Masculinities* 8, no. 1 (2005): 59.

The task of disciplining, toning, and strengthening one's body is painful. As Eden points out, she and other incarcerated women kept showing up for this practice of self-care as an act of will.[60] Incarcerated women endure the pain to experience a more toned, muscular body. Women are working toward feeling different both physically and psychologically. Ultimately, exercise can be a life-affirming practice, one that orients the body toward health and wholeness.

While women have constraints on the extent to which they can control their future, exercise does provide a valuable way to "work it out." Eden's description of exercise recounts a performance of resistance against a system that squelches mobility. Exercise counters women's sense of lacking control. Exercise is a form of subversive mobility, through which women can reassert power and take control of their bodies. In a system where bodies, especially Black bodies, are perpetual targets, care for the body is enacted against defeatism and victimization.

Exercise circulates hope. It nourishes the psyche. Enduring the "pain" of discipline requires a person to focus her attention on something other than what is right in front of her. The physical activity is life-affirming, for exercise mobilizes the human spirit's ability to endure pain. Participation in practices that sustain the self encourages strength and endurance that together embolden hope.

Resilience: Testifyin'

How does hope function in something as simple as exercise? Hope keeps life mobile, rather than incapacitated by restrictive prison practices and policies. While exercise centers the body as worthy of care, exercise also opens up the possibility for a more holistic well-being that transcends the body. Hope is a lived reality, manifesting in ordinary practices that help sustain the physical, emotional, mental, and spiritual aspects of life. As incarcerated women exemplify, resistance to death and persistence in life are performances of mobility that lead to hope and flourishing.

One way to locate hope in the lives of incarcerated women is to pay close attention to how their very bodies navigate the prison space. Embodying hope, through practices of resilience such as caring for the

---

60. Practices of self-care within prison span participation in exercise, group activities, art, and choir.

physical body, affirms that hope is holistic; hope cannot be partitioned off into only what one believes in one's head. Hope requires a capacity to *be* and to *move* in the world. It requires an affirmed selfhood. Even if one cannot speak or think hopefully, one's very existence, even one's physical body, has ways of embodying hope.

Female incarcerated bodies that live and move and have their being make a bold statement about hope. Often that statement is not articulated through words or profound theological treatises but is captured through their bodies. The body speaks loudly. It exuberates through subversive forms of protest such as exercise and self-care. Women's movements within prison give shape to hope. Hope, however, is not compliant, nor is it silent: hope is loud, disruptive, and even a bit transgressive. Hope is embodied resilience.

One example of such disruptive and loud hope is the *holler*, which comes from narratives of Black women who suffered abuse. Elaine Crawford writes:

> Holler is the primal cry of pain, abuse, violence, and separation. It is a soul-piercing shrill of African ancestors that demands the recognition and appreciation of their humanity. The Holler is the refusal to be silenced in a world that denied their very existence as women. The Holler is the renunciation of racialized and genderized violence perpetrated against them generation after generation. The Holler is a cry to God to "come see about me," one of your children.[61]

The bodies of incarcerated women holler! One of the most powerful lines I have ever heard about resilience is captured in a refrain created by a group of incarcerated women in a class I taught. They proclaimed over and over again a refrain they had written: "Hidden from existence, but I will not hide!" Controlled bodies resist being controlled by taking back control in whatever ways can be carved out. Overt and covert ways of surviving in prison involve the performance of hope in bodies that holler. The holler is lives screaming for recognition and respect from self, others, and God.

What might seem mundane in most people's eyes—engagement with food, exercise, and decorating space and bodies, for example—can really

61. A. Elaine Brown Crawford, *Hope in the Holler: A Womanist Theology* (Louisville: Westminster John Knox, 2002), xii.

be an attempt to stay alive. The women I interviewed for this project spoke of hope as reverberating most strongly when they could find pathways to live. Women learn the art of staying alive over and against attempts to silence them. *Embodied resilience is the activity of persisting in life while experiencing constant threats of emotional, physical, spiritual, and social death.* The act of coping, avoiding paralysis, embodies resilience. Embodied acts such as exercise demonstrate a capacity to care for the self amid disempowerment: to resist and persist, to move toward and against, sit between survival and flourishing, between life and death, between the cross and resurrection. To resist death is to make bold claims in spite of the social death that seems so prevalent for the women on the carceral continuum. I do not intend to minimize suffering and the scars women get from incarceration by my characterization of "staying alive" as a form of resilience. Rather, I seek to draw attention to women's survival as a testimony to God's grace.

Being alive is an overt, embodied demand for recognition, a refusal to hide or to be hidden to oneself and others. Being alive is an act not only of human resilience but also of God-given resilience. Even to have something as simple as breath in the face of death embodies life—a sheer recognition of divine activity. Incarcerated bodies "hold the holler," but they also hold a resilience that presses on against death-dealing circumstances. To be alive, to express one's embodiment as a woman on the carceral continuum, is a witness to God's grace. As Rosetta Ross writes, the very acts of speaking, writing, screaming, dancing, and singing testify to the sacredness of Black life; they testify to light breaking through oppression, male domination, and confinement. Being alive is a performance of hope. Bodies that have survived the violence of control and subjugation within prison testify to the resilience of the human spirit. Even unconsciously, women who have survived incarceration testify to the work of God. The act of surviving, of having breath in one's body, is rooted in an encounter with God, revealed through God's Spirit being active within one. It presupposes that God's Spirit will enable the individual to overcome seemingly insurmountable circumstances; for God will "make a way out of no way."[62] The ordinary things of life that many take for granted bear witness to God's grace. Ordinary things, such as markers, toilet paper, or a kind officer, become life-giving re-

62. Rosetta E. Ross, *Witnessing and Testifying: Black Women, Religion, and Civil Rights* (Minneapolis: Fortress, 2003), 14–15.

sources that sustain hope. Creativity becomes a tool that helps improve quality of life and that re-creates the prison experience. In the words of Indigo, *"Prison can be a phenomenal place if you re-create it."*[63] She shares further, *"Creativity—Imago Dei—this is where we are alike. Creativity is the first aspect of God [to which] we are introduced. The God factor in us resides in that creativity. Not in terms of the perfection of the expression, but the expression thereof."*[64] In other words, even the impulse to re-create oppressive contexts is a Godlike impulse.

Some women name God as present with them in their efforts to survive. Women identify God's presence as strength, as wise decisions, as light, as blessings. Even if the women do not see it, I posit that God is present even when they subvert the system for the sake of their own survival. According to Williams, God is present as women devise the resistance strategies that lead to their survival and to the resurrection of hope within the community.[65] Incarcerated women, much like Black women, direct their energies to create space where women can receive the much needed relational and emotional sustenance that bolsters each person's ability to survive, resist, and experience quality of life in prison. As Williams contends for Black women, I contend for incarcerated women: they do not act alone when seeking ways to flourish. Rather, the ingenuity and cunning that move women to pursue fulfillment for themselves and others is a move of the Spirit.[66] Some women talk openly about God's being the reason they made it through prison. Their understanding seems to encapsulate the large graces, such as making parole, as well as the small graces, such as a friend helping them out when they are sick. In all of these, I see God's presence. God is at work in creativity. God is at work in doggedness. God is at work in incarcerated women's bodies as they struggle through the daily realities of life. In other words, God is the origin and great mobilizer of resilience wherever it is enacted in people's lives. Their resilience invites the community to bear witness to the assaults women have faced against their humanity so that we can become partners in God's creativity as advocates, resisters, and companions alongside incarcerated women in their movement toward life.

63. Indigo, interview with the author, March 21, 2014.
64. Indigo, interview with the author, March 21, 2014.
65. Williams, *Sisters in the Wilderness*, 3, 208.
66. Williams, *Sisters in the Wilderness*, 3, 208.

God, Resilience, and the Prospect of Hope

Resilience is more than survival. It refers to internal resources for navigating difficulty. The act of navigating requires movement, which Westfield connects to resilience. She writes:

> In resilience there is "moving out/moving on," living, self-actualization, a growing together, a sense of ripeness, thriving, an experience of "go!" Resilience is like a room with many thresholds; a room with windows that open wide to vistas and views and that bring in fresh air. Resilience is where choice and location unfold into horizons, new dawns, rich possibilities. For oppressed, African American women, resilience is about finding ways of living within one's context and understanding the context so well that one reconstitutes the self while in chaos (but not out of chaos) to see oneself in a positive light while the world around would say the opposite. Resilience is the feeling of security, protection, and stability emerging from the midst of risk. Resilience is like a baby whose head and neck are held securely. Resilience is about mastering the terrain of the oppressive context so well that one re-creates and heals the self in the very midst of chaos.[67]

What Westfield identifies about the nature of resilience, the stories of the women I interviewed confirm. Resilience requires creativity. Resilience requires cunning. Resilience requires a force beyond oneself. Many women identify that force as God.

Westfield speaks about the resilience of Black women by describing resilience as something that bursts forth from adversity.[68] The reservoir of strength that women identify as essential to their ability to hope often leads to God-talk or intuitive knowing grounded in a sense of spirituality. Westfield names this internal fortitude "spiritual tenacity."[69] Describing the spiritual nature of hope, Laura says it this way: *"Hope has a spiritual connotation; it means letting spirit be in control."*[70] To let go requires a sense of knowing. Laura identifies that *"sense of knowing"* as

---

67. Westfield, *Dear Sisters*, 12.
68. Westfield, *Dear Sisters*, 8.
69. Westfield, *Dear Sisters*, 12.
70. Laura, interview with the author, February 25, 2014.

hope. That sense of knowing also appears to serve as a navigator through difficult circumstances.

Where is God when circumstances are hard? Toya describes the importance of "where" God is as significant to hope. God's absence, she shares, perpetuates a sense of hopelessness. In prison, she admits, God often felt absent.[71] Indigo, who is now a Christian but who grew up an atheist, talks a little bit about her own faith struggles. When hope is low, she doesn't question the goodness of God; rather, she questions the very existence of God. For her, nothingness is death. She says that when she struggles with her faith, her immediate question is, "*God, are you even there?*" Hope, as Indigo describes it, is therefore both "*tangible*" and "*relational.*"[72] God is present.

Often, women on the carceral continuum named God as central to their ability to make it through. For example, when I asked Myeshia how she could withstand her difficulties, she pointed to an internal fortitude rooted in faith and a strong sense of self. The song "Never Would Have Made It" by Marvin Sapp became a powerful indicator of Myeshia's resilience in prison. As Myeshia, with her powerful voice, sang a capella to words that resonated with her, she marveled at the fact that she was still alive despite the fact that so many of her cousins had completed suicide. The words echo the sentiment that God enabled her to get through, and she is stronger and wiser because of what she endured. In this song and in her interview, Myeshia located her strength and hope in God. In other words, her strength emerged from her ability to trust in God, not solely from her own efforts. Myeshia shared about her unwavering faith in God, which bolstered her spirit, enabling her to withstand the tough challenges that stood in her way while transitioning from prison.

The experiences of women on the carceral continuum force people of faith to wrestle with complex questions about where God is during incarceration and other experiences that might appear hopeless. Williams brings to light a truth about God which many of us must wrestle with when we think about hope, resilience, and carcerality. In the Hagar narrative of Genesis 16, God *is not* a liberator. God *does not* free Hagar from slavery; rather, God instructs Hagar to return to her masters, Abraham and Sarah. What God *does* promise Hagar and her descendants is survival, a survival that is perhaps linked to her use of the master's

71. Toya, interview with the author, September 15, 2014.
72. Indigo, interview with the author, March 21, 2014.

resources.[73] Liberation might be gained by human initiative, but it is not guaranteed. Further, God's promise of survival to Hagar does not presuppose an easy life.[74]

Women do not describe a God who is far from their situation, but one who is *in* their situation. Throughout the interviews, women themselves locate God throughout their experience that runs from survival to flourishing. The Spirit is present in beckoning one toward survival and mobilizing one to resist. God is present at the table, both as a guest and as a host, taking delight in women's gathering to create something satisfying. God is active in women's very being, with the breath/Spirit that keeps them alive, enabling them to embody the *imago Dei*. Pastoral and empirical theologian Annemie Dillen has proposed, "The belief that 'resurrection' is possible, not only after life but also in this life itself, together with the belief in the activity of the Holy Spirit, makes it possible for people to deal with the confusion," a confusion that might be characterized by collateral consequences, incarceration, and trauma.[75] In other words, hope may not wipe away confusion, but it does make it possible to work through the confusion.

Resilience Rooted in Hope

Resilience nurtures and sustains hope, and it is a manifestation of hope. Resilience performs possibility in the face of limitation, mobilizes in the face of disintegration, and breathes life in the face of death. In an exploration of how human sciences define resilience, philosophical psychologist Craig Steven Titus identifies three facets of resilience: coping, resisting, and constructing. *Coping* refers to how one's behavior adapts to manage current adversity. *Resisting* refers to an unwillingness to surrender to destruction. *Constructing* refers to the strengthening of a person's capacities as a result of adversity.[76] Myeshia's story illustrates

73. Williams, *Sisters in the Wilderness*, 20–21.

74. Williams, *Sisters in the Wilderness*, 4.

75. Annemie Dillen, "The Resiliency of Children and Spirituality: A Practical Theological Reflection," *International Journal of Children's Spirituality* 17, no. 1 (2012): 68.

76. Craig Steven Titus, *Resilience and the Virtue of Fortitude: Aquinas in Dialogue with the Psychosocial Sciences* (Washington, DC: Catholic University of America Press, 2006), 8–11.

how she coped, resisted, and constructed a future. For example, her life during prison strengthened her to face life after prison, enabling her to resist defeat and use budgeting to cope with instability and financial insecurity. In other words, resilience is about pressing through challenges so that one continues to live, resist, and grow. Resilience requires movement.

What is the source of resilience? The resilience of which many of the women spoke is rooted in hope. Their ability to cope, resist, and (re)construct rested upon an unwavering belief in possibility. For Myeshia, that possibility looked like hope in herself and in God that she would become financially stable enough to meet her basic needs. For Yvette, that possibility looked like hope in owning a home once released from prison. For Indigo, that possibility looked like hope in herself and her community of incarcerated friends to have a fellowship together by having a meal. Their hope in God, self, and others became a source to draw from while their hope for what could be served as a driving force. The "what" seemed to center on meeting basic needs in the here and now. Nevertheless, these hopes seemed to be encapsulated in a more enduring hope that transcends the "what" and presses toward a life that has meaning and purpose.

The exact source of resilience is a mystery. No one thing explains the "why" behind some women's ability or inability to be resilient. In their narratives, resilience flows from a combination of human initiative, divine activity, relationships, emotional regulation, environment, spirituality, and social supports. For some, it is the integration of divine intervention and human initiative. Resilience cannot be manufactured, although teachers, parents, and faith leaders can cultivate it. For many, resilience signifies depth of being, emerging from a repository of strength deep within the spirit. For others, resilience emerges as a disciplined practice of navigating challenges. That is, resilience emerges bit by bit over time. But resilience is not necessarily inborn, a trait that some have and others do not; rather, resilience is contextual and interactive. How women relate to their context influences their capacity for resilience.

Resilience nurtures and sustains hope because, at its core, it is oriented toward life. Though resilience does not always equate with flourishing, it does generate a hope that enables survival. When people on the carceral continuum choose to enact dogged, creative, and embodied resilience against the suffering they encounter, they perform hope. They become characters in this drama called life. Describing his experience of intense suffering in a concentration camp, psychiatrist Viktor Frankl captures the essence of hope in confinement by calling it "the art of living."[77] Frankl recounts how hope can come alive in the midst of suffering, resulting in joy:

> The attempt to develop a sense of humor and to see things in a humorous light is some kind of trick learned while mastering the art of living. Yet it is possible to practice the art of living even in a concentration camp, although suffering is omnipresent. To draw an analogy: a man's suffering is similar to the behavior of gas. If a certain quantity of gas is pumped into an empty chamber, it will fill the chamber completely and evenly, no matter how big the chamber. Thus suffering completely fills the human soul and conscious mind, no matter whether the suffering is great or little. Therefore the "size" of human suffering is absolutely relative.
>
> It also follows that a very trifling thing can cause the greatest of joys. Take as an example something that happened on our journey from Auschwitz to the camp affiliated with Dachau. We had all been afraid that our transport was heading for the Mauthausen camp. We became more and more tense as we approached a certain bridge over the Danube [to] which the train would have to come to reach Mauthausen, according to the statement of experienced traveling companions. Those who have never seen anything similar cannot possibly imagine the dance of joy performed in the carriage by prisoners when they saw that our transport was not crossing the bridge and was instead heading "only" for Dachau.[78]

Observers who witness the appalling conditions of another person's suffering, whether of a concentration camp or a women's prison, may never truly understand how that person is able to dance, move, exercise, cook, decorate, and live even while they suffer. But what has become clear to me through the interviews is that hope draws upon every form of life available in the moment. Life-oriented movement in the midst of suffering *is* divine activity. And the joy that bursts forth is a container for the reality of sorrows.

77. Viktor E. Frankl, *Man's Search for Meaning* (Boston: Beacon, 2006), 44.
78. Frankl, *Man's Search for Meaning*, 44–45.

Ultimately hope moves individuals away from helplessness and despair and toward life. Hope moves Indigo to imagine a recipe of fried chicken and enlist other incarcerated women to assemble and prepare good-enough ingredients. Hope fuels Eden to keep running, simply to feel as fully alive as she can and to hold depression at bay by stretching her body's capacities in prison. The move toward wholeness unleashes resilience against attempts to damage and destroy the human spirit. Hope emerges when agency is asserted in the face of perceived or actual helplessness. In other words, a person's will, emotions, and actions align with her orientation toward life when she sees life through a lens of possibility rather than a lens of helplessness. Indigo's ability to create food with other women counters alienation and isolation. Buying a car and budgeting are more than momentary successes for Myeshia; each success propels her forward, helping her to reintegrate into society. In other words, as a woman moves toward agency, she is better able to overcome the darkness that often characterizes the prison context.

Resilience is less about how the circumstance affects the self than about how the "I" responds while in the circumstance. When the circumstance presses against the "I," instead of sinking, the "I" adapts. Viktor Frankl notes, "When we are no longer able to change a situation . . . we are challenged to change ourselves."[79] Put another way, Frankl notes, "Everything can be taken from a man [or woman] but one thing: the last of the human freedoms—to choose one's attitude in any given set of circumstances, to choose one's own way."[80] Changing oneself in order to survive adversity embodies resilience; it stems from revising the way we see life and our relationship in the world. As pastoral care theologian Jan Holton identified in the case of the Lost Boys of Sudan, resilience is the practice of engaging in "strategies of coping that move one toward growth and flourishing," including "behaviors, beliefs, and even physical attributes adopted or adapted by persons and communities under conditions of duress that serve to negotiate the negative experiences of suffering."[81]

The suffering that persists for years and sometimes a lifetime for women on the carceral continuum challenges notions of hope and

79. Frankl, *Man's Search for Meaning*, 112.
80. Frankl, *Man's Search for Meaning*, 66.
81. M. Jan Holton, *Building the Resilient Community: Lessons from the Lost Boys of Sudan* (Eugene, OR: Cascade Books, 2011), 26–27.

flourishing.[82] Flourishing is typically situated in a narrative of self-actualization and the acquisition of material goods, but some people—in or out of prison—will never fully experience what society deems "the good life." Women on the carceral continuum who persist in life and resist death will rarely have the luxury of an easy life. That women on the carceral continuum must keep resilience as a companion on their journey can be a daunting reality. Some may never experience flourishing here and now. Instead, flourishing may remain simply a possibility as one embodies resilience. And it is this resilience—a form of mobility that moves away from helplessness and toward agency—that generates hope. Hope is sustained and secured through resilience, just as resilience is sustained and secured through hope. In other words, one's being is rooted in hope when one has a posture toward flourishing even when one's actuality is full of struggle.

Conclusion

Suffering is a shared human condition, but the suffering described throughout the narratives of women on the carceral continuum is compounded by its enormity and its persistence. Such women need an enormous hope that is able to hold them through the many challenges they face before, during, and after incarceration. Resilience—dogged, creative, and embodied—represents a form of hope for women on the carceral continuum that burgeons as it is enacted. It means, as London said to me in her swanky Atlanta office, that one has to be a person who exceeds all bounds, who surpasses expectations, and does so again and again.

---

82. Shelly Rambo identifies the suffering that remains in the aftermath of trauma, which survivors must continue to face. Rambo, *Spirit and Trauma: A Theology of Remaining* (Louisville: Westminster John Knox, 2010), 1-3.

Nurturing Connection

The Quest for Meaningful Relationships

Connection with others is critical to hope. The existence of humanity rests upon the interdependence of all human life. Relational understandings about what it means to be human counter Descartes's rational approach to existence ("I think therefore I am") and embrace the popular South African proverb known as *ubuntu* or "I am because you are" or "I am because we are." The well-being of "I am" is intricately connected to the existence and well-being of the "you." Many concepts of hope are rooted in privatized notions of hope, focused on an individual's longings and wants. What women on the carceral continuum bring to light, however, is that hope is inherently relational. Women may have individual wants and longings, but they often find their hope in relationship to something outside themselves and in connection with others. The relationships observed in prison and described in the prison context have led to my own poetic reflection on the power of relationships, which I think manifests in the stories of the women. These reflections are written below:

> Are relationships armed with the power to thwart death?
> To move between, among, and around despair,
> Ducking to avoid its deadly aim,
> Externalizing internalized rage.
> Shielding one from idle words
> That damage.
> Shapeshifting words
> So that death is killed
> And life is lived.
> Death and death-dealing can be thwarted.
> Death can be killed and life can be lived through connection.
> Are relationships armed with the power to thwart death?

To move between, among, and around despair,
Ducking to avoid its deadly aim,
Externalizing internalized rage.
Shielding one from death-dealing
Decisions, systems, and ways of being.
Overcoming disconnection
With something deeper, inexplicable,
But powerful enough to
Hold letting go and
To revive, restore,
And resurrect trust in something
Beyond the self.
Shapeshifting feelings of abandonment and rejection
So that death is killed
And life is lived.
Death and death-dealing can be thwarted.
Death can be killed and life can be lived through connection.

Hope as Inherently Relational

Prisons are designed to limit connection. When women first enter prison, interaction with their family, friends, and other social ties that existed prior to their incarceration are typically all cut, either through the challenges associated with overcoming prison's restrained communication guidelines or by the family members themselves. Even when family and friends do visit the prison, the carceral regime strictly regulates and restricts one's interactions, including physical touch and verbal communication. Such restrictions control both the physical interactions between persons and the objects that persons use to communicate to others. Letters sent to and from prison spaces, for example, are strictly monitored, presumably affecting the degree to which correspondents share their intimate feelings.

Connection is further blocked through the logic of punishment that isolates persons as a form of security and control. Perhaps the most extreme form of such punishment is solitary confinement, which can be inflicted even for trivial offenses.

Solitary confinement for being too young. Being too depressed. Being too mouthy. And . . . breaking the rules, too.

Not surprisingly, this extreme of nonconnection—solitary confinement—can prompt or exacerbate individuals' mental ill health.[1] Some incarcerated persons describe solitary confinement as *"a form of living death."*[2] Its negative effects can include suicidal thoughts, hallucinations, and irrepressible anger.[3] The negative impact of disconnection damages psychologically and leads to a loss of one's self.

While studies show that solitary confinement and other forms of extreme isolation do not in fact deter criminal behavior but do contribute significantly to psychological distress, prisons continue to use these tactics as a measure of control.[4] Some facilities use it for protection, not control, particularly in the case of juveniles who have been tried as adults. An example is sixteen-year-old Kalief Browder. After stealing a backpack with valuables in it, Kalief Browder spent three years in New York City's Rikers Island jail without being convicted of a crime. Most of that time was spent in solitary confinement, where he suffered extreme mental illness and eventually took his life.[5]

Practices such as solitary confinement and restricted physical contact compound the social isolation and prevent the fulfillment of the human desire for connection.

Ultimately, the parameters that establish how relationships are structured within prison settings complicate the ability to create and maintain meaningful relationships. Prison is a structured process of interaction and relationships of power. As such, it dictates *which* bodies can interact and *how* bodies can interact with one another. To transgress established boundaries typically results in punishment in the form of further disconnection. While there are reasonable explanations for why

---

1. Craig Haney, "Mental Health Issues in Long-Term Solitary and 'Supermax' Confinement," *Crime & Delinquency* 49, no. 1 (2003): 130–31.

2. Lisa Guenther, *Solitary Confinement: Social Death and Its Afterlives* (Minneapolis: University of Minnesota Press, 2013), xii.

3. Haney, "Mental Health Issues," 133.

4. Jayne Leonard, "What Are the Effects of Solitary Confinement on Health?," *Medical News Today*, August 6, 2020, https://www.medicalnewstoday.com/articles/solitary -confinement-effects; and Sara Rain Tree, *Solitary Confinement and Prison Safety: Solitary Watch Fact Sheet #4* (Washington, DC: Solitary Watch, 2023), 1–2.

5. Because of his death, many prisons, including New York, are now rethinking solitary confinement in prisons. David K. Li, "Family of Kalief Browder, Young Man Who Killed Himself after Jail, Gets $3.3M from New York," *US News*, January 24, 2019, https://www.nbcnews.com/news/us-news/family-kalief-browder-young-man -who-killed-himself-after-jail-n962466.

boundaries exist that limit opportunities for connection in prison, the fact still remains: to be human is to feel, touch, and engage others with one's emotions. To exist is to be in relationship with someone other than the self. Connection is a basic human need.

Hope, Affirmation, and Friendship between Incarcerated Women

The need for relationship is heightened in spaces like prison that have a dearth of meaningful relational connections. Yet despite the isolation incarcerated women encounter, many women manage to carve out pockets of space within prison where they can experience life-changing, hope-inspiring relationships that transform their lives. Nona, an incarcerated woman, shares her narrative of a friendship with Kristi, a death-row inmate who, she says, literally saved her life. She recounts:

> As long as I've known [Kristi], she has been out of normal population or what they call general population, held in a lockdown maximum-security prison where they normally would have people on lockdown with behavioral issues, mental health [issues], suicide watch, and I was all three of those things at one time [laughs]. So we were always near each other. We would yell to each other through the bars and the vents, and the ways that inmates learn to communicate with each other. . . . and they knew how close I was with [Kristi], so I worked her floor. I delivered her food trays and different things through the bars. She was not allowed out. . . . And the times that she would come out was when they allowed her to join the Theology Program and to be in the classes, and it humanized her, and it was just an awesome, awesome triumph of opportunity. . . . And so when all this was going on, and she's going to her classes, they stopped it. . . . Another warden came in, put her back in chains. So the program would come to her! While they were doing that I'm sweeping, I'm working around the lockdown unit, I'm talking to her, she is talking to me. Kristi says, "You're going to feel good if you could just get in this program. You won't want to cut yourself. You'll feel good. You won't care about what they have to say about you around here." . . . She was right. The Theology Program was literally my Department of Corrections. . . . It gave me something in the back of my head, too, to push me to do better. . . . Who cared if I sliced myself up? In fact, at one point I had a vein, and it was really bad, and I remember the officer's words, "Go ahead, kill yourself. We'll just take you off the count." And that was the

*moment I realized that I'm not plugged in. I'm not alive. I am not where life
is, and it's my choice that has me in this death, so God, can it be my choice
to get me to life? . . . I was so glad [Kristi, the other death-row inmate] was
a messenger of hope in my situation, and even in a lockdown unit, there
was freedom, and there was a messenger of liberty.* [6]

Kristi's words of encouragement were generative, creating a pathway
for Nona to experience hope. Kristi, the messenger of hope and liberty,
shared with Nona an opening to new possibilities. While this lockdown
space is meant to confine, Nona and Kristi did not let the bars confine
their ability to communicate; instead, they used the small openings of
the vent to meet each other's need for connection. Even openings as
small as vents can open up new possibilities. For Nona, Kristi affirmed
what she was beginning to awaken to: that her life mattered, regardless
of what the guards and others said.

As revealed in Nona's account, relationships provide spaces of affirmation, liberating one to be authentic. In the words of Robert Kegan,
as we create ourselves, "we look into the souls of our neighbors for ver-
ification."[7] Nona and Kristi created the space to look into each other's
souls, reawakening the possibility for new life, even in the prison. Although Kristi was eventually executed by the state, Nona makes clear
through advocacy and public engagement events the generative impact
that Kristi made in her life as a messenger of hope.

Nona and Kristi's story reiterates the fact that humans are meant to
be in relationship. Humans are meant to have significant others who
care about their actions and well-being. Similar to the biblical scripture
"iron sharpens iron," interdependency and connection sharpen the self.
All humans need help to become their authentic selves; it is not a solitary process. To borrow from Paulo Freire, "Hope is rooted in [humans']
incompletion, from which they move out in constant search—a search
which can be carried out only in communion with others."[8] Failure to
connect with others in a meaningful way feeds into a sense of aloneness
in the world, foreclosing even the possibility for help if needed. Human

6. Nona, interview with the author, January 30, 2015.
7. Robert Kegan, *The Evolving Self: Problem and Process in Human Development*
(Cambridge, MA: Harvard University Press, 1982), 1.
8. Paulo Freire, *Pedagogy of the Oppressed*, trans. Myra Bergman Ramos, 30th anniversary ed. (New York: Continuum, 2000), 91.

connections are divine. Human solidarity manifests the presence of God in a distinct way—"as an expression of the mystical body of Christ."[9] Without relationships, one can wither away. Even a hint of relationship can enable a person to blossom. Relationship thwarts death. Being in relationship *is* life.

Despite the vastness of prison, to those inside, prison becomes more like a community, what Sherry described as *"a small society behind barb-wire and razor."*[10] The work of carving out space for meaningful relationships within prison—a mobilization to know and be known—is a human endeavor, an act to become whole. Women claim that these relationships within the prison enable them to make it through the ups and downs of prison life. For Nona, her connection with Kristi was the saving grace that brought hope. Kristi and Nona's friendship thwarted death. Kristi's words were life-giving and enabled Nona to overcome suicidal ideation and hopelessness. Death and death-dealing can be thwarted even in the prison. Relationships give life.

Not Just Any Relationship

Yet not all relationships give life. Some reinforce one's existing situation or worsen it. In fact, when I asked one woman what prison teaches, she talked about how the social network in prison actually taught her how to be a criminal. Before coming to prison, she had not been involved in drug-dealing, theft, or other criminal offenses. In this instance, because of the women she met while in prison, she discovered new ways of being criminal. Prison, in other words, placed her in proximity to a counterproductive learning system. In short, not every connection is a positive one. Some connections drain life while others affirm it. Positive connections must be forged, and that takes effort.

For life-giving relationships are not easy to find. This is especially the case for women who transition from prison. Formal and informal conversations with women who seek to reintegrate back into society revealed that the need for authentic relationships remains. For those who struggled with depression during incarceration, lack of meaningful

---

9. Shawn M. Copeland, *Enfleshing Freedom: Body, Race, and Being* (Minneapolis: Fortress, 2010), 5.

10. Sherry, interview with the author, January 3, 2015.

relationships left a void, giving suicidal ideation and depression room to return with a vengeance. Others may have had family support but still no real grounding or place where they could be their authentic selves, as this vignette about Laura shows.

> No one else in the coffee shop knew that the last time I had seen Laura was in a prison classroom. Hugging without being surveilled by prison officers was something new.
>
> To my routine check in—"How are you?"— she responded, "Despite having a place to stay [with my family] and a job, I would rather be back in prison."
>
> "Why?" I asked, with a confused look on my face.
>
> "Because even though they are my family, they don't know me. In prison, I had friends that actually know me."[11]

For Laura, connection is about more than simply having someone to offer her a place to stay. Connection is about being known and accepted for who she is. She had felt such connection in prison, though to an outsider that might sound contradictory. As her words indicate, Laura often contemplated returning to prison *because* of the solid relationships she had built in prison, relationships she found impossible to replicate outside. She is not the only one. This is a common sentiment. Sherry also shares how she sometimes imagines being back in prison. She writes:

> Well, yeah, because I have a friend here recently, and I'll tell her different stories about me being in prison, and she'll be so sad. And she'll say, "We've got to create you some new memories." But it'll be fun stories I've told her. And she'll be like, "We've got to create you some new memories. I'm just so sad for you, because you're such an awesome person. I'm just so sad that so many of your great memories come from prison." [But] I'm not sad for me at all! And to be honest, right now, although I love my life, and that community, and those people I met in prison, I miss them. And I can't say if I could blink my eyes sometimes and go back and hang out, I totally would. So yes, although the rules were there and from time to time you get shook down and all that type of stuff to come along with the authority of prison, my wholeness of spirit overrode all that without a doubt.[12]

11. Sherry, interview with the author, January 3, 2015.
12. Sherry, interview with the author, January 3, 2015.

Laura and Sherry's yearning reveals the need for connection, the need to be fully known by another. That a person cannot find authentic relationships upon release is deeply troubling. This is why Laura could be out of prison yet still longing to be back in prison. It is not darkness for which she longs, but the relationships that seem to light a pathway toward hope. These connections seem to outshine space and time. To be out of prison and yet with very few relationships where she can be herself felt unbearable, even worse than being in prison.

What "saved" Laura, what prevented her from returning to prison, by her own recognition, is her desire to care for her godson, whom she loves. So while significant relationships are enough to create a desire in some women to return to prison, they are also sufficient to keep women out of prison. Laura's quasi-maternal love for and connection to her godson is a powerful force—so powerful that it drives and orients her decision-making, moving her away from anything that might cause her to recidivate.

Loss of Maternal Connection

Many stories of incarcerated mothers reflect this maternal drive. My connection with a woman named Shaunice helped me to understand the significance of maternal connection. One afternoon, as women were checking into classes, I noticed Shaunice sitting in the hall crying. This was my first time meeting Shaunice. Her face embodied the distress her heart felt. Yet I knew she could get in trouble with the prison officers if she did not come inside the classroom. "Come into the classroom," I invited her. And then I asked her, "Would you like to talk about what is going on?" She told me that she would have to drop out of the Theology Program if she wanted to see her child during visiting hours; she had to attend parenting classes, which took place at the same time as the Theology Program. The parenting class was a condition of child visitation.

This mom had to consider which class was most important for her at that moment and long term. Her entire decision-making process centered on the love she had for her child and communicating that love to her child. On the one hand, participating in the Theology Program represented an opportunity for her to prove herself to her child, to communicate that she could finish something of value, that she herself was valuable in the child's life, and that she considered education (her own and her child's) to be important. On the other hand, the parenting program might teach her concrete skills that would make her a better caregiver for her child.

Such decisions between competing programs within the prison forced women to weigh their options: a program that teaches one how to be a better parent or a program that stimulates one's intellect in the context of prison. In the short term, seeing her child might have more value for her child's healthy development and provide her with immediate gratification, while the Theology Program might enable her to model for her child the importance of education. Both programs are important for personal growth and development, which might contribute to her becoming a better mom. There was no best choice, no bad choice, just a tough negotiation between two equally important priorities that had the power to both mobilize and immobilize connection. She chose to see her child.

The desire for familial bonds, particularly between a mother and child, is a recurring theme in prison. And no wonder, since approximately 70 percent of the women in prison are mothers.[13] Yet women are often stripped of this opportunity for relationship when incarcerated. For a woman, surely no loss of connection is more tragic than the loss of connection between herself and her child. But of course, beyond the mother herself, maternal incarceration also affects the lives of children and their caregivers, who must learn how to navigate new challenges.[14] Children often do not understand why their parent is not around, and grapple psychologically for years, even a lifetime, with abandonment and rejection, which they can project onto other caregivers. On top of the psychological and behavioral challenges a caregiver might face, the caregiver experiences the additional financial burden of caring for a child. The loss of connection between a child and mother jeopardizes hope.

13. Julie Poehlmann, "New Study Shows Children of Incarcerated Mothers Experience Multiple Challenges," *Family Matters: A Family Impact Seminar Newsletter for Wisconsin Policymakers* 3, no. 2 (2003): 1.

14. Maternal incarceration refers to women who are mothers, particularly those who were the primary caregivers of their children before they were incarcerated. It could also refer to women who enter the criminal justice system pregnant and give birth to a child or children while incarcerated.

As shared in chapter 1, maternal separation has profound negative impacts on the children, some of which may last longer for the child than for the incarcerated mother. Many scholars liken the trauma of separation of a mother from her child during incarceration to that of death or divorce.[15] While studies show that maintaining a parental connection is critical for children of incarcerated parents, visitation and phone calls can easily become too costly to continue and can lead to the breaking of these familial bonds.[16]

So harmful is such a breaking of maternal bonds with a child that some scholars have even likened maternal separation to *natal alienation*—a term that Orlando Patterson uses in the context of slavery to describe the sense of powerlessness that denies slaves their birth right and their claims to any legitimate social order. Nor did repercussions end there: the slave's alienation placed automatic limits on their children's participation in society as well.[17] The term *natal alienation* therefore emphasizes the constraints and privations that the children of slaves faced because of their parent's or parents' confinement.

That children of incarcerated women today experience a similar form of natal alienation is merely one sign of the failure of the system to support the parent-child bond during incarceration, particularly for children who are left with little or no familial or financial support.[18] Natal alienation breaks the power of mothers to care for their children and for children to bond with and be cared for by their mothers. This and many other stresses on the children of incarcerated mothers reinforce a cycle of incarceration that severs the connection between incarcerated mothers and their children.

Shaunice's story above demonstrates how carcerality affects this connection between mothers and their children. In prison spaces, power is

15. Alison Cunningham and Linda Baker, *Waiting for Mommy: Giving a Voice to the Hidden Victims of Imprisonment* (London, ON: Centre for Children & Families in the Justice System, December 2004), 10.

16. Stacey M. Bouchet, *Children and Families with Incarcerated Parents: Exploring Development in the Field for Opportunities for Growth* (Baltimore, MD: Annie E. Casey Foundation, 2008), 5.

17. Orlando Patterson, *Slavery and Social Death: A Comparative Study* (Cambridge, MA: Harvard University Press, 1982), 6–8.

18. There are exceptions. Some cases may require maternal separation *for the safety of the children*. In such instances, I support the well-being of the child. Patterson, *Slavery and Social Death*, 6–8.

often mediated through relationships, limiting the types of interactions that take place between persons, even persons outside of the prison. This site of social interaction has direct implications for someone on the carceral continuum, meaning how a mother is affected by her immobility, by her incarceration. While she cannot be physically present for her children, she does typically seek other ways to remain connected, as Shaunice's story revealed.

But what about remaining connected to God?

Connection to God

"For me, hope is intrinsically tied to God, and when I feel disconnected from God, I lose hope."[19] Indigo's statement underscores that one's sense of connection extends to connection with a transcendent other. Many call this transcendent other "God." Indigo shares what she feels when God seems not to be present with her:

> *What I find is when I have faith struggles, it's not, "God—How come, God, you're not hearing me? How come, God, I'm not feeling a connection with you?" It's "God, are you even there?" Because I had that very strong atheist leaning [and] came to know God more when I was older, so my development of the concept of God didn't happen in my baby, toddler, childhood years when you're saying to your baby, say "Thank you, Jesus." I didn't have that. So Jesus—It's almost like being adopted when you're age nine or ten, and that's who you know as your parents. Something is still missing. So that's what I struggle with. So when I lose hope, I feel dead, I feel like there is nothing beyond what is visible, and thinking of the future and imagining the future becomes even more of a challenge, because even if you are atheist, you can imagine your future, but if your future imaginings are tied . . . to there [being] nothing, which is what atheist leanings taught me, it becomes even more challenging. So nothingness means complete death to me . . . and that absolute nothingness that this is the end, [that] there's absolutely nothing beyond this moment, that is what always comes up for me when there's situations in my life where I've lost hope.*[20]

19. Indigo, interview with the author, March 21, 2014.
20. Indigo, interview with the author, March 21, 2014.

For Indigo, this disconnection, or the loss of the felt presence of God, created a sense of nothingness. Indigo later explains how this loss of connection with God creates a sense of hopelessness in her and makes her question God. In this case, hopelessness, as she describes it, then led to her mental decline and poor decision-making, which seemed to lead inevitably to prison, where she was more willing to make "stupid decisions."

Disconnection carries feelings with it—feelings of abandonment and emptiness. How does one find the courage to hope when one is surrounded by emptiness? Indigo's disconnection from God seemed to provoke the anxiety of what Paul Tillich calls "emptiness or mean-inglessness," which then seems to foreclose courage and the will to live: "The anxiety of meaninglessness is anxiety about the loss of an ultimate concern, of a meaning which gives meaning to all meanings. This anxiety is aroused by the loss of a spiritual center, of an answer, however symbolic and indirect, to the question of the meaning of existence."[21] Such anxiety and such questioning can lead to all forms of darkness, including thoughts of ending one's life. Thus, hope requires a great deal of risk and courage to live life, especially in the context of darkness or death-dealing circumstances. For some women, this hope centers on God.

From Nothingness to God-Presence

Many women describe connection with a transcendent other to be life-giving. Of course, incarcerated women are not homogeneous, nor are their understandings of God. Yet because many of the women I interviewed opted into a theological studies program in the prison, it was not particularly surprising that all the women I interviewed, regardless of their faith tradition, expressed a clear belief in God. The content of that belief differed, as did its expression. But all the women I interviewed expressed an understanding of hope that also intersected in some way with their understanding of God.

Take Indigo, for example. She made a clear connection between her relationship with God and hope. Seeing, speaking, and imagining God's

---

21. Paul Tillich, *The Courage to Be*, The Terry Lectures (New Haven: Yale University Press, 1952), 47.

presence became a way for her to express her connectedness with God, and this gave her hope.

> I believe that in our relationship with God we receive hope. The other night I was feeling disconnected and as I laid down and went to bed, I said, "God, I've been running around. I haven't spent time with you. And even this — I'm saying this because I know I should, I know I should just pray and trust that you hear, but I just choose to experience you now as pure liquid love holding me in this bed, letting me know you are present, you are here, you are part of my life, you know everything I'm going through, you forgive me, you love me. I'm precious to you." And I felt like I was back in my mother's womb, and that experience just gave me hope again, like as long as God and I were cool, there's lots of hope. So feeling that connectiveness, which I did purely in an exercise that utilized my imagination, helped me reconnect . . . with God. [22]

In this instance, she connected with God through her imagination and belief about how God sees her. Feelings of love, trust, forgiveness, and being cherished transport her back to safety, to her mother's womb. Indigo makes a choice to experience God, and God's felt presence breeds "lots of hope." Her account above suggests that hope was not necessarily gone, but that the rigors of the day had seemed to block out her awareness of hope. The process by which she reconnected with God helped her to become more aware of hope and to experience a sense of peace, which she describes as her and God being "cool" with each other.

In her meditation, God seems to rescue her from the abyss by reminding her that there is something beyond the nothingness. God reestablishes her humanity and restores her hope by dissipating the threat of nonbeing. To speak of faith in a transcendent being while one suffers through incarceration is to call on a God who is not distant but *with* those who suffer. Indeed, many of the women I interviewed expressed that God is close to them. In this sense, faith is a gift that enables one to know that God is greater than the situation at hand, thus providing meaning for what may feel meaningless, and renewing one's hope, as happened to Indigo.

22. Indigo, interview with the author, March 21, 2014.

Hope as Transcending Darkness

To my question "What does hope look like when it is restricted?" Toya responded by writing the following poem.

> Darkness is all around
> It's on me
> It's in me
> At times, I close my eyes and think
> I recognize something
> Is it light?
> Darkness
> It's all around me
> It's on me
> It's in me
> It *is* me.
>
> —Toya[23]

Her poem illustrates how all-consuming darkness can be. Darkness closes in—first surrounding her, then settling on her, and finally in her. Toya uses darkness as a metaphor throughout her interview to describe prison. She is not alone in this. As evidenced in the poem, the experience of darkness becomes so pervasive that it is no longer outside of herself; it *is* her. The label of "sinful" or "criminal" perhaps confirms this sense of having a dark self, a label that society has already imposed on her. What is the light that Toya begins to recognize when she closes her eyes? Women who have to fight to not be consumed and obliterated by darkness need to be able to differentiate themselves from the darkness.

In Eden's case, this is exactly what God does: God provides a light that helps to transcend the overarching darkness that is in her life. When I asked her, "What does hope look like when it is restricted? What does it look like when it breaks free?" she almost immediately responded by producing a drawing. Eden's written description of the image is compelling. She writes:

There is a girl inside of the different stages of life, not having what she needed in the beginning. She's surrounded by all the different phases of life.

23. Toya, interview with the author, September 15, 2014.

> *This is Hope. She's the girl. And she's in the middle of it and she don't see a way out. Hope don't see a way out.*
>
> *But somewhere the sun shines. But the sun cries. So that's the reason I talked about God. There's no way you could have gotten . . . out of there. There's no way, because he didn't do nothing but lead from the cradle to the penitentiary, you see? There's no way in the world it could have happened. You can put it in words. I've given it to you, and you can put it in words, and you can use the little girl as hope. And that's pretty much the best way I can tell you, when you're locked in total darkness. Somewhere there's a little bit of candlelight. And it had to be God, because my life didn't produce light, and the choices that I made didn't produce light. It was like—I don't know what words you could use to describe it.* [24]

Her depiction of hope and God's transcending power raises the question, How does God transcend darkness? I am left with the same conclusion Barbara Brown Taylor draws from the scriptures in Psalm 139:12, "Darkness is not dark to God; the night is as bright as the day." [25] Here, God is both "the way" and "the light" that transcends the darkness in her own life. Eden's mystical experience with God enables her to see God as a waymaker or, as womanist scholars say, as "making a way out of no way." [26] In essence, God who transcends darkness is a God who makes passageways or provides light as women learn to walk in the darkness. Eden equates God's transcending activity with hope.

Hope as a Fresh Start

To identify with a God who is able to see one's humanity as finite and fallible and not as darkness is a source of comfort. Grasping for a God who transcends darkness is a fight to experience hope in one's own humanity. Indigo describes God's ability to transcend darkness as offering forgiveness and a fresh start. Referring to the criminal justice system, she says, *"You're telling me that permanently I will never have a fresh start? [That] I will never get over my sins[?] [That's] the antithesis of what my faith reflects.*

---

24. Eden, interview with the author, April 17, 2014.
25. Barbara Brown Taylor, *Learning to Walk in the Dark* (Norwich: Canterbury Press, 2014), 16.
26. Eden, interview with the author, April 17, 2014.

You sin, you repent, God forgives."[27] In this sense, forgiveness is a way to transcend darkness. A fresh start, then, becomes a way out of the darkness. When fresh starts are not granted, it is easy for women to remain in darkness and subsequently to begin to see their humanity as dark.

Women like Eden describe connection with God as a way to experience hope in their lives. God is a mediator, bridging the gap between hope and the typical circumstances of life. When women forge a connection with God, they also seem to forge a connection with hope. Theologian Paul Tillich similarly argues that the mystical experience provides one with power that transcends the anxiety prompted by the threat of death, the feeling of emptiness and meaninglessness, and condemnation. Such a mystical experience becomes a source of courage to face threats to one's humanity.[28] Similar to how theologian Jürgen Moltmann describes his experience as a prisoner of war, the incarcerated women came to know "God in the dark of the night—God as the source of hope."[29]

Connecting with God thus became a way for Eden to renew existing hope, but it also gave her hope when hope seemed to be nonexistent. Hope seems to be only a connection away. Thus, when individuals begin to see and know themselves in relationship to others, and more particularly to God, they move toward a more wholesome sense of self. One's identification with another—and particularly with God or the transcendent—offers self-affirmation. To identify and to be in relationship with the divine is itself powerful, offering pathways that reorient one toward hoped-for ends, meaning, and fresh starts. This reorientation ultimately enables women to let go—of the need to control, the need to have everything figured out, the need to be perfect. For some, that letting go is a form of "surrender."

Hope as Letting Go

What does surrender look like in a setting in which women are forced to relinquish their rights? Laura tells me about her connection with God and hope:

27. Indigo, interview with the author, March 21, 2014. For the full quotation, see pp. 91–92, above.
28. Tillich, *Courage to Be*, 155–57.
29. Moltmann, *Experiences of God*, 8–9.

To me, hope has a spiritual type of connection. People always say, "Surren-
der and let God do things," but if you're doing everything in hopes of this
and in hopes of that, then you're the one doing everything. That leaves no
room for the spirit to do anything if you're the one trying to always con-
stantly do everything that you hope for.[30]

For Rochelle, being in relationship with God actually gave her a way
to let go and trust completely in God to do things that will help bring
about a hoped-for outcome for her. For Rochelle, letting go of things that
she cannot control anyway is a way of hoping, of trusting. She describes
how God functions in her life to enable her to hope:

When you start over and things happen that you didn't necessarily plan or
you could not have put in motion yourself, and when that happens over and
over and over again, you just realize how limited you are. And so, if this can
happen without me, maybe it's a question of agency as well.

But I think about everything that's happened to me post-[prison]. Those
are things that I had an idea that I might want to do, something with pol-
icy. But, I had no idea how to get there, and then an opportunity comes
along that I would not have known how to reach. . . . And then you look
back at your experience and the classes that you had or the people that you
met. You realize, there's no way I could have orchestrated that. And it just
happens over and over. And, when it continues to happen, you just realize,
boy, [laughs] there's something out there that makes things work that I
really didn't understand.[31]

For these women, seeing God as one to whom they can surrender
their lives provoked hope and opportunities. In a space that forces certain forms of surrender, another woman talks about how in this instance letting go of the desire to know everything is empowering. As
described in chapter 1, Laura writes: "*I don't understand everything, but*
I'm so happy I don't. . . . And that comes with the whole empowering feeling
you get from a certain type of surrender for me."[32] Hope enables people to

30. Laura, interview with the author, February 25, 2014.
31. Rochelle, interview with the author, July 21, 2014.
32. Laura, interview with the author, February 25, 2014. For the full text of this
quotation, see p. 41, above.

let go of "knowing" the future and be okay with trusting the God who is beyond the future (while also within the present).

Hope as a Sense of Knowing

Language falls short in describing exactly how God works in the lives of women along the carceral continuum. Yet when women make connections between God and hope, they describe hope as a "sense of knowing" that is more intuitive than factual, a knowing that is transcendent, that could not easily be expressed in words. When I asked women to describe hope, several talked about hope in a mystical way. Take Rochelle, for instance. She talks about the mysterious nature of God in this way: "*I think for me it's just a sense of how God works in ways that you don't understand. And, I think a lot of it is really mysterious and—can we use those words, mysterious, and unfathomable? And, just wanting to be in the right position, in the right place.*"[33]

Many women describe the hope that emerges from God as mysterious, mystical, and inexplicable. At the same time, God works through people and circumstances which can be encountered in tangible, visible ways. For Rochelle, the fact that she can work in the job she always dreamed of, even after being incarcerated, is something she attributes to God. As she sees it, her role is about being in a place to receive, but it is God moving through people and circumstances that actually brings about the hoped-for job. The fact that Rochelle realizes her own limitations points to the need for a God who can work in the places she cannot control. That God can reach beyond her own limitations and does so over and over again provides her with a sense of hope, even though God's ways remain "mysterious and unfathomable" to her. God's activity is not always discernible; but if one seeks for God, one may find God moving in mysterious ways. Or, as Rochelle makes clear, if a woman looks back over her life, she may be able to discern the movement of God. Further conversation clarified that, for many women, that sense of knowing is rooted in spirituality. Some even identified it as an unwavering confidence in God that began to wane when they no longer felt connected.

Hope does not dissipate suffering or make reality disappear. Rather, the women told me, faith in a transcendent other can be a useful re-

33. Rochelle, interview with the author, July 21, 2014.

source for coping with and managing problems, conflicts, and emotions. More particularly, they spoke of the human-divine encounter as contributing to positive emotions toward others and the world while also enhancing their sense of well-being. Even in moments when meaninglessness and despair seem to prevail, in the words of Tillich, the women demonstrated that "their courage to be is reduced to the acceptance of even this state as a way to prepare through darkness for light, through emptiness for abundance."[34] In other words, one's relationship with God helps transform one's feelings and perceptions so that one knows the world in a more open and optimistic—one could say hopeful—way.

Yet that optimism and openness may be grounded in a renewed sense of purpose and meaning despite being in an unstable, unjust, and sometimes unkind world. The affirmation women feel from God actually frees them to participate in the world in ways that sustain them while at the same time countering the confinement the world seeks to impose upon them.

To be clear, faith in God did not presuppose faith in religious institutions. In fact, religious institutions seemed to contribute to rather than relieve some of the stress women on the carceral continuum felt. These women sometimes discussed those associated with the church in a negative light. Sometimes the church became a source of shame, silence, and inactivity. Yet women seemed to draw a clear distinction between the church and God, not conflating God with those who treated them in unloving ways. On the other hand, when people associated with the church engaged the women graciously, the women saw this as evidence of God in their lives. Further, despite their sometimes negative experiences with the faith community, the women did not want to do away with the church. Rather, they saw the church's role as crucial in providing acceptance, advocacy, and support for them.

Our relationships with others create pathways to hope. As evidenced in the conversations with women on the carceral continuum, so do our relationships with a transcendent other. In the interviews they revealed their ways of clinging to God, ways that provide them with a sense of security. In turn, this sense of security gives women the courage and comfort to let go of their own need to be in control. Letting go allows them to find their security in something beyond themselves. Many of the women expressed clear relational connections with God that encouraged them to be hopeful.

34. Tillich, *The Courage to Be*, 159.

Institutional Connection

Many people would not understand how a $112 paycheck evokes hope. But for Indigo, a returning citizen, her connection to employment matters beyond the amount of money she receives. Likewise, Rochelle says, *"Three days after I came home, I received a job. That was hope for me."*[35] Hope looks like something tangible. Hope looks like a job and a paycheck.[36]

Outside the prison, women are often immobilized in their connection to institutions. How one is connected to the system is often mediated through parole or probation rather than through positive interactions with the criminal justice system. At the same time, education, social services, assistance for public housing, and employment opportunities are often housed within institutions that erect barriers, making it nearly impossible for incarcerated and formerly incarcerated women to connect to the services they offer. Paradoxically, the society that requires formerly incarcerated citizens to be productive is the very society that erects barriers to their participation. Institutions lock women out of the very spaces they need in order to thrive and sustain themselves in everyday life. At the heart of institutional connection is understanding that one's social *and* physical locations have implications for one's ability to imagine and realize particular visions.

The existence of structural evil, which arises from within society because of how humans interact, sheds light on why some groups of people have easier access to institutional connection than others. Those with easy access experience privilege as a result of their connection, a privilege that enables them to flourish and prosper—largely understood as having financial stability and material goods. In other words, those who have easy access to education and career prospects find it much easier to meet basic needs such as food, shelter, and transportation. While characterizing prosperity and flourishing solely on the basis of one's material circumstances is insufficient, such circumstances do matter to most people's well-being. The ability to connect to educational, corporate, and financial institutions becomes a pathway to secure the financial capital to live. Social and institutional capital, then, becomes a means toward mobility. Capital provides a form of power or influ-

35. Rochelle, interview with the author, July 21, 2014.
36. Indigo, interview with the author, March 21, 2014. For the full context of Indigo's statement, see chapter 4 on p. 119.

ence that gives women strength to tear down walls that block advancement. Thus, institutional connection is an essential navigational tool for women on the carceral continuum.

Bridging Opportunities: Social Networks, Proximity, and Institutional Connections

Institutional connections are critical for helping women who are returning to society to concretize hope. Mobilities scholar John Urry points out in his exploration of the ways in which lives unfold through social networks, that movement, particularly travel and connections, extends people's social networks. Conversely, lack of mobility and connection leads to inequality of all kinds.[37] The lack of mobility that is characteristic of incarceration, then, demonstrates how lack of connection through immobility contributes to inequality. At the same time, the bridging that takes place through social networks can make a drastic difference in life opportunities for those who are incarcerated and those recently released. Connections to others bridge connections to institutions. Indigo helps us to understand the importance of social networking and proximity to people that connect women to housing, jobs, and other important essential services. She says:

> I'm reminded in so many ways of this blight on my character or my life. When I came out [of prison], I stayed with a friend. I was supposed to stay with them in their finished basement for some time, but she had people coming from out of town and asked me—over the summer, if I could go stay with a friend for a couple of weeks because she had company. And a couple of weeks became eleven weeks, and I really felt put out. And, I was staying with my pastor, who had never signed up for that, and so I did everything I could to find a place to stay. And I found an older lady near school who has Parkinson's, and her family . . . wanted someone in the house with her at night in case she fell. So, for $200 a month, I had a room in her house. And now, her family has decided to put her in a home, and so they gave me three weeks to vacate the place, and so in the middle of the craziest amount of school stuff, I have to move. So on Sunday I'm moving. Well, the way it

37. John Urry, "Social Networks, Mobile Lives and Social Inequalities," *Journal of Transport Geography* 21, no. 1 (2012): 24.

relates to this is I went to six different places, three apartment complexes, three houses, individual people, and they all, because of my background, wouldn't give me a place to live. So I couldn't even find a place to live [even though] I have the money now with the school loan. I struggled with taking out the school loan—should I? shouldn't I?—because it's just more debt for my future, but I decided to take it out to just pay my rent for one year. That was the only amount I took out, and I couldn't get a place to live. So . . . a friend of a friend who knows what my background is, is letting me come and live in their house. [38]

She got a job because a friend in the courthouse recommended her. She got a place to live because a friend of a friend knew someone who was looking for someone to stay in it while she was gone for the summer. Entry into the university happened because of the recommendations from the teachers who came into the prison each week.

Institutional connection requires a level of proximity with women on the carceral continuum. Women who are or have been incarcerated are among the most vulnerable. Those who are in a position to *see* and *hear* from these women are more likely to see and hear them for who they are, rather than how most of society designates them. In other words, proximity has a spatiotemporal element. Proximity is about being engaged in the nitty-gritty of understanding the who and why. To know that women are more than their crimes and deserve opportunities to lead fruitful lives requires people to *see* women for who they are and to hear the narratives that underlie some of the decisions they have made. Proximity prompts empathy and a will to act on behalf of others.

In his own work with death-row inmates, public interest lawyer Bryan Stevenson uplifts the importance of such proximity:

Proximity has taught me some basic and humbling truths, including this vital lesson: *Each of us is more than the worst thing we've ever done.* My work with the poor and the incarcerated has persuaded me that the opposite of poverty is not wealth; the opposite of poverty is justice. Finally, I've come to believe that the true measure of our commitment to justice, the character of our society, our commitment to the rule of law, fairness, and equality cannot be measured by how we treat the rich, the powerful, the privileged, and the respected among

38. Indigo, interview with the author, March 21, 2014.

us. The true measure of our character is how we treat the poor, the disfavored, the accused, the incarcerated, and the condemned.[39]

For Stevenson, being in proximity to death-row inmates early in his law career shaped his understanding and approach to law. Stevenson recognized that proximity and justice are intimately connected. Justice mobilizes laws that are just toward those who have limited power, those who have been immobilized by their place or status in society. Stevenson's career is an example of how those in proximity to incarcerated women are often the ones who become mobilized to contribute to the mobilization of those same women.

The act of seeing and listening is not unlike the ministry of Jesus, who became incarnate for the mere purpose of identifying with and securing redemption for those he loved. The writer of the epistle to the Philippians identifies what makes for meaningful connections:

> In your relationships with one another, have the same mindset as Christ Jesus: Who, being in very nature God, did not consider equality with God something to be used to his own advantage; rather, he made himself nothing by taking the very nature of a servant, being made in human likeness. And being found in appearance as a man, he humbled himself by becoming obedient to death—even death on a cross! (2:5-8 NIV)

Jesus's physical engagement with the people kept him emotionally engaged. A passage from the Gospel of Matthew confirms the way proximity often works:

> Jesus went through all the towns and villages, teaching in their synagogues, proclaiming the good news of the kingdom and healing every disease and sickness. When he saw the crowds, he had compassion on them, because they were harassed and helpless, like sheep without a shepherd. (8:35-36 NIV)

Jesus's ability to *see* people depended on his daily engagement with their issues and concerns. What he saw prompted compassion in him.

39. Bryan Stevenson, *Just Mercy: A Story of Justice and Redemption* (New York: Spiegel & Grau, 2014), 17-18.

With his example in mind, one of the most biblical things an institution or those who work within an institution can do is to engage in close relationships with those who are disenfranchised and vulnerable. Proximity to the disenfranchised does not result in coercion, whereby one feels forced to move in a particular direction because of guilt and obligation. Rather, it results in *compassionate mobility*. Compassionate mobility compels a person or institution to act on behalf of and in partnership with others, particularly those with less power, because of love and direct engagement with the lives of others. Compassionate mobility moves *from* a place of direct physical engagement with others *to* a more intimate knowledge of persons, and from there *to* heightened awareness of the circumstances surrounding others, and direct engagement with the systems that make it difficult for others to move freely in the world. Compassionate mobility is both prompted by and prompts meaningful relational connections that ultimately mobilize hope and help. Hope is communal in nature.

Proximity not only drives compassion, it also effects change. As Rochelle said in response to my interviewing her,

> In order for society to really get it right, that they have to do more of what you're doing. They have to talk to people who's been through it. . . . Because a lot of times they like to go from people. . . . They like to look for those who's done something huge, like come home and got a master's degree, got a PhD degree. And while that's fine in life, what's really good is dealing with the naked people—[what] I call people such as ourselves who got it right, didn't go and get no master's, didn't go and get no PhD, just got it right. We're the naked people. And I think in order for society to fully understand and get it right, they have to do more of what you're doing, [Sarah]. They have to talk to those who ha[ve] been through it, who ha[ve] lived through it, who understand it, who['ve] processed it, who['ve] tasted, who['ve] seen] it, who['ve] witness[ed] it. I think society ha[s] to look at it from that perspective, and I think when they do it from that perspective because they have a tendency to not trust adults completely or fully believe that naked people really know what it is that they're discussing, but we do, because we've lived through it. We've been on the other side. We saw it with our own eyes. We witnessed it with our own souls, so we know what it is that we saw and understood and did, and I think when society realizes this, I think that you'll see a lot more changes in life.[40]

40. Rochelle, interview with the author, July 21, 2014.

Knowing when and how to help effectively emerges from allowing those who have been incarcerated to be experts in the transformation of the systems that make it difficult for returning citizens to live in society. Those who have tasted and seen what incarceration is like can offer the truest holistic perspective on the external and internal challenges they face.

Beyond the Privatization of Hope: Community and Connection

Rochelle, a returning citizen who now works with politicians making changes within the criminal justice system, speaks here of the difference that is the communal nature of hope.

> I think a lot of times we think of hope as something that's internal, and I don't think it's necessarily always internal. . . . I think it's a biblical thing. Hope is not just sitting around waiting for things to change. Hope is not always an individual making things change. Hope is sometimes a community making things change, and even when you think of the criminal justice system and the difficulties in transitioning from prison . . . there are things that are the responsibility of the community as well, and so I think when you've got an individual who has expectations of things getting better and you have a community with the same expectations, that's just a total difference.[41]

Hope looks like the community taking responsibility for changes that need to be made. When the community makes changes, the community pays attention to *the criminal justice system and the difficulties in transitioning from prison.*

Many concepts of eschatological hope are rooted in privatized notions of hope. Yet hope has never been a private endeavor. What the women make clear is that hope is not just an individual's wanting and waiting; hope is a collective aim to bring about what is wanted and the type of world we want to have. Hope looks like the community's providing help when help is needed. It is rooted not merely in individual generativity but also in communal and institutional generativity. When we realize that hope is not just what the *self* wants but what *we* want,

41. Rochelle, interview with the author, July 21, 2014.

then we also realize that hope is more public than private. Existential hope is about this public form of hope—about inviting institutions and others into our ways of realizing the visions and expectations we have for ourselves and the world. Existential hope holds systems accountable for the obstacles they create that prevent people from reaching their hoped-for futures.

Connection leads to offering and accepting help. Help, according to William F. Lynch, is a critical component of hope.[42] This help is often found within the context of relationship. For the women in these stories, it is typically teachers, friends, pastors, and chaplains who offer help. Western society adopts a self-help philosophy that refuses to acknowledge that some people can actually be helpless. Western society is so bent on not admitting one's own helplessness, suggests Lynch, that society also won't admit that others need help.[43] The recognition that helplessness exists seems itself to be perceived as a weakness. Yet there are moments when humanity is helpless, for that is the very nature of humanity. Lynch puts the situation like this: "Being helpless, being unable, that is, to help himself, [a person] suddenly finds himself confronted, at so critical a moment, with a culture, and sometimes with a medical situation, which tells him that he must help himself, that the help must come from within."[44] Women on the carceral continuum expose the notion that hope is solely individualistic as a false notion of hope. Rather, hope is rooted in connection to something outside the self.

The relational nature of humanity requires the community to pay close attention to those who have been exiled or rejected. Relational humanity presses toward generative behavior that manifests in care-oriented actions. Helping one person within the community provides possibilities for the entire community. Thus, help is a communal task rooted in hope; it is not a task relegated to the government or specific individuals within a community. It requires all hands to be invested in the being and becoming of others. Connection signifies communal possibility. It recognizes that the diminishment or edification of one affects all. Restorative hope both invites and challenges. Hope invites institutions and the larger community into the joy of helping others,

42. William F. Lynch, *Images of Hope: Imagination as Healer of the Hopeless* (Baltimore: Helicon, 1965), 42.
43. Lynch, *Images of Hope*, 76–78.
44. Lynch, *Images of Hope*, 77–78.

particularly those on the carceral continuum, to realize the visions and expectations they have for themselves. At the same time, restorative hope holds systems accountable for the obstacles they create that defer hope.

Conclusion

Connection restores hope along the carceral continuum. Multiple stories from the women interviewed emphasize that the type of connections one makes and sustains in life matters. When women forge life-giving relationships, those relationships offer sustaining power. As I have shown throughout the chapter, connection with others, God, and institutions holds great value for women on the carceral continuum. The value of who we are is based on God's creating us; the fruit of who we become is a result of our living into our authentic selves in the context of authentic relationships. Ultimately, relationships between humans as well as relationships with the divine contribute to a sense of well-being and restore hope during difficult times.

I centered this chapter on interpersonal connections, transcendent connections, and institutional connections. But women also identify connection with the self as a critical aspect of hope. In the next chapter, I pay attention to connection with the self by focusing on identity. Restorative hope centers on an awareness and acknowledgment of who we are as valued selves while also taking into account who we are becoming. We shall see that for those women who identify as Christian, what emboldens their hope is knowing that the possibilities for becoming do not rely solely on self but on partnership with God.

CHAPTER 4

Overcoming Identity Paralysis

Carceral Stripping and the Quest to Be Somebody

The criminal justice system requires women to surrender the very things that gave them a sense of identity prior to prison. In very concrete practices, the criminal justice system strips a woman of her identity. From the point of a woman's entry into the prison system, the process of depersonalization begins. During the arrest and initial imprisonment, women must remove their clothes, shoes, electronics, and any other physical items they have with them when taken into custody.

Not only are the physical artifacts of their identity removed, but through incarceration women also lose their careers, their families, their sense of control, and their physical freedom. Criminologist Shadd Maruna identifies this loss of personalization as the *initiation phase* in a larger ritual of incarceration.[1] He explains: "The prisoner undergoes a 'civil death,' losing former citizen rights and liberties, but also a distinct set of ritualistic admission procedures—undressing, strip-searching, and disinfecting the individual, assigning him or her a new institutional uniform, haircut, and living quarters and 'obedience tests' meant to break the individual's personality, including forced verbal acts of deference."[2]

All these practices are identity-depriving. They distance a woman from her identity. Depersonalization, a time marked by the enforced shedding of things that had been identity markers, contributes to a woman's sense of identity loss. A woman begins to ask herself, Who am I apart from my career, my social status, and my possessions? This jarring process of identity deprivation coincides with her forced introduction to her new identity.

1. Shadd Maruna, "Reentry as a Rite of Passage," *Punishment & Society* 13, no. 1 (2011): 13.
2. Maruna, "Reentry as a Rite of Passage," 11–12.

*When I discovered I was going to prison, I couldn't cope. I had a breakdown.
I lost hope. . . . Prison was a death sentence in my psyche. When I was faced
with this thought of prison, I literally wanted to kill myself. . . . Up until
the moment I was sentenced, I was still under this delusion that I wasn't
going to prison. So I left my computer running at home. Everything was like
oh, I'm going out. I'll be back. I was in denial. And so from the sentencing
hearing, I went straight into prison, into jail. I wasn't allowed to go home
and pack up my house. . . . There was no time to say, oh my God, I'm going
to prison. I never had that, because I just refused to deal with that thought.*

*So then I was sitting in this courthouse jail cell . . . and all that was going
through my head was, "I'm going to prison, I'm going to prison, I'm going to
prison." And so we go through this whole process. I finally get to my room,
and I'm just numb. . . . Going through the motions. It's just so unbelievable,
even now, it is so unbelievable. It was otherworldly.*

*You have to understand [that] my father was a professor. My brother is a
professor. My sister works in academia. We don't have people in our family
that go to jail. [laughs] We're not drunks. I've never even smoked weed in
my whole entire life. I've never had anything happen other than a speeding
ticket. I didn't even have a DUI. . . .*

*So you go to your room, you carry your mattress, you carry your sheets,
you carry your—I think you have one change of clothes, your rubber slip-
pers, you send everything [else] home, and they give you everything down
to your underwear. So there is absolutely nothing I came in with (except my
glasses) that was from the outside. So all your creature comforts are gone.*[3]

Indigo paints her being sentenced to prison as a "death sentence" in
her psyche. Denial became a barrier to facing reality, and reality felt
surreal. Who she was and who she was supposed to be didn't match
up with her going to prison. And yet Indigo's sentencing left her with
no choice: her computer and home, artifacts of her identity, she had to
leave behind. Whatever Indigo's physical artifacts communicated about
who she was could not function quite the same in prison. The cultural
capital that once served as a marker of economic, occupational, and
social status holds no weight within the prison. Indigo's death sentence
is not physical but social.

3. Indigo, interview with the author, March 21, 2014.

Carceral Identity

Women are stripped of the things that mark their identity; at the same time, they are also pressured to embrace an identity that is distinct from their own. Prison has its own culture. Women must conform to the norms within the culture in order to survive. Prison culture includes the unspoken rules to which incarcerated women must adhere in order to fit in. The criminal justice system introduces Indigo, for example, to a new class in society—the so-called criminal class. She has to embrace a *carceral identity* to conform to prison culture in order to survive incarceration.

A carceral identity, however, pressures incarcerated persons to become something other than themselves. Performance becomes a necessary tactic of survival during incarceration. To be seen as weak or soft, for example, makes one an easy target for others. Therefore, a woman must wear a mask that dissuades ridicule and potential violence and present as someone she is not.

Women perform this new identity not only for their peers within the prison; they must also perform it for prison officials. Toya, a returning citizen who was interviewed, shares her experience navigating a carceral identity. In some circumstances that means "playing tough," while in others it means "playing perfect."

"Playing tough" is often driven by the need to survive in prison, resulting in Toya's attempt to follow the unwritten prison codes.[4] This *prisonization* is the process by which newly incarcerated individuals accept and adapt to the sociocultural norms of the prison. Even when people come into prison with few to no values that resonate with the informal inmate code, they either embed themselves in the prison subculture or risk becoming the target of serious bullying.[5] These codes include not looking weak, vulnerable, or frightened; defending oneself in the face of disrespect; and at times even bullying others to prove one is tough. The performance of invulnerability offers status within prison culture

4. Toya, interview with the author, September 15, 2014. Toya is a pseudonym.

5. Craig Haney, "Psychological Impact of Incarceration: Implications for Post-Prison Adjustment," written for the conference "From Prison to Home: The Effect of Incarceration and Reentry on Children, Families and Communities," University of California, Santa Cruz, December 2001, 9-10.

while at the same time numbing emotions that would typically lead to compassion and care.

On the other hand, prisoners recognize that "playing perfect," which is primarily behavior geared toward guards, chaplains, and other prison officials, gives one access to certain privileges and favor. For Toya, this means intentionally trying to distinguish herself as a model inmate in front of the guards, meaning conforming to prison rules, using deferential language, and complying absolutely with the "written codes" of the prison.

Wearing these roles becomes a way to gain privileges, maintain safety, or simply fit in. No wonder that women perform multiple (and at times conflicting) identities in order to navigate the prison context! These competing priorities mean navigating the prison contexts in ways that mask one's true self. As Toya noted, *"I had to transform into different people at times to fit in."*[6] She talked about playing roles like *"being on top of the world, being the one that had it all together, and then [the] one that was bad, and just being mean [and] hateful towards people that didn't even deserve it."*[7] While neither of these roles characterizes Toya's natural demeanor, performing these roles became part of the carceral identity that sometimes subsumes her authentic self. While Toya is fully aware that this is not her real identity, she also understands the prison as a place that does not welcome her true and full self.

I asked Toya what happens when people do not change in order to survive in prison. She shared:

> If you don't, I feel that you'll be taken captive, seriously. I feel that if you don't have some form of changing to, well, adapting, if you don't change or perform in a certain type of way, you will feel lost. . . . Feeling alone, not fitting in and stuff and you don't fit in, because you're not like everybody else. So you start having second thoughts about yourself and who you are as a person, and you seep into a depression.[8]

In short, at the same time as women seek to secure their own safety and well-being during their incarceration, the prison space is foster-

6. Toya, interview with the author, September 15, 2014.
7. Toya, interview with the author, September 15, 2014.
8. Toya, interview with the author, September 15, 2014.

ing identity deprivation. Toya feels lost in her own skin even when she seeks to fit in.

Many women in prison are like Toya in being able to give and be only parts of themselves in that space. To be known intimately is a longing that they must surrender in order to survive.

This constant identity-shifting is a form of captivity, in which a woman can easily lose herself. While safety required protecting her authentic self, and moving between identities became a navigational tool for Toya's survival, the inability to lay hold of an authentic identity also has dire consequences. The incongruence between the public persona that women wear (of necessity, as a way of preserving their life) and the personal identity that constitutes who women really are can easily become blurred in the constantly shifting image negotiations in prison.

The Loss of Dignity

The prison strips women's bodies as well as their identities. The carceral identity includes wearing a prison uniform. Even within the prison, women may be assigned to wear a variety of uniforms. These uniforms become ways of marking status within the prison context. For example, a prison uniform can communicate how long a person has been in that particular prison. Or it can communicate whether or not women are on suicide watch. It also can communicate whether a woman is a low or high security risk. While the goal of these color-coding practices is safety in the prison, the practice also has the effect of separating and categorizing women. To deter crime, the prison uniform publicly humiliates and shames those who break prison norms. It is an identity marker that points to the criminality, offensiveness, or troublesomeness of particular women.

Yet the women describe something else as more shameful even than wearing the status-identifying prison uniform: the stripping of the prison uniform. The criminal justice system uses strip searches to deter crime and to maximize security in the prison. Thus, by nature of their incarceration, all women are subject to strip searches—frequently. Most members of the public are aware that women are subjected to a mandatory strip search when they enter the prison for the first time. But that is hardly the only occasion for such a humiliating act. Anytime women transfer between prisons, have visitors, return from court, or return from temporary release, they are also subject to full searches. Mandatory drug tests and cell searches also always warrant a strip search. Why? One of the most common reasons why officers strip-search women randomly is because they are suspected of having contraband. Contraband can range from more innocent but prohibited items such as glitter, markers, and tape to more illicit items such as cell phones, alcohol, or weapons. On the one hand, many things that seem inherently harmless can easily become weapons to harm oneself or others; thus, restrictions against contraband reinforce safety in the prison. On the other hand, often women are placed in lockdown or are wrongfully strip-searched for contraband as a means of reinforcing the prison's power over them. Besides such instances, random strip searches take place. Those who are considered high security risks undergo even more searching.

When guards strip the prison uniform to enact routine strip searches within the prison, women face physical and psychological stress. What intensifies the stress, however, is the fact that routine searches can happen even when one has not committed a breach. Recall Nona, a formerly incarcerated woman, who described in detail her experience of being strip-searched:

> One of the worst things about being incarcerated is having to take off all of your clothes in front of somebody and . . . to pull your butt apart, bend over and cough for them to examine all of you and leave you there just to put back on a uniform that has a number on it. . . . If you don't know you—If you don't have a good name to call you, you don't have a hope to link onto to say "I'm somebody even as I'm doing this," or "God you said I'm—." If you don't have a Bible verse to quote, you will be left there stripped, only to be given nothing. . . . You must have somewhere else to go.[9]

Strip-searching requires women to expose their genitalia and anus to complete strangers. Beyond exposing private parts, women expose stretch marks, fat tummies, birthmarks, and other aspects of their bodies they might be embarrassed to expose. Stripping their bodies shifts the gaze to their naked bodies as a spectacle to deter crime, maintain law and order, and reinforce their status as people who are under state

9. Nona, interview with the author, January 30, 2015.

control. Physical discomfort, loss of control, and hypervisibility are all made public through strip-searching, making it a form of public shaming. Further, women who have been sexually assaulted or who have experienced some form of abuse experience increased mental and emotional stress because of such strip searches.

Nona, at a transitional center during the time of the interview, talked about how, despite transitioning out of the prison, being compelled to return to this site where one's clothes could be stripped off at any moment for any reason was a continual reminder that she is other, not trusted, a person under someone's perpetual gaze. She writes:

> Even at the transitional center, I think an incredible part of, again, the duality of it, was that here I am . . . getting on MARTA, the train, the bus, handling currency again, working a job, feeling normal, wearing clothes, having a zipper, and having pockets, and then going right back into the place the same day. Like Cinderella, I told my mom, "I feel like my carriage turned into pumpkins and rats at the end of the day when I would have to take those same jeans, same thing I did with the brown uniform, my clothes off every time you came in that building, every single time, every day." I worked Monday through Friday, and then I went home for twelve hours on a merit pass on Saturdays. Even when I came back from pass, at the end they could still do it at any time while you were in [the prison], and it just—I don't know—I don't —I don't know what to do, how to explain that. If you don't have hope, what that can do to you.[10]

The strip searches enacted when a woman returns to the prison space function as a reminder that she has been marked forever as criminal—someone who needs to be thoroughly searched and evaluated before crossing over into society or back into prison.

The Stripping of Agency

Carcerality manifests in multiple ways, including the loss of agency. Sherry, a returning citizen, describes the restrictions one feels when one is physically confined within the prison: *"You don't have any rights. You don't have a voice. Basically you're just told to do things when someone*

10. Nona, interview with the author, January 30, 2015.

else wants you to do them, not when you want to do it. You can't go to the refrigerator and look in. You can't sit on your porch if you decide. You can't decide, 'I don't want to have this today. I want to get something else to eat.' It says that you were behaving so awfully and so badly that society decided this is the best place for you. You're powerless."[11] Rights and privileges that were once taken for granted no longer exist when women are incarcerated. A woman's sense of agency, her ability to make decisions about what she will eat, where she will sit, and how she will engage in her daily tasks—these are all stripped away.

Even when a woman is finally released from prison, she faces the collateral consequences of her incarceration and its stripping of her identity, not least because through this carceral stripping she has now become accustomed to her carceral identity and has to rebuild her identity as a person no longer behind bars but forever marked by having been incarcerated. These consequences make it difficult to obtain employment and housing, some of humans' most basic social needs. The myriad complications of this decarceration process manifest in the intangible bars that still exist. There is also an internal decarceration process that takes place, in which returning citizens must learn *how* to be physically free even though they haven't quite made the mental transition to freedom. For example, one woman described her release by saying, *"You are still incarcerated in certain types of ways. You need to learn how to separate yourself from the bars. It's very hard doing that. Because right now, I feel like I'm still behind bars. Mentally I'm still behind bars."* This freedom doesn't feel complete since one can be free of incarceration but not free of the impact of being incarcerated. For example, while one may be technically free, one may still be on parole, which creates unique circumstances of confinement and possible reincarceration. The lines between physical and psychological incarceration then easily become blurred, pointing to the carceral continuum.

11. Sherry, interview with the author, January 3, 2015. Sherry is a pseudonym.

The Ritual Movement of Incarceration

Incarceration is a cultural performance.[12] Understood like this, incarceration becomes a way for incarcerated individuals to move from the status and identity of human to the status and identity of criminal with few means of ever systematically going through a process of rehumanization.[13] Within incarceration, dehumanization takes place in a systematic way that shapes one's views of one's humanity as well as others' external views of one's humanity. In other words, punishment becomes a systematic process of dehumanizing individuals during their arrest, trial, strip searches, and other practices within incarceration. Once incarcerated, women become static in an identity that is marked by criminality. The movement back to citizenship, humanity, or a meaningful existence is either not clearly marked or else strewn with barriers that make citizenship, humanity, or a meaningful existence almost impossible to achieve.

Once women enter the system, they are constantly moving in and out of these cultural rituals, whereby perpetual separation from larger society seems much more realistic than reintegration into larger society. These multiple losses often leave women in crisis, bewildered, and unable to demarcate their own identities. They have been stripped of their current sense of being and have had limitations arbitrarily placed on who they can become.

A Static Identity

When police arrest a suspect, they arrest more than her body: they arrest (literally: "stop" or "halt") her development, her humanity. Incarceration

12. I borrow from the language of Victor Turner to describe the process of incarceration as a cultural rite or social drama. Within this cultural performance or social drama, as Victor Turner has identified, four stages take place: breach, crisis, redress, and reintegration or schism. Victor Witter Turner, *Dramas, Fields, and Metaphors: Symbolic Action in Human Society* (Ithaca, NY: Cornell University Press, 1975), 23–59. The social drama begins when someone breaks a rule (breach) in which sides are taken either for or against the rule breaker (crisis). Actions are then taken to repair the breach (redress). Successful repairs result in returning to the community as normal, while unsuccessful repairs result in separation from the group. This seems like a fairly linear process; yet for women on the carceral continuum, this process can be taking place on many levels at the same time and can easily place hope in crisis along the continuum.

13. Maruna, "Reentry as a Rite of Passage," 11–12.

ritualizes human confinement through practices that diminish a sense of humanity and give rise to a myriad of feelings that counter hope.

One question that emerges along the carceral continuum is this: What type of identity have I embraced and have others assigned to me because of my incarceration? Incarcerated women have difficulty breaking out of the box of other people's perceptions and expectations because they have somehow internalized these same perceptions and expectations. A person's sense of identity sometimes experiences constraints that impede her ability to become more than who others have named her to be.

A Shame-Filled Identity

The public censure and the disavowal that women receive from society because of their incarceration often leave permanent marks that become reminders of pain and guilt. Rituals of punishment, in fact, brand these marks into a person's psyche as well as the imagination of those watching. In the past, executions served as a public ritual. The executed received the marks of condemnation on their bodies; they became public spectacles that were intended to serve as a reminder to deter others from deviance.[14] Officials invited the community to the grand performance. The community could feel a sense of justice by watching those who committed crimes pay for their actions. In more recent years, punishment has shifted from the material reality of the body to the immaterial reality of the soul. In the words of Michel Foucault, "The expiation that once rained down upon the body must be replaced by a punishment that acts in depth on the heart, the thoughts, the will, the inclinations."[15] Even though punishment is less public, it is no less ritualized. The public gaze shifts from the body being a public spectacle of condemnation through execution to the courtroom scene, where criminal selves are placed on trial and sentenced for their crimes.[16] Not only is the behavior of the criminal placed on trial, so, too, is the criminal's soul.[17]

14. Michel Foucault, *Discipline and Punish: The Birth of the Prison* (New York: Pantheon Books, 1977), 8.
15. Foucault, *Discipline and Punish*, 16.
16. Foucault, *Discipline and Punish*, 9.
17. Foucault, *Discipline and Punish*, 18.

Trials function as a ritual of blaming. They publicly shift one's gaze toward a specific individual and hold them responsible for criminal activity. Rituals of punishment then escort persons into this diminished status, sometimes marking both the body and soul as condemned. Indigo confirms the impact of the courtroom conviction on her state of mind. *"Prison was a death sentence in my psyche,"* she says.[18] Blaming, in turn, shapes discourses around punishment.[19] Passing through the trial into prison is a ritual space that signifies loss of social spaces and a change in status.[20] In *Good Punishment? Christian Moral Practice and US Imprisonment*, James Logan describes alienation, even that which women on the carceral continuum might experience, as a consequence of sin, while also recognizing that the category of "criminal" assigns inferior status to those who have committed crimes.[21] It moves persons from the status of innocent and fully human to one who deserves punishment and is less than human.

Shame is the invisible cost of ritualized punishment and often lives beyond the public gaze. To escape shame in the face of false visibilities and a condemned self is difficult. Women on the carceral continuum experience this condemnation externally and internally, and it follows them even upon their release. One woman talked about how she kept shrinking back in public spaces because she thought people knew she had been incarcerated when they looked at her. Moral exclusion and shame led sociologist Harold Garfinkel to name punishment practices as "status degradation ceremonies" whereby a person's entire identity is shaped by these practices.[22]

Punishment rituals trigger internal misgivings, often resulting in the residue of shame. The feeling of condemnation and shame unfortunately robs women of hope. Particularly in the prison context, the assumption is that these women, labeled criminals, deserve to be exposed. Yet shame is mostly invisible. The exposed self is left in a perpetual

---

18. Indigo, interview with the author, March 21, 2014.

19. David Garland, *Punishment and Modern Society: A Study in Social Theory*, Studies in Crime and Justice (Chicago: University of Chicago Press, 1990), 68.

20. Catherine M. Bell, *Ritual: Perspectives and Dimensions* (New York: Oxford University Press, 1997), 36.

21. James Samuel Logan, *Good Punishment? Christian Moral Practice and U.S. Imprisonment* (Grand Rapids: Eerdmans, 2008), 26–32.

22. Harold Garfinkel, "Conditions of Successful Degradation Ceremonies," *American Journal of Sociology* 61, no. 5 (1956): 420.

state of hiding that which was exposed, even when that exposure is no longer evident.

The moral exclusion of prison is difficult, but the procedures done within prison scar a woman's humanity, leaving her (sometimes forever) in a state of crisis about who she is and who she can become. It also places her into a posture where she is constantly forced to prove her humanity.

A Stigmatized Identity

Punishment rituals come with clear consequences both for how we understand punishment and how we come to know those who have committed crimes. Not only do rituals of punishment rob women of hope in themselves; they also rob society of hope in these women. Rituals of punishment mark women in the public's eye, often causing society to limit their perspective on a woman's ability to be productive. An incarcerated or formerly incarcerated woman experiences this type of human arrest, where her very being is deliberately stunted and always in question. "Criminal" becomes part of her identity, rather than a time in history. In fact, society continues to place someone on trial even when she is released. She may have served her time, but she is forced to continue to pay for her crime. The burden of proof always rests on her to prove to society, her family, and faith communities that she is "better" or "productive." What makes this particularly difficult is that society not only places these expectations on formerly incarcerated people—but then also takes from them or denies them access to the resources they need to provide the evidence that they can be productive.

When people fail to reintegrate people into society in a way that enables them to obtain the economic and social capital necessary to make it through, they lose hope. Indigo remarks, "*As a community, you are creating a perpetual cycle of non-feel-good, despair, the opposite of hope when a person cannot pay the price for their crime and come out and say, okay, I have a fresh start.*"[23] Far too many times, women's anticipation for release spikes, yet they experience severe disappointment when they realize that they will remain barred from participating in society. Those who struggled with mental health before and during their incar-

23. Indigo, interview with the author, March 21, 2014.

ceration encounter the monster again, sometimes even having to fight off thoughts of suicide.

Criminality applied to one's humanity creates a type of identity that prevents incarcerated and formerly incarcerated persons from moving beyond the criminal act(s) they committed. Identity confinement places a person's humanity under lock and key. In this frame of reference, a person's being is static and unchanging. A person is the same today, yesterday, and forever. The fragmentary glimpse into a person's past becomes the truth by which society identifies incarcerated and formerly incarcerated women. It locks a woman in her mistake by emphasizing a fragment of her life, namely her criminal act(s), and applying it as if this is the "truth, the whole truth, and nothing but the truth." She is not her name but her Department of Corrections number. She is not her transformation but her murder or drug use or kidnapping charges.

The carceral stripping represents depersonalization, loss of authenticity, and loss of dignity and results in an ultimate loss of self that disrupts hope. Further, women's embrace of a carceral identity only alienates them even more from the possibility of forward movement. As long as women are under confinement within the criminal justice system and embrace a carceral identity, their identities are under threat. If they are not careful, the carceral identity will mark not only who they are—their being in the here and now—it will mark who they are becoming.

Restorative Hope Moves Us from Stasis

The question Nona raises after the physical clothes on her body are stripped is one of identity. *"Who are you"* once you've had your butt pulled apart and examined multiple times over? What Nona tells us is that one's identity must be more than what is happening with one's body in the current moment. One must not be left as a stripped body but must have the internal resources that enable one to remove oneself from that place, even if it's in one's imagination. In her words, *"you have to have somewhere else to go."*[24] Movement, whether physical, emotional, or imaginative, must transport women beyond the current circumstance so that the momentary experience of strip-searching does not leave them frozen in place with powerlessness.

24. Nona, interview with the author, January 30, 2015.

Reclaiming Agency

How do women move from powerlessness when the odds are stacked against them? Being out of prison brings a rude awakening when women are faced with the real social challenges related to the identity marker of "criminal."

> *So today I received a paycheck of $112, and this is hope for me. I got out of prison May 9th last year. I've not been able to find a job, and it's March 20th, and this is the first paycheck I've received since I got out of prison. And it's amazing. I'm pretty sure it's the least amount I've ever made in my whole life. But it's hope that there'll be more. In two weeks, there will be another paycheck; and it doesn't matter the amount. I get to tithe off it. I get to share from it. I get to put gas in the car and food, and I've been faced with some of those lacks. . . . For me, my struggle with coming out of prison has been mostly self-esteem type things. But the paycheck says somebody wants you to do a job. Somebody sees value in you and you're contributing and you're being productive. So even being able to be productive is hopeful.*[25]

Something as simple as getting a paycheck of $112 inspires hope, moving one from powerlessness. The money doesn't give hope: the sense of being a productive self does. In this instance, hope emerges when a person can see him- or herself as a contributing, productive citizen in the world.

When a woman leaves prison, she bears an incredible burden to prove she is a productive citizen. Participating in life in a meaningful way becomes a powerful way to restore a sense of agency. Yet it is also clear that such agency is not restored easily or at once. In her comments, Indigo describes this burden:

> *Hope is a fresh start. Hope is me saying, okay, you know what? I was a terrible money manager. I need to come out, reevaluate my skills, find a different skill set, don't deal with money. . . . I don't deal with money anymore, but I need to find a fresh start so that I can develop skills or utilize skills I already have to be productive and to give back to the community.*
>
> *But I don't have a fresh start, and that's what has been devastating for me in reentry[:] reentry doesn't give you a fresh start. I've been told no for jobs. I've been told no for housing. So I'm still incarcerated but free.*

25. Indigo, interview with the author, March 21, 2014.

I'm still in prison. Even the room in the old lady's house, which she was a Jewish lady, so unless I cooked kosher food I really wasn't allowed to cook in her kitchen, and so I was back in a room, and there were days I felt like I'm back in prison. Nobody has come to see me at that house and I've lived there about eight months now, because I can't receive company there, but that was the best living situation I could find for myself.

But the point is, if you don't allow me to work hard, yes, work hard and get a job, and get a place to live, then you have told me I'm in prison, and as long as I'm in prison, what hope do I have? This is permanently going to be on my record. You're telling me that permanently I will never have a fresh start? I will never get over my sins. It's the antithesis of what my faith reflects. You sin, you repent, God forgives. Community in the area of criminal justice should reflect that. There's no deity that doesn't forgive. So even with Catholics when you're supposed to do penance, I did my penance. So at what point do I get restored back to my community? If I'm not restored back to the community at large, how can I have hope?[26]

Re-crafting one's narrative upon release, for many women, includes confronting what it means to be "productive" in a society that limits where and how they can produce. This is particularly important in a society in which one's ontological value is more often quantified based on what one can earn and possess rather than on who one is. These values seep into the thoughts and hopes of women and begin to mark how they see themselves.

Restoring a sense of possibility in oneself often takes women's seeing themselves as contributing in a meaningful way to society, unrestrained by status and despite the pain and suffering that characterizes so much of life. Participating in society offers a woman an opportunity to move away from the labels or expectations placed upon her; it also offers her a sense of agency and the ability to reframe what it means to contribute productively in the world.

Reframing Productivity

The term *productive citizen* often denotes one's ability to work for pay. Unfortunately, that may not be an option for women who are

26. Indigo, interview with the author, March 21, 2014.

incarcerated or recently returned to society. Yet women also find new ways to describe their ability to contribute to the world. Laura, for example, does not perceive her ability to work a good job as her sole contribution to society. Rather, her confidence exudes from a deeper place—the essence of who she is as she interacts with others in the world. In other words, Laura centers her hopes on being a loving being. She commented:

> My hopes. I just want to continue—I don't know. I don't have like an aspiration. . . . I just feel I'm here to be a loving being, so that's my aspiration, to be a loving being. . . . There's no place that's associated with that. There's no title that's associated with that. There's nothing for me that's associated with that. If I end up being a loving being, being a janitor somewhere, I'm okay with that. If I end up being a loving being in a position somewhere, that would be great, too.[27]

In another interview, Laura speaks further about this theme:

> Once you've begun to realize things about yourself. You have to figure out how to maneuver with that information things that you've accepted about yourself. . . . Like with my family. . . . I'm a people pleaser and I wanted everyone to be good. That's just my personality. And I was always falling short, not because of me but because of their expectations, not my expectations. . . . So I had to release myself from their expectations, and I know the consequences of that is that when they call, I might not be able to run to their assistance. So I know they may feel X, Y, and Z. But I have to allow them to be who they are so I can be who the fuck I am.[28]

What stands out about these comments is the fact that Laura's sense of a meaningful existence is not based on a particular position but rather on a particular state of being. She bases it on her capacity to live according to her own standards. She admits that this is difficult, but she finds meaning in being who she is rather than an externally imposed identity. Hope arises from the possibility that meaningful existence can emanate from being one's authentic self wherever that

27. Laura, interview with the author, February 25, 2014.
28. Laura, interview with the author, March 16, 2016.

may be, regardless of position or title. It allows the possibility of re-framing meaning.

Reframing Meaning

Restorative hope describes the natural quest that humans undergo—the quest for meaning. Robert Kegan describes meaning-making as a human activity. He writes: "Meaning is, in its origins, a physical activity (grasping, seeing), a social activity (it requires another), a survival activity (in doing it, we live). Meaning, understood in this way, is the primary human motion, irreducible. It cannot be divorced from the body, from social experience, or from the very survival of the organism. Meaning depends on someone who recognizes you. Not meaning, by definition, is utterly lonely. Well-fed, warm, and free of disease, you may still perish if you cannot 'mean.'"[29]

To exist without meaning is almost like not existing at all. Frankl raises a similar question in *Man's Search for Meaning*.[30] He asks, Why say yes to a life in which human existence is constrained by pain, guilt, and death? Is there any inherent meaning in a life marked this way? By extension, is there inherent meaning in an incarcerated woman's life? His response centers on a person's ability to find meaning; he would even say that this is a person's entire motivation for existence.[31] When a person finds meaning, that person gets a glimpse of who she is and who she is becoming. In this sense, despair results not from the presence of suffering but rather from suffering without meaning.[32] One who cannot find meaning in life, perhaps, does not have a life worth living.

Authentic selves find a sense of meaning that is all their own, which enables them to fulfill the plot to their own narrative. Meaning and connection to a sense of purpose in life create the content for the plot. One's "will to meaning," or concrete meaning for one's personal existence, contributes to the agency needed to live out the plot.[33] Meaning lays the internal groundwork needed to sustain life amid hardship. If

29. Robert Kegan, *The Evolving Self: Problem and Process in Human Development* (Cambridge, MA: Harvard University Press, 1982), 19.
30. Viktor E. Frankl, *Man's Search for Meaning* (Boston: Beacon, 2006), 137.
31. Frankl, *Man's Search for Meaning*, 99.
32. Frankl, *Man's Search for Meaning*, 104–5.
33. Frankl, *Man's Search for Meaning*, 99.

one of a woman's primary purposes for existence is to discover meaning, it is no wonder why incarceration seems to confine one's humanity. Anything that threatens one's sense of meaning in life actually becomes a direct threat to her sense of being. Nevertheless, the disequilibrium that occurs internally as a result of incarceration tends to coalesce around meaning-making. In this space of existential questioning and meaning-making, one's authentic self is formed or is forced to emerge. For meaning does not occur on a "one size fits all" basis but is tailored to an individual and her particular narrative. The quest for meaning, in fact, is a being-in-process. To be clear, life presents challenges that may cause a woman to question her sense of meaning and place hope in crisis. Authoring one's life, nonetheless, is about making meaning of the circumstances in which one finds oneself. Put succinctly, "[wo]man should not ask what the meaning of [her] life is, but rather [she] must recognize that it is [she] who is asked. . . . Each [woman] is questioned by life; and [she] can only answer to life by *answering for* [her] own life; to life [she] can only respond by being responsible."[34] Thus, the task of a burgeoning authentic self is to hold fast and remain faithful to fulfilling one's personal quest for meaning. Frankl calls the task of remaining faithful "responsibleness," where one is always asking the questions "for what, to what, or to whom [she] understands [herself] to be faithful."[35]

The very act of reframing one's story is thus an act of restorative hope, an act in which people are invited to author their own narratives. Thus, an authentic self is rooted in this process of meaning-making that is both connected to the things around them and is also completely distinct and separate from the things and people around. In other words, hope within the framework of restorative hope "is not about the doing which a person does; it is about the doing which a person is."[36] Women who have learned to author their own lives refuse to accept society's expectations for their lives in exchange for their own.

34. I changed the gender to signify that the words also apply to women. Frankl, *Man's Search for Meaning*, 109.

35. Frankl, *Man's Search for Meaning*, 109–10.

36. Kegan, *Evolving Self*, 8.

Redemptive Possibilities

At the heart of centering hope on a person's potential is the understanding that we are all people on a journey toward becoming. Restorative hope values humans for who they are while also recognizing that humans are on a journey. This *human-in-process* perspective is the understanding that we are not today who we were yesterday, nor will we be tomorrow who we are today. Humans are not static beings. Our very human becomingness speaks of possibility and purpose. This perspective ultimately leaves room for a person's identity, both personal and communal, to change amid a world that is in constant flux. Rather than simplifying how one understands what it means to be human, hope embraces a more complex and nuanced perspective of anthropology. Hope does not discount sin, crime, or the capacity for someone to do evil. Instead, it recognizes that all humanity, whether incarcerated or not, participates in individual and systemic acts that can be deemed sinful, criminal, or evil, thus requiring a greater need for redemption for all humanity. All must see themselves as criminals in order to receive the beautiful act of redemption. Restorative hope tends away from focusing solely on discourses of personal responsibility and tends toward a discourse of second chances.[37]

When one sees possibilities for what others can become, new possibilities are birthed and pathways opened. Eden connects her birthing process with hope and second chances. Eden says:

> I was born dead. I was turned the wrong way, breeched. . . . I was just blue . . . and they were getting ready to prepare me a death certificate. But an old doctor happened to walk by and he looked. He heard the layman talking, and he said, "Well, this child is not dead." He picked me up . . . hit me about four or five times real hard, you see? And they said I leapt up. That was hope. That's an unusual thing of hope, but that was hope. That was hope in one of its greatest forms.[38]

The declaration that *beings* whom some may have declared dead are actually alive represents the importance of second chances.

---

37. Maisha T. Winn, *Girl Time: Literacy, Justice, and the School-to-Prison Pipeline*, Teaching for Social Justice Series (New York: Teachers College Press, 2011), 136.

38. Eden, interview with the author, April 17, 2014.

Whereas the facts may communicate death (i.e., the lack of oxygen), the truth may actually be another reality not yet realized. In this case, the truth was she perhaps appeared to be dead but wasn't, or that she was momentarily dead and needed to be quickly revived. She goes on:

> And hope, to me, also looks like this. I know the people that I lived with and the ones that I left in prison, there are some good people that would be good in society. So, even though it wasn't my plan to do reentry work, it has become my passion.
>
> Hope that we as human beings can see the larger picture is asking a lot, because there's so many things that's going on out here. But all I want them to see—and this is where my hope comes in—is see someone giving an honest second chance. And, that's not easy. That's not easy at all.[39]

Restorative hope is the belief that a person is always more than what you can see with your eyes. Even in the face of the most preposterous criminal actions, human hope leaves room for restoration in the very essence of a person's humanity. It embraces a human-in-process perspective that counters identity paralysis. To counter an identity that has been stripped, degraded, and fragmented, restorative hope recognizes humanity as resilient, authentic, and relational.[40]

Retrieving Self-Worth

Women in Eden's prison recognized the world and humanity as complex and imperfect. They embraced imperfection as part of life and learned

39. Eden, interview with the author, April 17, 2014.

40. The categories of *resilient, authentic,* and *relational* emerged from coding the manuscripts from the interviews conducted with research participants. During the coding process, I compared the manuscripts to search for consistent patterns or reoccurring themes that surfaced among them. When I noticed phrases or narratives that relied heavily on depending on and connecting with others, I coded that as relational. For phrases, repetitive words, or narratives that centered on being oneself or being able to realize one's full personhood, I coded that for authenticity. Lastly, I coded narratives and themes that centered on traversing through great difficulty as resiliency. Because all three themes repeated throughout all the interviews, I concluded that these themes were critical in building hope with women on the carceral continuum.

to see themselves through a lens of generativity rather than imperfection. Toward the end of her interview, Eden described precisely this internal transformation of self-worth: *"I told you when I looked in the mirror, I didn't see nothing but a reflection. Now, I see [Eden] when I look in the mirror. I see the creation of God. I see a strong woman that is a door to the hopeless."*[41] She describes her authentic self as one who has come to see herself clearly, both the good and the bad. Her self-image transformed from a reflection in a mirror to a *being* created by God with a specific meaning in life—to be "a door to the hopeless." When I then asked her what prompted her to see her authentic self, Eden responded:

> *Truth. Truth. Truth. I deal with a lot of people that they hadn't got to that point yet of truth. They don't deal with truth. . . . You see the good, bad, and the ugly. And you accept it. You change that which you can . . . when you fall that far you're bound to have scars, permanent scars. They don't go away. Permanent things don't go away. You live with them. And permanent scars have a way of reoccurring. They have a way of reoccurring, especially when you are getting a checkmark for a new lesson that you've learned.*
>
> *I'm just as good as the next person. There is no better than, there is no less than, and each one of us in the women, there's enough stuff in us to make a lady and a tramp. In a gentleman, there's enough in him to make a gentleman and a rogue. I've come to learn that. None is perfect but the Father. That's a beautiful lesson, Sarah, that a lot of people—some of us won't never learn that lesson. Forgiveness. We have to learn how to forgive yourself.*[42]

Forgiveness of herself demonstrates "the courage to accept acceptance."[43] This acceptance of self provides a shield against the labeling that dehumanizes and diminishes hope. In other words, her authentic self is grounded in the fact that despite the inadequacies of herself and others, and despite suffering in the world, her being is still one that has been created in God's image and thus her being is worthy of forgiveness and new life. An authentic self that knows what it means to be forgiven enables participation in healthy relationships with others. A person,

41. Eden, interview with the author, April 17, 2014.
42. Eden, interview with the author, April 17, 2014.
43. Paul Tillich, *The Courage to Be*, The Terry Lectures (New Haven: Yale University Press, 1952), 163.

nevertheless, becomes more hopeful as she is able to be her authentic self-in-community. In other words, as Greg Ellison argues, a hopeful self needs to be seen and heard.[44] This seeing and hearing typically occurs in relationship with others.

In prison, being seen and heard and hearing and seeing others fully happens in numerous ways. For Toya, her participation in the choir opened doors for her to invite others to glorify God with her, reaffirming the fact of God's presence dwelling within those who are incarcerated. For Nona and Toya, participating in the Certificate of Theological Studies Program provided a community where the human exchange of knowing and being known took place through writing, learning, and dialogue. Others found creating and sharing art to be a meaningful way both to contribute and to express one's true self. Participating in weekly chapel as a means to connect with God for some became a space in which to demonstrate their talent to speak or sing while also encountering God more deeply. All these ways shape women's perception of themselves and others in prison.

A carceral identity confines one's identity to society's expectations. These expectations influence how others ascribe value to women on the carceral continuum; they also influence how women internalize their own value and worth. Shame and stigma can take people captive, preventing them from being and becoming their best selves. Circumstances within prison create multiple instances in which women have to learn to move away from what they have been called or how they have been identified by society in order to experience a sense of hope. Falling victim to identity paralysis represents a real threat. As the examples throughout this chapter have demonstrated, in order for women to move forward, to experience hope, and to reclaim a healthy sense of self, they have to break free from a static existence. And women on the carceral continuum do break free. They reject shame and stigma. They abandon identity deprivation, taking small steps to reclaim dignity, agency, and worth through a renewed sense of identity.

44. Gregory C. Ellison, *Cut Dead but Still Alive: Caring for African American Young Men in Today's Culture* (Nashville: Abingdon, 2013), 90.

Self-Authorship and Agency

In carceral spaces such as the prison, it is easy for one's own voice to be muted when external voices dominate so much. Self-authoring is particularly important in contexts along the carceral continuum where authoritarian voices tend to be White male voices, or the voices of prison officers who are a paycheck away from being in prison themselves. Unlike parental voices, there is no guarantee that these external authority voices in prison settings have the woman's best interest at heart, nor is there any indication that their guidance is integrity-based.

Self-authorship enables the woman's voice to make clear determinations about her life—to regain control of the plot of her own narrative. Self-authorship pushes one to embrace an authentic identity by refusing to *be* under the authority of someone else's plot and narrative for one's life. While prison forces conformity in so many ways, self-authorship enables women to say "No!" to negative identity recruitment while also recognizing their ability to make conscious choices about their identities for the sake of survival. Everyone may not have chosen how their narrative began, but everyone has a choice about how their narrative can develop.

Identity, Hope Building, and the Prospect of Becoming

Hope shifts the question from What did you do? to Who are you? and Who are you becoming? It asks, Who am I? Who might I become? Hope sees the question of *being* as central to self-understanding and to one's own consciousness. To be human is to be complex. It is to possess the capacity to do great harm and great good. The paradoxical nature of the essence of what it means to be human beckons us to come to grips with the multifaceted essence of human nature. Embracing this complexity and living into one's authentic self is a way of embracing freedom.

When a woman cannot be her authentic self, she embraces a host of false selves. The constant performance of a false self may become a serious inhibitor in restoring hope in the possibility of becoming more. While women must perform false selves to survive, as Toya named, women must also find spaces in the prison to be true to themselves. Those spaces in which women feel like they can be themselves become restorative spaces that help women build and sustain a sense of self.

Women identify these spaces in a number of ways, including through exercise, cooking, choir, and the classroom. Exercise, for instance, becomes a way of maintaining control over one's body. The choir becomes a place where one can express oneself both socially and spiritually. Cooking becomes a way to invite others to a place of creativity and sustenance. The classroom becomes a place to enrich one's mind and demonstrate one's mental capacities to oneself and others. All these are powerful ways of transforming a woman's self-understanding while at the same time transforming how people might view her.

Further, this task of learning to be one's true self becomes critical as one reenters society. Not learning how and to whom it is safe to expose oneself can become dangerous. For most formerly incarcerated women, that means cutting off relationships that encourage them to live into the inmate codes on the streets. For Myeshia (whom we met in the previous chapter), that meant leaving behind friends who tried to get her to hustle. For Indigo, that meant recognizing her generativity even in the small amount of money she was able to bring into the house. Hope looks like small miracles that take place in the everyday lived reality of women on the carceral continuum.

Human confinement shuts down the possibilities of becoming more than we are by saying that we are who we will be, that there is no possibility of growth or change. Hope is grounded in the affirmation "I Am Because I Can Be Who I Am While Becoming Who I Will Be." The promise of becoming is hopeful in light of *being*-in-the-moment constantly moving toward a *being*-in-the-future. This future being is at once distinct from the being now but also the same being. Hope, on the other hand, affirms an open-ended process of becoming. It refuses to lock our identities in particular boxes based on our actions or current circumstances. Restorative hope affirms who we are while also pushing us to be who we will become. In this sense, restorative hope is rooted in the concrete reality of a person in the here and now while also being invested in the being-to-come. Restorative hope refuses to be constrained by and content with the boxes others impose on one. The affirmation of a safe, nonvolatile space does not motivate a person to become; the risk of losing oneself to the expectations and definitions of others motivates a person to become, and the possibility of not having a sense of meaning and purpose in life. Restorative hope does not accept the illusion that only a select few are in the process of becoming while everyone else has arrived at the limit of their becoming. Instead, the understanding that others are likewise in a state of becoming motivates hope for a world that can be different, as one makes meaning out of one's life.

Conclusion

Within prison, women are isolated from the things, people, and practices that made them who they were prior to incarceration. In other words, the practices used to sustain law and order usher a woman into a process of losing herself so that she becomes unfamiliar even to herself. To overcome hopelessness, she must overcome the threat of a static existence. The narratives of the women interviewed prove their ability to overcome, whether that means embracing a false, partial, or full sense of self. Women move beyond the crisis of identity loss and shame by finding creative ways to rebuild their identities. This identity-building ultimately restores hope in themselves and others. Hope is sustained and nurtured when women recover and reframe an authentic sense of identity that counters the carceral identity that incarceration seeks to impose.

CHAPTER 5

Theological Teaching in Prison

The Quest to Create Spaces of Hope

To restore hope entails curating space in which women are invited to be their authentic selves, to be in relationship to others in a life-giving way, and to be challenged to grow. Such space creates a context for resilience and for sustaining hope. Spaces in which a woman can appear, become, and connect are critical especially on the carceral continuum when she finds herself in a circumstance of intense existential questioning and meaning-making. Such spaces invite introspection, dialogue, and resources as means to help such women reframe their stories. Such spaces offer women a moment of noncarcerality.

For women who are subject to a constant and highly judgmental carceral gaze, the Certificate in Theology classroom in which I taught seemed to be one of the few places where they felt a sense of freedom to be themselves.[1] Why? Because in it women are actually seen; they are not just physically visible, but professors see and embrace their emotions, experiences, and possibility. Women do not have to embrace a carceral identity in order to survive; these spaces provide them the opportunity to be themselves. The pressure to embrace a carceral identity does not disappear, but the alternative space expands opportunities for women to be more authentic in the carceral context. Having spaces within the prison that give them something to put their hope in or to look forward to contributed to a sense of resilience and optimism. Course syllabi, then, became a way to communicate the possibilities of what we could explore together as a learning community.

---

1. Jennifer McBride describes her own experience teaching in prison in her books *You Shall Not Condemn: A Story of Faith and Advocacy on Death Row* (Eugene, OR: Cascade Books, 2022) and *Radical Discipleship: A Liturgical Politics of the Gospel* (Minneapolis: Fortress, 2017).

Course Outcomes as Beginning with the End in View

As in all my courses, on the first day of class I announce the course objectives listed in the syllabus. "By the end of the class, students should know Erikson's seven stages of psychosocial identity development," I say. These objectives center on the information I want them to gain from the content of the class. Following Western modes of education, I prioritize the mind and intellectual knowing.

Teaching in prison broadened my understanding of what to include in such objectives and desired outcomes. It opened my eyes to the fact that these students—indeed any students—bring more than their minds with them to each class: they bring their bodies, experiences, and emotions, too. If I measured success in this class according to whether a student left with theoretical knowledge about identity formation, then I as a professor would have missed something crucial about what each student brings with her into the space and takes from it. Rather than simply expecting them to leave with particular scraps of theoretical knowledge, I began to wonder, What if the classroom could be a place where success looked like people beginning to grow? What if the appropriate question is not What will my students know by the end of the class? but Who will my students have become by the end of the class?

Of course, I had always known that such formation mattered, but I had never explicitly claimed that I wanted my classrooms to form who my students would become because of my class. Teaching in the prison has helped me to shift the question of class objectives and outcomes from what I want them to know into who I hope they become as a result of taking this class. It has also prompted me to ponder what practices, patterns, processes, and course content I need to integrate into a particular course to orient students toward that telos.

So when I entered the prison classroom, I embarked on a journey of learning how to ask new questions and write new objectives for my class. My assignments thus had to align with these new objectives, creating spaces in which students felt they could freely explore, discover, and revise who they are and who they are becoming. Students' explorations and revisions of themselves opened my eyes to the enormity of their task.

Creating a Space for Identity (Re)Formation

The assignments for my reenvisioned course invited students to reflect on their identities and the lived experiences that have shaped them. Shantel's, Jane's, Lesley's, and Christina's poetic explorations are representative.

Trapped Inside My Mind

Why am I not the alright person?
Is this not the right time?
I forgot who I was.
I must find me again.
This isn't who I am.
My life, my love, my dreams.[2]

During class, Shantel illustrated through her poem what it feels like to be lost, to be in a place of despair and hopelessness, to be unsure of who she is and is becoming. Her declaration is about finding herself again. Finding oneself restores hope. For her, the classroom created a space where she could find herself.

"What have you learned in this class about your identity that you did not know before?" I therefore asked students in the course evaluation. They responded:

- "I learned not to be shy, but to open up more and go after my goal to help teenagers."
- "I learned about my parents [after reading *Becoming Abigail* by Chris Abani] and the struggle with grief she experienced after her mother's death. I have struggled with my identity for the last thirty-five to forty years."
- "Before this class, I never really did any soul searching. Lately, I've been trying to figure out what events in my life have made me, me."
- "I learned that there are parts of my identity that I was covering up.

---

2. Shantel [pseud.], "Trapped Inside My Mind," Exploring Spirituality and Identity course, prison in Atlanta, Certificate in Theological Studies Program, October 26, 2012.

I knew about my gifts and talents, but tapping into the experiences and circumstances that make me . . . *me*."

In short, the course enabled each woman to be introspective and thus to develop and hear her inner voice amid the competing voices in the prison. Course dialogue, readings, and activities prompted the question, What makes me *me*? Assignments helped students to explore their inner selves. One assignment, for example, invited students to walk down memory lane. It tasked them with bringing to class something to illustrate their most formative memory. Women shared about grandma's biscuits and bedtime prayers. They also shared about divorce, death, love, and loved ones. These were the memories that shaped and made these women who they are. Exploring these memories helped them respond to the question, What makes me *me*?

As a site of identity formation, teachers in the classroom do not convert or form students in their own image; rather, the classroom becomes a place in which students can explore their own identity as it is, and as it is becoming. In her exploration, Jane, a student in the prison classroom, conceives of herself as a memory:

When I Am Only a Memory

I sit there next to God looking down at all the people that loved me. I want so much for them to know I'm safe and sound with God in heaven. All the things I did in my life—helping teenagers that was facing time, preaching the Word of God. Remember me is all I'm asking. Remember the good I did. All the lives I saved. How much it meant for me to be there for someone's child that was facing time. Being there every step of the way. Remember me.[3]

Such powerful and touching introspection sparked another assignment. I asked my students: "How do you want to be remembered when you die? What type of legacy do you want to leave behind? When others talk about what you are like once you are gone, what types of things do you want them to say?" These were among the prompts I gave them to write their own eulogies. My instructions included the following:

---

3. Jane [pseud.], "When I Am Only a Memory," Exploring Spirituality and Identity course, prison in Atlanta, Certificate in Theological Studies Program, October 26, 2012.

Writing and delivering a eulogy is truly an honor. It is an opportunity for you to bring the deceased person back into the minds of those in attendance. Your words will paint a picture of the deceased through the memories, anecdotes, and the stories you tell. A eulogy allows the audience to remember the person—who they were, what they did, and what they enjoyed about life. In this activity, you are not writing about someone else; you are the person you are sharing about.

Students eagerly engaged the eulogy-writing activity. Once completed, I invited each person to share her eulogy in front of the class, which they likewise did eagerly.

Eulogy Assignment Example 1

She was a mother, a wife, a poet, a friend.
Loyal and true until her final end. She made a lot of mistakes.
And caused so many heart aches.
She found forgiveness for all her wrongs.
And found a way to express it in song.

(Song break—in class, she would sing a melody as she presented)

The timing was perfect for her to go.
But now she's in Heaven.
This we know.

(Song break—in class, she would sing a melody as she presented)[4]

Eulogy Assignment Example 2

Dear Mama,
I once had a home in you, until I was evicted that November.
It's true. Your sixth child . . . leaving behind a world of warmth . . .
Mama, I was lost until I got found! I was mute, but I got sound!
And when I was a prodigal, went up and down, and laid in that pig's pen with nobody around

4. Lesley [pseud.], eulogy, Exploring Spirituality and Identity course, prison in Atlanta, Certificate in Theological Studies Program, December 14, 2012.

I prayed to heaven, and touched his crown. My smile lifted from the ashes of my frown. I got liberated. No longer bound. To be, eternally in the warmth of peace. My tomb is another womb, but I'm born again . . .[5]

Time and Identity Formation Intersect

When I first crafted the assignment, I was simply inviting the women to explore who they wanted to be. Writing a eulogy, I thought, would be an interesting way to explore what matters most to them in their lives. I wanted the assignment to remind them that their past need not determine their future. But as the women began to present their eulogies to the rest of the class, I realized much more was happening: the activity became a space for them both to reflect on and to share their authentic selves within their learning community. The women not only reclaimed their pasts through these assignments; they also reauthored their futures. They used the assignment to confront their past selves, affirm their present selves, and claim ownership of their future selves, all at the same time.

Teaching in prison made me acutely aware of the way in which sites of identity (re)formation create space for a person's past, present, and future to intersect. These moments of intersection offered these women a sense of agency over their lives, an opportunity to choose how they would show up in the world. They were in an active process of writing and learning their future into being.

Class as a Space of Contemplation for Self-Knowledge and Formation

One of the benefits of prison is that it can be a setting for one to reflect on one's life. This is especially so in classrooms that expect students to engage in introspection and reflection around course material. As Kaia Stern notes in her research on prison education with men, introspection can be a faith act that reminds incarcerated persons of their dignity and provides a sense of freedom.[6]

---

5. Christina [pseud.], eulogy, Exploring Spirituality and Identity course, prison in Atlanta, Certificate in Theological Studies Program, December 14, 2012.
6. Kaia Stern, *Voices from American Prisons: Faith, Education and Healing* (New York: Taylor & Francis, 2014), 146.

Contemplation represents the process of the self *knowing* the self more genuinely. Contemplation may be characterized as a "theology by heart," whereby the self gives primacy to the interior life in its quest to establish and maintain a solid internal foundation.[7] Amid the voices that compete for one's attention and loyalty, contemplation attends to the often-muted voice that yearns to become comprehensible to the self. The emphasis on reflection and contemplation is really an invitation to become intimately acquainted with oneself and so to become authentic. As educator Maxine Greene reminds us, "To be yourself is to be in process of creating a self, an identity. If it were not a process, there would be no surprise. The surprise comes along with being different—consciously different as one finds ways of acting on envisaged possibility. It comes along with hearing different words and music, seeing from unaccustomed angles, realizing that the world perceived from one place is not *the* world."[8]

For some women, the Theology Program offered a context in which, in response to my invitation, they could develop and clarify their sense of their selves and their emergent voices.

Coming to Know Oneself

My role in the classroom is invitational: I invite learners into the process of meaning-making within the learning environment. I'm less interested in finding out, What did you learn from what others have said or from the reading you read? and more interested in learning, How are you coming to understand and make meaning out of what you have heard and read in this class? How does this new understanding fit into your world? This approach recognizes that learners are not only coming to know the content; learners are also coming to know themselves in relation to the content.

To be clear, sometimes the process of coming to know oneself can be messy. One comes to know the good, bad, and ugly that marks the condition of being human. For example, in a prison focus group conversation we were talking about identity and self-image, and Laura began to share about her own process of becoming comfortable with who she is. She

7. Elaine L. Graham, Heather Walton, and Frances Ward, *Theological Reflection: Methods* (London: SCM, 2005), 18.

8. Maxine Greene, *Releasing the Imagination: Essays on Education, the Arts, and Social Change*, Jossey-Bass Education Series (San Francisco: Jossey-Bass, 1995), 20.

said, "*I'm a people pleaser and I wanted everyone to be good. That's just my personality. And I was always falling short, not because of me but because of their expectations, not my expectations. . . . So I had to release myself from their expectations.*"[9] Critical to this act of becoming more authentic and developing a sense of voice is this process of differentiating herself and her own standards from those of others. To become authentic is not to become perfect but to be on a quest to become more whole, honest, and transparent with and about oneself. In a sense, that is also a quest to be more just with oneself.

Women in my course named injustice in a variety of ways and places, including in journal entries, informal conversations, and class dialogue. The act of naming injustice in a system like prison that is fundamentally unjust is a manifestation of resistance. However, what stood out to me more than anything was not the critical knowing around structural injustice within the criminal justice system; it was the critical knowing about themselves and their circumstances. They claimed knowledge about the difficult things in life, and they faced those hard truths courageously.

Education that invites imperfection into the classroom space reinforces the idea that humans are always engaged in a process of becoming. In other words, the story of one's life is not complete but continues to be written. In what ways might the classroom become a safe space in which to fail? A safe space in which to transform failure into growth?

Restoring Hope through Self-Authorship

Hope serves as a robust pedagogical lens by which to clarify who we are and how we become. Hope manifests in the movement from being a person formed by others to being a person formed by one's own sense of self. It is the process of moving from one state of being to another that produces integrity in one's identity. The underlying question in restoring human hope in pedagogy is, In what ways can we invite the person's essence into a learning environment that both affirms who she is but also challenges her to become who she can become? Through restorative hope pedagogy, I propose that hope manifests through processes of self-authorship as students actively engage in creating themselves.

---

9. Laura, interview with the author, February 25, 2014. See her full comment in chapter 4 on p. 120.

The question of authorship becomes particularly important in prison settings that reinforce human confinement. Carceral settings tend to operate on an "obey what I tell you to do, believe what I tell you to think, be who I say you are, and imagine only what I say is possible" basis. To be immersed in a setting in which external authorities are the primary means by which one is expected to organize one's experiences and shape one's identity has severe consequences for one's formation. However, when such persons are immersed in prison learning environments, they find some room and some permission to engage in a process of becoming. That process of becoming entails differentiating what they believe about themselves, others, and God from what others have told them to believe. Self-authorship emerges from a human hope that refuses to remain content and constrained by others' expectations.

To illustrate human hope amid threats to confine one's being, I draw on Marcia B. Baxter Magolda's theory of self-authorship. *Self-authorship,* a term first coined by Robert Kegan and then expanded by Baxter Magolda, is a constructive-developmental approach to meaning-making and the development of self.[10] I resonate particularly with Baxter Magolda's theoretical framing of self-authorship which goes beyond the cognitive developmental approaches to self-authorship and takes seriously the relational and circumstantial impact of external influences in the making of self. Self-authorship, she says, is "characterized by internally generating and coordinating one's beliefs, values, and internal loyalties, rather than depending on external values, beliefs, and interpersonal loyalties."[11] In other words, self-authoring people assume responsibility for their thoughts, emotions, and actions.[12] Baxter Magolda's theory, like my own, understands the interlocking influences that contribute to the development of an inner self. Epistemological (How do I know?), intrapersonal (Who am I?), and interpersonal questions (How do we construct relationships?) are key questions to which learners respond on their journeys to self-authorship.[13]

10. Robert Kegan, *In Over Our Heads: The Mental Demands of Modern Life* (Cambridge, MA: Harvard University Press, 1994), 185.

11. Marcia B. Baxter Magolda, Elizabeth G. Creamer, and Peggy S. Meszaros, eds., *Development and Assessment of Self-Authorship: Exploring the Concept across Cultures* (Sterling, VA: Stylus, 2010), Kindle location 137.

12. Baxter Magolda, Creamer, and Meszaros, *Development and Assessment of Self-Authorship*, Kindle location 137.

13. Marcia B. Baxter Magolda, *Making Their Own Way: Narratives for Transforming Higher Education to Promote Self-Development* (Sterling, VA: Stylus, 2001), 3–8.

Learners move from following external formulas that others (parents, prison authorities, etc.) have given them to a transitional space (known as the *crossroads*) in which learners seek to integrate the self influenced by the expectations of others with the self influenced by their own values. At the crossroads, learners see a need to develop their own values but are not quite ready to do so. From this transitional space, learners move toward self-authorship. Self-authorship refers to the phase in the journey toward self-knowing in which learners choose their own beliefs, values, and identity, rather than necessarily mimicking external influences.[14]

Because self-authorship is grounded in the work of a being coming to voice, self-authorship is a manifestation of hope. Self-authorship represents the process by which one becomes. To be an author of one's life refers to a person's ability to make decisions about her own life based on her internal voice rather than seeking to accommodate to others' demands. In other words, to be an *author* of oneself is to take *authority* of one's voice, one's identity, one's relationships, and one's narrative. This reclamation of self-ownership shapes one's life trajectory. Self-ownership and self-authorship refer to the realization that while several external influences may contribute to who one is and is becoming, it is the author who has agency about who and how others will contribute to her life. It is the author who chooses how she will be seen and will see herself.

Meaning-Making as a Means to Self-Authoring in the Classroom

In the following poem, Sherry expresses her journey toward such self-authorship and self-ownership by realizing what it is that gives her life meaning.

Trapped Inside Myself

Ah, I feel like givin' up 2 day, NUMB
Yeah, empty
I feel like givin' up, But LUV
TRAPPED INSIDE MYSELF—LUV
Episodes of reality

14. Baxter Magolda, *Making Their Own Way*, 71–105.

Get 2 ME
Loose ME, LUV
Life's raw deals feels calloused
My worthlessness
TRAPPED INSIDE MYSELF—LUV
Zeroes feel nothing—NOT A 'THANG'
But pain, divided LOVE
Deadened pain
ME, A body battlefield of landmines
Cuts, scars of past abuse
In time, ooze—moan luv
The WAR, TRAPPED INSIDE MYSELF
Dreams scream Luv's silent cry
A silent cry 4 ME
NO ONE here hears!
But LUV, Trapped N-side myself
LOVE—echoes, Love ME, LUV U
Sings Love MEEE 2
Trapped inside myself
LUV's echoes blast a claim & survive the
Shame game 2 blame, LUV
Life ain't bad I L-O-V-E-S ME
Mad, sad, bad
LOVE TRAPPED N-Side, ME
ME! Myself
The think tank 2 live
ME, I motivate myself Luv
Power, strength
Trapped inside myself
Even hurt, I survive
LUV
Choose, change, Xcept
I challenge LOVE
2 maintain, sustain, 2 recognize ME
LUV
UC the Love jewel my,
Inside, shining light
TRAPPED INSIDE MYSELF

LUV, courageous
Victor of the mind battle
4-self release, cleanse, re-do ME
TRAPPED INSIDE LOVE 4 ME,
L.O.V.E.S. U
Feel thoughts of LOVE hugs
Recall feelin' LOVES snug joy
NEED 2 LOVE[15]

Educators have a unique challenge in working with learners who have been socialized to believe that only external authority figures have voices worth hearing and following. To assist learners to come to voice, educators first need to help those learners to know themselves; for to understand and value one's internal self are key tasks in restoring hope. Assignments that invited students to participate in artistic activities were particularly helpful in encouraging them to express their true identity beyond that of their prison number, to become more fully visible to their professors and classmates.

The results of two assignments in particular stood out to me. One is from a woman who remained incarcerated at the time of writing, while the other was the work of a woman who participated as an interviewee. The first is a letter written to a young girl. The incarcerated woman describes to this imaginary girl how she's been where the girl is. Having been locked up for sixteen years, since the age of seventeen, she tells the young girl she wishes she had had someone to talk to at the point at which she encountered her challenges.[16] The letter then tells some of the lessons the woman has learned while incarcerated. The wisdom shared in the letter could itself be an avenue for transformation for young girls. The letter is generative. The words of encouragement, transparency, and hope shared in the letter embody resistance against the criminal justice system. They are an attempt to reroute the pipeline away from prison.

Another response to an assignment is a poem written by Sherry entitled "Trapped Inside Myself." In the poem (above), Sherry writes about feeling

15. Sherry [pseud.], "Trapped Inside Myself," Exploring Spirituality and Identity course, prison in Atlanta, Certificate in Theological Studies Program, October 2012.
16. Because this woman is still incarcerated, I cannot share many details of the letter.

"NUMB," "empty," and "like givin' up." "But LUV." Love seems to be the force that repeatedly intervenes as she experiences "life's raw deals" and her own "worthlessness." Love motivates and encourages her to survive.

These examples illustrate the ways in which practicing art unearths one's own capacity to survive. As students created art, this class seemed to allow the artists to feel themselves, to recognize gifts in themselves and others, and to participate in a process that helped heal past hurt. Given the chance to reflect on and contemplate their lives, women in the course essentially made new meaning about themselves and their experiences.

Been, Be-ing, and Becoming in the Quest for Meaning

Meaning-making is the work of the interior self; thus, it is important for educators to acknowledge inner formation as critical to restorative hope pedagogy. Meaning-making is a significant ontological aspect of self-formation. It protests against human confinement and stagnation and announces a self that is open to formation and more developed meaning-making capacities. Says developmental psychologist Robert Kegan, "The activity of being a person is the activity of meaning-making. There is thus no feeling, no experience, no thought, no perception, independent of a meaning-making context in which it *becomes* a feeling, an experience, a thought, a perception because we *are* the meaning-making context."[17] Truly, meaning-making cannot be separated from the self who is becoming; meaning-making drives how a person experiences and makes sense of the world. At the same time, meaning-making is complex, for a person can identify her socialized self and enact agency even while she herself is being co-constructed with the world and relationships around her.[18]

Restorative pedagogy enables learners to resist the tendency simply to submit to authority—in this case that of the teacher. Instead, restorative hope pedagogy encourages learners to develop a sense of personal integrity that enables them to exercise agency and authority over their own selves, and over the thoughts and decisions that the self makes.

17. Robert Kegan, *The Evolving Self: Problem and Process in Human Development* (Cambridge, MA: Harvard University Press, 1982), 11.
18. Kegan, *Evolving Self*, 32.

Educators invite learners into the process of meaning-making within the learning environment.

Self-authorship is ultimately a process of coming to see, know, and be oneself in a way that creates inner peace. Restorative hope pedagogy encourages self-authorship by creating spaces of theological reflection and contemplation. Critical to the development of self-authorship are periods of reflection so that a person (in this case, students) can integrate her experiences with what she is coming to know about herself and the world. Concrete practices of such reflection and contemplation include journal writing, spiritual autobiographies, and letter writing, as well as the aforementioned eulogy assignment. Such "turn-life-into-text" forms of writing become a "living human document" on which the self can reflect.[19] A self that is more grounded can be critical of competing voices while also being discerning of her own voice. This moves ontological valuation from the hands of others to one's own hands. One no longer measures one's being against other people's standards and values but against one's own internal standards.

While people are constantly making meaning throughout the day, contemplation provides an opportunity for one's internal voice to rise above the other voices that seek to impose meaning. Contemplation provides space in which to listen to one's inner self and to discern the things that matter most in life. Acting on one's discernment—self-authorship—is based not solely on cognition or one's consciousness: rather, such self-authorship focuses on building a solid internal foundation so that a person learns to listen to and trust her own voice amid external influences.[20] Contemplation builds an interpersonal intelligence and enables a person to understand their self so that the self can function effectively in the world.[21]

Though people might associate it with mystics and mysticism, contemplation is no disembodied experience. To have a strong internal foundation means embracing one's whole self—body, soul, and spirit. To this end, one's ethnic and cultural identity becomes a critical frame for restoring hope.

19. Graham, Walton, and Ward, *Theological Reflection*, 18.
20. Baxter Magolda, *Making Their Own Way*, 155–91.
21. Howard Gardner, *Multiple Intelligences: New Horizons*, rev. ed. (New York: Basic Books, 2006), 9.

As part of self-authorship, a woman learns to name herself, her beliefs, and her contexts. Each student becomes more conscious of her
ethnic identity and her body, using both as resources to know herself
more intimately. In turn, this leads to increased self-definition, self-
determination, and self-awareness, all of which provide her with the
internal resources to differentiate between the multiple selves that she
has created to obtain approval from parents, teachers, and peers. To
practice self-contemplation is to learn to be alone with oneself so that
one can discover who one is most fully. Such contemplation and discovery enable a student to reposition her consciousness, so that she regards
her body as an embodiment of hope.

Now, many of the women I interviewed are Black, and such a
bodily difference can easily lead to self-fragmentation. The fact that
Black bodies and Black consciousness still exist in a world that has
attempted to exterminate all forms of Blackness is astounding. The
resilience of Black existence transcends confinement. Contemplation
creates opportunities for fragmented selves to regain or restore their
coherence and integration. For the goal of self-awareness is not an
elevated sense of self but a more grounded and true self. This is particularly important in situations of danger and death, like prisons, as
Eden narrates next.

Creating a Space of Resilience and Resistance
against Death by Being Self-Aware

Several of the women I interviewed openly named injustice as part of
their coming to self-awareness. Doing so armed them with the resilience
to fight against injustice in the world. Critical knowing helps inform
this type of resistance. Non-critical knowing feeds into selves that are
complicit in their own dehumanization, while critical knowing informs
people about the odds stacked against them.

> Of my culture, of me being an African American, I understand that foul
> play was involved in the beginning. Yeah, yeah, I do, and that's very im-
> portant. And I'm not just talking about slavery. I'm talking about the things
> that has been set in place for control. Having that knowledge gives me an
> opportunity to persevere against it.

> *When I was younger and participated in that schematic, that scheme of things, when I say that scheme of things, it was as if well, you come out the ghettos, and something is supposed to happen to. . . . A perfect example, I can bring it up to speed today. Now they are testing children, African American children, and according to those test scores they're building prisons. I know you've heard about that. I'm not making it a color thing, I'm just telling you there are certain things that's in place that it only upgrades, it doesn't go away, and knowing that gives me reason to persevere from a knowledgeable perspective and not just to prove anybody wrong, but to prove that it's okay, that it's okay to live. No, I don't go around holding no banner being no . . . trying to . . . I don't have any points to prove. It was just a knowledge [that] will allow you to be able to work in an area where your awareness is up, and you understand what's going on, you understand the permanent scars that you've chosen for yourself, the gulf . . . where you are like a leper.*
>
> *You've set yourself apart from people [by] the choices that you've made, but you can change even that. You can't take that record back. You can't take that decision back. But you can create a life. . . . It's okay to live and let live. I can't hate you because your choices were better than mine. Whatever your choices were, they were yours, and whatever my choices were, they were mine. And we can coexist.*[22]

Eden pointed out that before understanding how the system worked, she actually participated in the system; now, however, she recognizes some of the structural patterns that contributed to incarceration, poverty, and injustice—hers and others'. One clear example of these structural patterns is the relationship between education and prison; those who fall into the "nonknower" status (on the basis of the testing she mentioned) are already deemed lost or prison worthy, often long before they have committed any crime. She uses this newfound recognition of racist structural patterns not to sidestep accountability and responsibility for choices she has made, nor even to prove the system wrong, but to "persevere against" the system.

Eden's ability to name injustice in the world as well as her place in it is a skill—of critical knowing. It is clear from our conversations that Eden, like many of the women interviewed, would attribute her capacity

---

22. Eden, interview with the author, April 17, 2014.

for critical knowing to some of the prison education programs where contemplation and meaning-making were central aspects of the course. Critical knowing includes not merely knowing about the system but learning from one's mistakes. This type of learning that produces critical knowledge of how to respond to the issues of life is significant for both personal and social transformation. For upon release, Eden actively shared this critical knowing with others to help build resilience and perseverance in others and ultimately to put them on a different course than the pipeline to prison. Eden clearly believes that if people become more critically aware, they may make different choices. Thus, restorative hope pedagogy embraces critical knowing as a way to build resilience against suffering in the world. What Eden shared about herself, her world, and her agency in the world demonstrates a critical knowing that emerges from hope and self-authorship.

Chapter 2 identified resilience as the ability to bounce back and sustain oneself despite and through difficult circumstances. Resilience is a protective factor that often generates a sense of well-being and hope.[23] It is, as Nancy Lynne Westfield describes, "about mastering the terrain of the oppressive context so well that one re-creates and heals the self in the midst of chaos. It is mastering the ability to see oneself in a life-affirming light while the world around would shroud her in a shadow."[24] Hope, then, includes simply choosing to live and be in a world that is unstable, unjust, and often unkind. This embodied resilience, particularly in the lives of women on the carceral continuum, seems to be most alive when women decide to resist death and persist in life. Such resistance to death makes bold claims against and in spite of the social and emotional death that seems so prevalent against women's bodies and lives.

It is difficult to pinpoint specific things that build resilience, especially within education. Further, whether resilience is an inborn personality trait or something someone learns over the course of encountering great difficulties is still a matter of dispute. However, the women's comments reveal that one can form a sense of resilience when

23. George A. Bonnano, "Loss, Trauma and Human Resilience: Have We Underestimated the Human Capacity to Thrive After Extremely Aversive Events?," *American Psychologist* 59, no. 1 (2004): 20–28.

24. Nancy Lynne Westfield, *Dear Sisters: A Womanist Practice of Hospitality* (Cleveland: Pilgrim Press, 2001), 8.

one has critical knowledge about structural and personal situations that make hope precarious amid crisis. Having such critical knowledge can then prompt a person to embody resilience and weather her challenges. Within restorative hope pedagogy, resilience emerges organically when persons are able to author their human-being-ness in relationship to self, God, and others. Further, critical knowing is an epistemological resource from which restorative hope pedagogy can draw in pursuit of embodying resilience.

Critical Knowing as a Tool for Resilience

At the heart of resilience is a deep desire to respond to hardship by drawing on the life-force one has within oneself. Besides that, awareness of injustice (or critical knowing) can often elicit from a person a response to combat such injustice. Critical knowing means more than just head knowledge; it also requires the capacity to "read" the world—to decode the world and systems in the world, including one's place within that situation.[25] When learners know and understand their world, they have a better chance of using their voices to name their (unjust) world, and of doing something about it. The Theology Program, for many of the women in the course, prompted critical knowing through the dialogue that took place in the classroom. This dialogue featured content from course material but also invited women to share from their own personal narratives. In the words of liberation educator and critical pedagogue Paulo Freire, "Dialogue is the encounter between humans, mediated by the world, in order to name the world. . . . Those who have been denied their primordial right to speak their word must first reclaim this right and prevent the continuation of dehumanizing aggression. If it is in speaking their word that people, by naming the world, transform it, [then] dialogue imposes itself as the way by which they achieve significance as a human being."[26]

To name the world, particularly in the context of a learning community, is an act of resistance. It counters the muteness that marginalized selves are taught to maintain. The act of naming, then, facilitates both a critical

---

25. Paulo Freire, *Pedagogy of the Oppressed*, trans. Myra Bergman Ramos, 30th anniversary ed. (New York: Continuum, 2000), 87–134.

26. Freire, *Pedagogy of the Oppressed*, 88.

knowing of oneself and a critical knowing that the learning community can claim as a whole. The task of teachers is to create this space in which students can name, reclaim, and ultimately voice their protest against the backdrop of paralyzing silence or a silencing society. When learners share their voices, their truths, and their perspectives, they shatter the unconscious identity confinements that we as teachers and students ascribe to persons in the learning community. Multiple shared voices in the learning community open the door to consider the complex nature of humanity and the interlocking influences, including one's own perception of others, that detain other selves and their action upon the word.

Critical to this idea of naming is voice. How teachers navigate voice in the learning community is therefore of primary importance. Those who invite voice into the learning space can use voice as an entryway into understanding the vast racial, economic, and structural injustices experienced by learners in the room.

Critical pedagogue Peter McLaren provides resources for thinking about the different voices that appear in the learning environment. He suggests that voice refers to "the cultural grammar and background knowledge that individuals use to interpret and articulate experience."[27] In the context of critical knowing, voice refers to the development of consciousness and authorship in institutional and structural settings.[28]

Voice, as a pedagogical concept, relies on its situatedness in history and culture as mediator; in other words, one's voice depends on interaction with others. McLaren claims that there are three voices that are heard in learning environments: the school's voice, the student's voice, and the teacher's voice.[29] The student's voice mediates and forms reality. Critical knowing positions one's heart and imagination toward hope. McLaren explains: "Hearts gesturing toward hope create an arc of social dreaming; that is, such a gesture amounts to hope bolstered by critical reason and that turns on action; it is a hope bound to a vision of what could be possible, a vision fired by righteous anger. It is a vision that accounts for the totality of capitalist exploitation yet does not become totalizing in its own right."[30]

27. Peter McLaren, *Life in Schools: An Introduction to Critical Pedagogy in the Foundations of Education*, 4th ed. (Boston: Allyn and Bacon, 2003), 245.
28. McLaren, *Life in Schools*, 247.
29. McLaren, *Life in Schools*, 245.
30. McLaren, *Life in Schools*, 297.

Critical knowing refracts the world by disrupting what has tacitly been accepted as normal.[31] More than an act of imagination, it is an act of reimagination. It promotes students' and teachers' reimagination of their relationships between each other and in the world. It reconstitutes power relations by naming the way in which ideologies have configured selves in favor of perpetuating the status quo—a status quo that favors some and ignores others. The reconfiguration of self, then, happens when someone's heightened consciousness has come to a critical recognition of the forces of oppression and when that person has come to recognize the possibility that she herself can be a builder of just futures.

As a professor, the prison classroom taught me to grasp for critical knowing. It is not only a way of knowing that I hope will inform my students' ways of engaging the world: I also want critical knowing to inform my engagement with students in the classroom. Within the prison, this means demonstrating genuine care for students in the classroom as well as being receptive myself to the care students offer. It means calling students what they want to be called rather than simply what the prison says they should be called. Sometimes, it means advocating for students beyond the classroom. It means referring to students as "theologians" rather than simply as "students." It means understanding that we are all one decision away from doing something that could land us in prison right beside the women in my classroom.

Critical knowing enables us to name the globalized oppression at the intersection of race, class, gender, and sexuality by identifying the structural injustices and hegemonic ideologies that normalize the submissiveness and inactivity of marginalized bodies, voices, and modes of knowing. In oppression's place, critical knowing calls people who have been oppressed to become actors on this grand stage of history by unmasking the character of various "-isms" that would rather remain hidden. Critical knowing rejects the claim that systems, including dominant epistemologies, are value free and neutral and instead identifies these frames of reference as actors that have often been working behind the scenes to rig systems and situations for their own benefit. Critical knowing calls into question America's metanarrative that deems some humans to be protagonists, heroes, leading actors in life and others to be merely "supporting" characters or "extras."

31. McLaren, *Life in Schools*, 257.

Critical race and womanist pedagogues are committed to using race as a central organizing framework for identifying and naming some of the practices and policies that teach learners to marginalize particular bodies and ways of knowing.[32] Critical knowing, then, is not just about recognizing structural injustice; it's also about coming to conscious awareness of one's own biases and prejudices, which impede deep connections and perpetuate the status quo. In other words, critical knowing is just as much about unlearning as it is about learning. The unlearning that inherently takes place in hope-filled and self-authoring spaces requires hard truths to be declared. Those who speak these truths about the structures of injustice may be the very ones others fear. These painstaking truths may be difficult to hear, but typically they are also the truths most likely to cause transformation. This is not new knowledge in the academy.

In the midst of a long struggle, womanist voices, Black theological voices, and other religiously and socially marginalized voices are still carving out space at the table. The academic community has often provided such voices their own space, in an effort to create the appearance that they are listening, rather than make room at the existing table of academic and theological discourse. Why this reluctance? Because to bring their scholarship to the table calls into question the very epis-

32. To remain within a particular scope, I want to acknowledge but not provide a robust analysis of these critical race pedagogues whose work helps shape the conversation in educational arenas. These scholars have much to offer to the thinking and rethinking of religious education: Bryant Keith Alexander, *Performing Black Masculinity: Race, Culture, and Queer Identity*, Crossroads in Qualitative Inquiry (Lanham, MD: AltaMira Press, 2006); Michelle Fine, *Off White: Readings on Race, Power, and Society* (New York: Routledge, 1997); Keith Gilyard, *True to the Language Game: African American Discourse, Cultural Politics, and Pedagogy* (New York: Routledge, 2011); Stephen Nathan Haymes, *Race, Culture, and the City: A Pedagogy for Black Urban Struggle*, Teacher Empowerment and School Reform (Albany: State University of New York Press, 1995); Zues Leonardo, *Critical Pedagogy and Race* (Malden, MA: Blackwell, 2005); Glenda MacNaughton and Karina Davis, *"Race" and Early Childhood Education: An International Approach to Identity, Politics, and Pedagogy*, Critical Cultural Studies of Childhood (New York: Palgrave Macmillan, 2009); John T. Warren, *Performing Purity: Whiteness, Pedagogy, and the Reconstitution of Power*, Critical Intercultural Communication Studies (New York: Peter Lang, 2003); Lois Weis and Michelle Fine, *Construction Sites: Excavating Race, Class, and Gender among Urban Youth*, Teaching for Social Justice Series (New York: Teachers College Press, 2000); Menah A. E. Pratt-Clarke, *Critical Race, Feminism, and Education: A Social Justice Model*, Postcolonial Studies in Education (New York: Palgrave Macmillan, 2010).

temological, axiological, ontological, and methodological assumptions that higher education in particular and a carceral society in general espouse. To avoid this challenge, the academy mutes the voices of particular scholars and types of scholarship and makes invisible particular bodies. Yet as critical knowers, these voices continue to raise questions. Their questions serve as a sociopolitical tool of hope that promotes awareness, accesses new possibilities, protests compliance, and explores the self.[33]

This critical knowing manifests, for example, in womanist theological and pedagogical discourses around hope. Womanism represents the multiple and at times richly contradictory voices of many Black women in the academy. Black women, in particular, had to be creative to develop new strategies to become and to be heard in the midst of dehumanization. Thus, womanists took on the "rigorous intellectual exercise [of] defining, determining, defending the Black women's revolution of self-actualizing in a death-dealing context."[34] They became self-authoring in a theological enterprise that had always sought to author them. The intellectual rigor invested in differentiating the womanist voice from the normative White male theologians, from White feminists, and from Black male theologians expanded the modes of knowing that Black women and other bodies could engage within the academy. Their survival and expansion into third- and fourth-wave womanists demonstrates that womanists have successfully written themselves into historical repertoires of theological discourse. Notwithstanding the oppression dealt by a carceral society, a womanist epistemology of hope integrates an ethical consideration of care for self and other; this knowing has the capacity to care even for those who have oppressed them.[35] Hope, in this sense, manifests in womanists' ability to provide spaces of epistemological hope for Black women while also inviting those who have typically "othered" Black bodies or womanist modes of knowing into a theo-epistemological revolution of wholeness. Womanists also helped open up the conversation for the primacy of the body as an epis-

33. Nancy Lynne Westfield, "'Mama Why . . . ?' A Womanist Epistemology of Hope," in *Deeper Shades of Purple: Womanism in Religion and Society*, ed. Stacey M. Floyd-Thomas (New York: New York University Press, 2006), 137.

34. Stacey M. Floyd-Thomas, "Introduction: Writing for Our Lives—Womanism as an Epistemological Revolution," in *Deeper Shades of Purple: Womanism in Religion and Society*, ed. Stacey M. Floyd-Thomas (New York: New York University Press, 2006), 3.

35. Westfield, "'Mama Why?,'" 134–35.

temological resource for knowing. Overall, the vast body of pedagogical resources that underscore the importance of critical knowing affirms a key aim of restorative hope: to prepare resilient beings that are open to and pressing toward social and personal transformation.

Critical Pedagogies as Nurturing and Sustaining Hope

As a teacher in prison, I therefore frequently made space in which women could reflect and share. One of the most transformative moments in one course was when the generative theme of suicide emerged. Bar one, every incarcerated woman in the course had either attempted suicide or engaged in activities of self-mutilation to gain some type of control over the pain they encountered on a daily basis. In fact, one student shared how she and seven of her cousins had made a pact to complete suicide before they turned eighteen. The obituary she brought to class reminded her of these seven funerals that were held in her church. That day in class was the first time she had ever told others of the pact. Doing so made her realize that she was alive! After she had told her story, a thick heaviness shrouded the classroom as woman by woman shared their battle scars. As the sharing came to a close, the heaviness was still there. I invited the women to stand and, as a community, to embody some of those suicidal feelings. I invited everyone to look around, and then to move from that position of embodying suicidal feelings to one that embodied life. We discussed what it felt like physically to move out of that position. At this moment, I reminded the women that they are survivors. We realized that the movement helped shift the atmosphere. It helped invite a spirit of life back into the classroom.

In response to this moment, I then asked the students to complete an impromptu assignment: to create an anthology of writings that spoke directly about and to their narratives of resilience and survival. I realized they had something important to share with others who might be entertaining thoughts of suicide. Because they were still alive, I wanted to know, "How did you make it through?" "What would you say to other young girls who may be wrestling with the same thoughts?"

Several of the poems acknowledged that suicidal feelings and ideation often left one feeling trapped. For example, Toya shared a poem about this wrestling match between death and life in a poem entitled "Trapped Inside."

Trapped Inside

Why do I feel trapped inside my tears?
My tears, my emotions, my pain,
I try to hide.
In whom can I confide?
I take strokes of hurt and anguish in strides,
Grieving like someone just died,
Why do I have to hide
Behind my pride?
Thoughts of suicide consuming my mind.
Do I want to live or die?
I can't try . . .
I won't decide.
Who will decide?
Am I yours or mine?
The devil's?
Christ's?
Who paid the price
For this
Thy life?
Is it all in my mind?
A reason to live
I cannot find.
Who wants to turn back the hands of time?
Water to wine
Hard to define
Why . . .
I die everyday on the inside.
Life is cruel
Like a rising tide.
Death is peaceful like a solemn ride.
Why in this life do I abide?
Oh, how I've cried and cried . . .
Why God?
Oh why do I want to die?
By and By
By suicide . . .
Bound and tied . . .
Chained . . .

Side by side . . .
The grave is deep and
Oh so wide.
A coffin inside my soul resides
Is it your lifeless body trapped inside?
Once you decide whether you want to live or die,
Just remember after your death,
Many others will cry
And cry
And wonder why you didn't try . . .[36]

Lisa responded to her with a poem called "Open Your Eyes."

Open Your Eyes

I know how you feel.
I've been there before.
Lonely, sad, and dark.
Trapped behind a door
Of your mind,
Which has kept you from seeing a way out.
Keeping you locked inside
A world of fear and doubt.
But you can't give up.
You're truly not alone.
There is a God in Heaven
Who sits on a throne,
Who loves you more than you know.
Death, destruction, loneliness and demise
Are not what he wants for you . . .
Open your eyes!![37]

In another poem, Laura invites those who might be experiencing the same feelings to awaken to a new awareness about the many blessings that exist around them:

36. Toya [pseud.], "Trapped Inside," Exploring Spirituality and Identity course, prison in Atlanta, Certificate in Theological Studies Program, November 9, 2012.
37. Lisa [pseud.], "Open Your Eyes," Exploring Spirituality and Identity course, prison in Atlanta, Certificate in Theological Studies Program, November 9, 2012.

To Be

"Don't miss out on your blessings,"
I heard someone say.
I closed my eyes.
I dared to ask.
Is there a particular time or place
I'm supposed to go to wait for them?
I decided not to ask.
I opened my eyes.
A homeless man sitting on a piece of cardboard.
His beard, salt and pepper with a hint of brown.
Unkempt.
His hair, a tangled heap of curls.
His eyes, a dark and mysterious blue.
There was a scruffy dog, spotted,
with his head comfortably laying on the old man's lap.
His tail wagging almost effortlessly
to the beat of the saxophone
coming out of the battery operated, static laced,
handheld radio laying beside him.
Sitting
Enjoying the beautiful music,
fully experiencing the sunlight on their bodies.
The rat race around them continued.
A businessman in his finest three piece suit
hurried by, rushing off to his meeting,
Preoccupied with the details
of his looming presentation.
He didn't feel the sun.
He didn't hear the music.
Dare to be the music causing them to listen.
Dare to be the sun causing them to feel.
Cause them to open their eyes and see.
Dare to be heaven.[38]

---

38. Laura [pseud.], "To Be," Exploring Spirituality and Identity course, prison in Atlanta, Certificate in Theological Studies Program, November 9, 2012.

Despite the difficult questions they raised in their writing, God's activity resonated as a predominant theme in it. We created an anthology for the course that we titled *Learning to Live: Rethinking Suicide*, in an effort to reflect this. The purpose of this anthology as part of the Exploring Spirituality and Identity Course through the Arts was to give the women a space to engage critical reflection and then to offer a generative voice to other young women who may be having similar thoughts of suicide. While I did not set out to assign this type of activity, the act of creating space for my students to share their experiences resulted in something more substantial in our learning community and seemed to demand some kind of creative follow-up assignment. Note how the assignment I gave was not centered solely on what they knew but also on what they could offer to others.

Overall, participating in the Exploring Spirituality and Identity course gave students an opportunity to build their confidence in a way that contributed to a sense of stick-with-it-ness or resilience. Laura, who for the first time ever wrote a poem in this course, talked extensively about how she saw the transformation that happened in our classroom. She shared that she saw *"transformation in other people's view of themselves, like where at one point they may have come in with this bad stuff, and then in the midst it's like something happened."*[39] She went on to speak of how she thought the course had prompted a process of transformation in a student she knew well. She shared, *"I saw like a happiness in her when she was talking about her artwork. I saw like when people appreciated it and people were like that's awesome, I saw like a boost of something in her, even though she might go back and complain about her shitty circumstances, just for that moment, I still saw that boost in her."*[40] In this sense, the very act of participating in art—art-making and art-sharing—countered her circumstances so that, in the moment, she could experience a boost. These boosts contribute to resilience; they proclaim life and resist death, at least for that moment. They are meaning-making experiences. Indeed, critical knowing takes place when participants have an opportunity to name injustice or when observers have an opportunity to become critically aware of a grace that transcends pain, even for a moment.

39. Laura, interview with the author, February 25, 2014.
40. Laura, interview with the author, February 25, 2014.

Faith Formation, Spaces of Resilience, and Metaphysical Knowing

What was particularly significant for one student named Sherry was the practice of drawing, a skill that was reawakened through her participation in the Theology Program. Drawing, she shared, has sustained her throughout her incarceration, enriching both her faith and her imagination. She perceives drawing as an actual weapon with which she fights. Her real battle, she shared, was on behalf of her family: "*I feel like I incarcerated my family.*" The impact of incarceration on families results in women's guilt and shame. For Sherry, drawing became a means to navigate her own guilt of the impact of her incarceration on her family, a way for her to fight on behalf of her family.

In particular, she talked about how the Exploring Identity through the Arts course enabled her to open up. She tended to draw scriptures in order to visualize them. She described one image of a woman wearing armor. She communicated that looking at the completed art helped her gain insights. She said, "*You don't actually see God, but the winner. It helped me remember my place and where God is in the picture.*" She continued, "*It doesn't take a large person to win the battle.*"[41] As evidenced in the imagery, Sherry saw herself as resilient warrior capable of winning this fight called "incarceration." Overall, she says, "*The Theology Program helped a lot because [until I took it] I never really knew I was standing on faith.*"

For Sherry, like others, the Certificate Program became a space in which she could expand her imagination and faith. "*The Theology Program was wonderful and happened at the perfect time. It really put me back into studying and understanding the Word for myself. It put me back into self-reflection, and it was wonderful. It put me back on track in my prayer life and study of the Word.*"[42] Connection to God ultimately increased her resilience in the face of the difficulties of incarceration and separation from family.

The courses provided an opportunity for women to explore their faith. In prison, faith can quickly become a weapon against the carceral system.[43] What I mean is that women find connection to God in ways that empower and infuse them with strength to persevere against the

41. Sherry, interview with the author, January 3, 2015.
42. Sherry, interview with the author, January 3, 2015.
43. Stern, *Voices from American Prisons*, 148.

system and to see themselves differently within the system. This is particularly the case when they have an opportunity to discard harmful images of God and embrace new ones. Several of the women talk about how the classes in the Theology Program help them explore their image of God and challenge some of the religious doctrines and traditions that had confined them in the past.

Sherry's narrative reminds us that not all knowledge is rational. Intuition, memory, imagination, and faith play a role in how one comes to know. While these metaphysical epistemologies are often deemed uncritical, in fact, in regard to one's ability to hope these sources of knowledge are critical. Most closely related to this idea of metaphysical knowing is the concept of existential intelligence. Although originally termed "spiritual intelligence," Howard Gardner shifted the language to "existential intelligence" in response to his own inability to talk in depth about the content of such intelligence.[44] Within existential intelligence, questions about one's humanity, the nature of God, death, and life emerge. According to Gardner, existential intelligence refers to "the capacity to be able to locate oneself with respect to the furthest reaches of the cosmos—the infinite and the infinitesimal—and the related capacity to locate oneself with respect to such existential features of the human condition as the meaning of life, the meaning of death, the ultimate fate of the physical and psychological worlds, and such profound experiences as love of another person or immersion into a work of art."[45]

Metaphysical knowing is also an activity of the whole self, even though it privileges understanding the unseen.[46] While Gardner cannot adequately explain the "spiritual" or mysterious in concrete terms, he values its existence as a significant form of knowing. To discount this knowledge is to discount countless mystics and those embodiments of hope that have been the bedrock of diverse religious traditions. In other words, this mode of knowing does not have to legitimize itself; it exists with or without approval from dominant modes of knowing.

Metaphysical knowing draws on resources outside the self to understand the deep meanings of life. In this sense, intuitive-spiritual

44. Howard Gardner, *Intelligence Reframed: Multiple Intelligences for the 21st Century* (New York: Basic Books, 1999), 53–54.
45. Gardner, *Intelligence Reframed*, 60.
46. Gardner, *Intelligence Reframed*, 54.

knowing takes precedence over detached forms of cognitive knowing.[47] Overall, to acknowledge that there are other modes of knowing that contribute to our experiences and feed into how we come to hope is critical in restorative hope pedagogy. This is particularly significant for those teachers who understand what they do as a sacrament that mediates the holy.[48] Whether the teachers serve as an embodiment of metaphysical engagement or intentionally invite God's Spirit into the space to engage with students on their own terms, they clearly draw upon resources outside of themselves to help embolden the teaching and learning moment. Within religious education, it seems central to the task to acknowledge the metaphysical as a resource for knowing and for connection that influences teachers, students, and the learning environment itself.

Creating Space for Connection in the Classroom

One of the markers of incarceration is isolation. In contrast, connection is a marker of hope. The Theology Program counters carceral isolation by providing spaces in which women can connect with each other and those (from the) outside. These connections within the class invite women into a space in which they can share their authentic selves and become agents that construct knowledge. As evidenced in chapter 4 with the interaction between one of the participants in our program and the death-row inmate, connection with one another inspired hope. Also, witnessing the humanizing impact of the Theology Program on her fellow inmate created a desire in the death-row inmate for that same type of connection. In this particular case, once Nona got into the program, she never received another disciplinary report. The program itself did not make her choose to refrain from activities that would get her a disciplinary report; she made this decision herself. She chose participation in this learning community rather than the isolation that she had previously experienced in lockdown. Connection is a human desire that pedagogies of restorative hope fulfill.

47. Norman Harris, "Afrocentrism: Concept and Method," *Western Journal of Black Studies* 16, no. 3 (1992): 154–59.

48. Mary Elizabeth Moore, *Teaching as a Sacramental Act* (Cleveland: Pilgrim, 2004), 30–31.

Connection: Authoring the Self-in-Community with Others

Community is often a context in which a person can develop and claim her sense of self and her emergent voice. While it may appear that I have made the primacy of self central to self-authorship, my understanding is much more nuanced than that. Self-authorship requires contemplative and communion-oriented practices; however, self-authorship also requires a communal context in which a learner claims her voice. Having voice is significant apart from others; yet it becomes even more relevant and transformative in interaction with others.

Self-authorship pays particular attention to strengthening one's internal voice rather than simply listening to the external voices around. To possess a strong inner self makes learners better participants in the mutual construction of knowledge that happens when all learners make meaning. As Carol Lakey Hess notes, beyond simply self-expression (although important), voice refers to "the ability to express oneself *and* the right to be heard; it means knowing one's mind *and* will and trusting that one can express oneself in one's community. Voice is one's feelings of 'presence, power, participation, protest, and identity.'"[49] To disregard and dismiss a person's voice is to disregard and dismiss what a person knows, how a person sees, who a person is, and the possibilities to be transformed by that person. To trust one's own voice and to understand that voice as a meaningful contribution to the world is critically important in this formative phase of the self-in-community. The communal affirmation that the learner and her voice is significant, however, also contributes to the process of self-authorship. Being in community does not mean that dissenting selves won't emerge from within the community; instead, the self remains assertive in her truth-telling, humble in her truth-seeking, and assured in her truth-sharing.

Yet there is more. Authors do not simply write themselves into being; they also write the world into being. Their lives help shape history and the metanarrative of the world. Their lives become words against the backdrop of a larger narrative that they are helping to shape. In one sense,

---

49. Carol Lakey Hess, *Caretakers of Our Common House: Women's Development in Communities of Faith* (Nashville: Abingdon, 1997), 69, quoting S. Reinharz, "Toward an Ethnography of 'Voice' and 'Silence,'" in *Human Diversity: Perspective on People in Context*, ed. E. J. Trickett, R. J. Watts, and D. Birman (San Francisco: Jossey-Bass, 1994), 183.

a person's life is a text that continues to be written. The author decides which main characters will be a primary part of her plot and how the main characters respond to the major events that take place in her life. Considering that one narrative life intersects with other narrative lives lends itself to an intertextual reality—that our lives always affect the lives of others. We are constantly being written into the stories of others as we engage others with our lives. In this sense, self-authorship presumes an intertextual authority, where one not only writes one's own life into being but also helps as others seek to revise and reenvision their lives.

One's voice enters the class when educators welcome the narratives of learners into the space. As learners engage in storytelling, story-linking, and sometimes the process of re-storying, teachers and the learning community listen attentively. The process of articulating voice is formative, not only because it illustrates a self-in-the-making but also because it demonstrates a world-in-the-making. Teachers partner in the process of self-authorship by creating spaces that welcome the learning community to engage one another in authentic, life-giving ways. The learning space becomes sacramental by mediating the presence of God and by making the God-in-others more visible. To claim one's own life as not fixed is one thing; but to claim one's own being as an artist who can bring color to a dull and bleak reality opens up a whole other world of possibilities where one can see, know, be, and do in the world differently.

Connection: Restorative Hope as Relational Knowing

Because restorative hope promotes connection rather than individualism and competition, we must name the importance of relational knowing that undergirds restorative hope pedagogy as an epistemological resource. Restorative hope pedagogy views relationships as a significant epistemological resource for the construction of knowledge and new meaning. The primacy of relationships in restorative hope pedagogy recognizes that being in community offers a way to access and sustain hope in the midst of crisis. Relationships ultimately contribute to the knowledge of self, knowledge of other, and knowledge about subject matter by enabling persons to know themselves apart from others while also knowing themselves in relationship to others. According to Gardner, relational knowing represents an interpersonal intelligence that enables one to understand other people and how they work in order to employ that knowing in relationships.[50]

Relational epistemology assumes that we come to know things subjectively. In other words, we come to know what we know from within various contexts. Multiple perspectives help verify what we know. To know others in relationship apart from one another requires some degree of differentiation. Relationships provide a significant context in which learners can differentiate themselves (their thoughts, philosophies, practices, and essence) from others. This differentiation from others is not a way to privilege autonomy and individualization over dependence and community; instead, it values the unique self that brings diversity to a space. This unique self becomes "iron [that] sharpens iron" in the midst of a community of other unique selves. Those in relationship are willing to ask hard questions that provoke new insights and lead to new structures for meaning-making. Being around other beings helps one become clearer about one's own sense of self while also challenging oneself to become more. In other words, to know oneself is to be oneself in the midst of community. This birth into a more formed self manifests human hope within the context of relationship. When two beings engage in dialogue around a particular subject matter, they approach each other from their respective epistemological standpoints; this epistemological standpoint shapes the content of dialogue and provides the milieu for a robust discovery of new meanings. The fruit of their engagement is new or more clearly defined ways of looking at the subject matter, as well as new ways of seeing the other. The task of the educator, then, is to encourage diversity and difference rather than uniformity and fused selves. As persons come to know themselves more clearly, they also have the opportunity to know others more clearly, and this clarity often precipitates encounter.

Connection in the Prison Classroom: A Learning Activity

One activity in particular demonstrates a communal encounter that occurred in my Identifying Spirituality through the Arts course. What I observed throughout the course is that this "I see you" and "I hear you" dialogue emerged organically when women shared their art with the class.

50. Gardner, *Multiple Intelligences*, 9.

The understanding that testimony reaches out for a sacred community undergirded the design of the session entitled "Establishing a Sense of Identity in Contested Spaces." In response to four significant questions, the women created identity maps. They responded to the following set of questions: (1) Who do I say I am? (2) Who do others say I am? (3) Who does God say I am? And (4) How do I want others to see me? Following their identity maps, we gave each woman the silhouette of a face. Their task was to draw eyes on the face that reflected their response to the questions above. The guest visual artist made connections between the "eyes" and the "I," feeding into a paradoxical understanding of visibility. Namely, how others view us may be completely different from how we want them to see us and ultimately how we see ourselves.

After they completed their identity maps and drawings, we asked each person to share her visual art, using the four questions as prompts. What stood out to me about this session is how the students yearned for a response from the class. They did not merely want to present what they thought about themselves; they wanted verbal responses from the class of how the class perceived them. When an adequate response was not given, the women actively sought the community's response by asking them questions about the community's perceptions of who they are. Out of all the sessions, this session of call and response became one of affirmation, vulnerability, and confidence-building. After this session, I noticed the ways in which the confidence of particular students increased. One student was so inspired by the words of the learning community that she overlaid her journal with eyes. When she showed the journal to me, she just smiled and shared the transformative impact of the class session on her confidence.

Ultimately, the performative aspect of sharing art became complete for the women when the community affirmed it. Even more than an affirmation of the art, it served as an affirmation of the reality of the experiences and transformation that each woman named in her art. Within the prison, surveillance complicates this idea of visibility. Not only are they always aware of being visible to their peers, they are hyperaware of being seen by the guards. The paradox, however, is that their peers and the guards can see them physically but are not able to see them holistically. Performing testimonial-art and sharing it enabled a more holistic visibility. Ultimately, it was the acknowledgment of being seen and heard as more than bodies in beige jumpsuits that allowed the women to see and hear themselves more deeply. In other words, the practice of sharing art created a communal encounter as a result of which they felt free to share their authentic selves with others who also shared their authentic selves.

This form of relational epistemology invites unique selves into conversation with one another and results in new forms of consciousness that welcome new ways of seeing subject matter and subjective selves. To find common ground offers opportunities for collaboration in the struggle for a more just society. Relationships help mediate hope in a learning environment by providing affirmation, accountability, and a stage on which to rehearse agency. Communal encounter places learners in contact with others so that connected knowers gain empathy in a way that shifts and expands how they perceive one another.[51]

The competitive nature of Western pedagogies sometimes prevents the formation of genuine bonds in the classroom, blinding learners from seeing the deep dissonances and resonances in others as a resource for knowledge. Further, the desire to avoid conflict in the classroom may lead to silence and disengagement rather than an invitation to grow and learn. Instead, Western ways of learning teach difference and disagreement as a negative that needs to either be converted or denied value. Restorative hope pedagogy counters this perspective by seeing disagreement as an entry point into deeper engagement with the subject matter or person. Practices of critical visibility, empathy, hospitality, and respect in the learning environment become key factors in avoiding stagnation and distance in the learning community when difference and conflict emerge. Seeing-the-self-in-the-other while at the same time seeing-the-self-as-uniquely-other enables people to come to know people, places, philosophies, and practices differently.

Conclusion

Like us all, women who are incarcerated desire to connect, love, grow, be creative, and develop. The theology classroom curated spaces of connection, resilience, creativity, and identity formation that enabled women to do exactly that.

---

51. Mary Field Belenky et al., *Women's Ways of Knowing: The Development of Self, Voice, and Mind*, 10th anniversary ed. (New York: Basic Books, 1997), 115.

Conclusion, Implications, and Future Research

Where Do We Go from Here?

I have explored how hope functions in the lives of populations in confinement, specifically women on the carceral continuum. I defined *restorative hope* as a way of seeing, knowing, being, and doing that takes seriously the present and future possibilities for personal lives and the world. Building on these insights, restorative hope pedagogy is a broad-based learning rooted in how we see, know, do and be in a world whose hope is in constant crisis. My conclusions have been developed from the ground up—from descriptions and illustrations by individuals who have been incarcerated and are (largely) now released. Due to the exploratory nature of this study, I highly recommend further studies that build on these insights about hope, prison education, and transformative pedagogy. This final chapter begins with a summary of the major implications from this study and the contributions it makes to thinking about how we offer theological education. It concludes with some questions raised by the study and suggestions for future research.

What images invite us to see women on the carceral continuum in a holistic way? There must be other images for these women besides the heroic reintegrated citizen.[1] Dreams besides the "American Dream" must inform how we measure success. If the only image of reentry that women see is an image of heroic reentry, to which very few returning citizens have access, then we reproduce a sense of hopelessness for women on the carceral continuum. Given the many tasks that are seemingly impossible to overcome, even small achievements are "suc-

---

1. Robin Steinberg, "Re-Entry for Dignity and a 'Productive' Life," lecture, Shepherd Higher Education Consortium on Poverty Symposium, Virginia Military Institute, Lexington, VA, July 31, 2017.

cess." A woman getting a job and staying at that job is a measure of success. A woman figuring out how to get all her fines paid on time with a job below minimum wage and still getting a car is success. But ought we to measure success by achievements that most people would not be able to accomplish easily, like obtaining housing, transportation, and employment with a livable wage? If not, by what ought we to measure success—by what we see from the women or by how well the society to which she returns reintegrates her?

To be clear, my notion of seeing is not privatized. Nor is my understanding of hope. What we see and how we see are interdependent. Moreover, hope requires society to see women on the carceral continuum differently. In other words, it's not only women on the carceral continuum whose imaginations ought to move away from failed visions and move toward possibility. Society should also be moving in this direction, learning to see the world as it could be, learning to see such women as capable and generative citizens.

Society's movement toward seeing women as generative citizens opens the possibility of building connections that help nurture resilience. Myeshia's story of dogged resilience highlights this layer. Resilience does not operate on its own but emerges from other foundational supports. In this case, connection and resilience work together to build and sustain an *endurance* that allows Myeshia to move forward despite the circumstances. The connections with her friends, God, her former chaplain, a benefactor, and a local ministry, alongside her own sense of authenticity, create the inner fortitude to endure and adapt in her process of reintegrating back into society.

While Eden admits that hope is not without challenge, she clearly states, "*I could have quit a long time ago and just say whatever. But that's not an option for me. I see hope in us sitting right here. It's educating you, yes for your school, but it's educating you as a person, that there is a possibility that a person that has been incarcerated can be utilized out here.*"[2] Eden identifies hope in the interaction that takes place when one learns to see an incarcerated person differently. One's seeing incarcerated persons differently has implications for the impasses they encounter. Society's seeing differently perhaps can move society to a place where it is more willing to remove the collateral consequences, which present impasses

2. Eden, interview with the author, April 17, 2014.

and make it impossible for women on the carceral continuum to move in the world.

To speak of the collateral consequences women face after prison invokes Shelly Rambo's theology of remaining.[3] By highlighting trauma, Rambo sheds light on the pain and suffering that often go unnoticed. While she is referencing the aftermath of violence, I want to draw attention to the aftermath of incarceration. Women's experience of freedom and reintegration into society is not typically an experience of death to resurrection; rather, it is an experience in which suffering remains.

Overall, the women I taught in prison and interviewed for this book did not describe hope's development as a linear process that took place over a predetermined set of time in a predetermined way. Instead, hope developed in a cyclical way; hope went through seasons of highs and lows. The driving force behind hope is its fundamental reorientation toward life, in which one is moved either from a place of stasis or from a downward orientation toward a life-giving orientation and toward life itself. In other words, hope is not just a movement toward and against something that is of this world; it is also a movement toward self-transcendence.

The indomitable nature of the human spirit, revealed in the stories of women along the carceral continuum, shatters arguments that locate resilience in mere creativity or sheer determination. Resilience combines the best of multiple forms of connection that enable women to resist and persevere. It also draws attention to the seemingly impossible task that awaits women at several points along the carceral continuum. Resilience is part of life. But the type of resilience that's required for those on the carceral continuum is an act of repeated navigation that women have to revisit as they pick up the pieces of their lives.

Implications for Restorative Hope: New Directions

This research seeks to understand the concept of hope more deeply. The work of refining the perception of hope beckons researchers to ask questions about the things that really matter in people's everyday lives. Three primary implications emerge about the nature of restorative

3. Shelly Rambo, *Spirit and Trauma: A Theology of Remaining* (Louisville: Westminster John Knox, 2010), 1–8.

hope: that restorative hope is holistic; that restorative hope is rooted in both the here and now as well as the not yet; and that restorative hope creates space for identity formation, connection, and resilience.

Restorative Hope as Holistic

The restorative hope lens acknowledges that one's experience of hope is intricately connected to one's very humanity. Thus, when crises emerge that affect one's sense of human-being-ness, such as the physical, social, maternal, psychological, and spiritual crises named in chapter 1, the whole self faces severe threats to hope. Because these existential crises deal with so many aspects of the self, it is important to recognize the existential nature of hope. Hope is not simply a function of the mind but includes the way women see, know, are, and live life. Seeing, knowing, being, and doing participate in a dynamic integrative process that must be seen in connection with every other aspect.

In doing so, I've pressed toward a holistic understanding of hope that takes seriously the multidimensional needs of all human beings. Behavioral psychologist Abraham Maslow helps us to think about human needs holistically. Maslow's hierarchy of motivational needs can be divided into physiological, safety, social, esteem, and self-actualization components.[4] Maslow places these needs on a hierarchy whereby the lower-level needs (such as safety and physical needs) must be met in order for people to fulfill the higher-level needs (such as self-actualization). In later years, Maslow even added the motivational need for self-transcendence over and above self-actualization; *self-transcendence* takes into account a person's need to connect to something beyond the self or to engage in altruistic behavior.[5] Theories of human need emphasize the importance of taking into account one's needs from a holistic perspective; the body, soul, and spirit of a person are equally

4. Abraham H. Maslow, "A Theory of Human Motivation," *Psychological Review* 50, no. 4 (1943): 370–96. Please note that there has been intense criticism of Maslow's hierarchy of needs in recent years. I plan to publish on these concerns in relation to the needs of incarcerated women. However, for the sake of this book, it is important to know that these "universal" needs exist and sometimes drive the motivations of individuals.

5. Abraham H. Maslow, *The Farther Reaches of Human Nature* (New York: Viking, 1971), 259–69.

important and should be equally cared for in order to experience sub-jective well-being. This subjective well-being is closely related to experiences of hope. This more holistic approach to hope gives a way for us to view hope as an intervention along the carceral continuum that helps to build resiliency and grit in tough circumstances. Restorative hope creates possibilities for the whole self. The concept of restorative hope, then, encompasses tending to and seeing the whole person—body, soul, and spirit. It counters tendencies to view women as just their behavior or just their experiences or just their *you name it*. Instead, it recognizes that our lives are on a continuum, and that a variety of internal and external stimuli affect how we are and where we are in the process of becoming who we are.

For many scholars, the "where we are" for women on the carceral continuum has to do primarily with one's ability to desist from crime. In *Making Good: How Ex-Convicts Reform and Rebuild Their Lives*, criminol-ogist Shadd Maruna notes significantly that the "where we are" can be measured by how returning citizens see and speak about themselves in relation to the future. Maruna never uses the language of hope, yet his research wrestles with some of the same dimensions of my research. I would even go so far as to propose that his characterization of a "re-demption script" falls into the category of hope-talk. In his seminal ethnographic research with male inmates in Liverpool, England, he uses life-story interviews to explore how those released from prison can transform their lives and desist from crime. Maruna interviewed over fifty male inmates, including both active offenders and desisters. Desisters, or those who no longer commit criminal acts, constructed a self-narrative that redeemed the past and articulated a meaningful future. Maruna categorized these narratives as a redemption script. On the other hand, active offenders focused on immediate pleasures and needs. They lacked agency and could not articulate a meaningful future. Even more specifically, his use of life-story interviews suggests that how one interprets and subsequently stories one's life shapes one's behavior. Important to understand about the redemptive sequence, however, is its heavy reliance on a "tragic optimism," whereby the men reached back into their past to redeem their criminal selves rather than wres-tling with the possibility of who they are apart from criminality. In this sense, the redemptive script lacks the critical consciousness, personal accountability, and self-reclamation that restorative hope explores. In short, people can desist from crime and experience a future with hope in spite of the social, economic, and political barriers that exist. Hope builds on the idea of envisioning and articulating a meaningful future as well as a meaningful today.[6]

Restorative Hope as Rooted in the Here and Now and the Not Yet

Furthermore, hope-talk in carceral contexts shifts the conversation on hope. We need not discuss hope as if it were solely a here-and-now experience grounded in the present context, nor solely an already-but-not-yet experience grounded in the future. Instead, it is a both/and experience that may take root in the present or the future. In the present, hope is rooted in fights against injustice to one's humanity and that of others. In the future, hope is rooted in the promise of new possible worlds and new possible selves. Both perspectives invite incarcerated women to act upon themselves and the world to bring about transformation. Further, when hope in the present is difficult to find, the embodied resilience of the forebears or those who become images of hope actually holds weight. The past, then, becomes a rich resource for evoking hope. Each point in time—past, present, and future—offers treasures to be unearthed on one's journey toward hope. Overall, time becomes a major consideration in experiences of hope, ultimately illuminating that the here and now holds just as much value as the already but not yet.

Restorative Hope as Creating Space

Women on the carceral continuum taught me that within pedagogy, hope is primarily about creating space. In the prison context, ways of seeing, knowing, being, and doing became ways to experience, sustain, and maintain a sense of hope in one's life. Thus, restorative hope is itself a generative praxis that gives birth to authenticity, connection, and resilience in women. In a world that uses a wrong-until-proven-right framework to make women prove themselves, sites where becoming, appearing, and communal encounters are prioritized or inherent in the space generate hope for women along the carceral continuum. These insights

---

6. Shadd Maruna, *Making Good: How Ex-Convicts Reform and Rebuild Their Lives* (Washington, DC: American Psychological Association, 2001), 54.

about what generates and sustains hope in women have implications for how we think about and employ religious education and theological education more broadly. Theological education aims to remind students of the possibilities in themselves and in the world around them. From the understanding that all have inherent worth and value, spaces within theological education should also invite students into recognizing their own authentic identity, enable spaces where students can encounter and connect with one another, and build the resilience necessary in students to face a world that is constantly shifting and changing. When education stops meeting those aims, we must reevaluate what it is we do.

New conversations are beginning to emerge from seminaries throughout the United States that take seriously the institutional role of a theological education that integrates issues concerning the mass incarceration crisis. These institutions sit in a unique position to explore some of the distinct benefits and challenges of providing theological education in prison settings. Does theological education, in fact, offer different outcomes, have different goals, provide different benefits than other credit- or non-credit-bearing course offerings within prisons? These questions also help us to reimagine some of the ways we approach teaching more broadly.

Beyond the Bars: Implications for Education in Noncarceral Settings

Beyond the prison context, this research leads me to believe that the wrong-until-proven-right epistemological framework also functions in noncarceral spaces. In particular, I have begun to reflect more intently on the way in which epistemological valuation drives our educational agendas from elementary school through university. While valuing knowledge is important and necessary within educational contexts, I have become increasingly concerned with the costs of placing such a high value on what one *knows* that the possibility of who one *is* may be lost. I would like to share these preliminary reflections in my observations on how a wrong-until-proven-right framework functions in both secondary and postsecondary environments as well as the academy. My overarching claim is that because wrong-until-proven-right cultures measure value based on epistemological valuation, learners in this culture learn to be competitive in order to receive value. However, their value is based on a performance of knowledge rather than a performance of being.

For example, test taking from the schoolyard to university becomes a rite of passage that proves one's knowledge. Children learn how much they know by how well they do on the test. Kids who do poorly on tests are stigmatized as slow, behind, or developmentally challenged while those who perform well are rewarded for their knowledge. In other words, some are ritualized into a *knower* status while others are placed in a *nonknower* status. The nonknower status can make it difficult to trust oneself; it can also create a need to prove knower status, an attitude which ultimately drives competition and individualism. The categorization of nonknower and knower feeds into a utilitarian society that uses knowledge to determine one's usefulness in the world. Those who know more can do more; those who can do more yield more value. This epistemological valuation that is based on external voices imparts a sense of hopelessness to non-knowers. Nonknowers begin to view their capacity to know through the lens of others. In a society that rewards knowledge, the capacity to know has direct implications for the capacity to be. The rewards-based system lavishes networking opportunities and other social capital on the knower. While rewards are a good thing, I worry that the capacity to know in a rationalistic way can become so easily fused with the capacity to be. In this sense, a person's value rests not in their ontological being; it rests in the value placed on the epistemological self, or better yet, the content in a person's head.

In academia, I want to play out an all-too-familiar scene. Similar to a courtroom scene, a wrong-until-proven-right culture places particular learners in the roles of defendants, judge, prosecutor, and jury. For example, defendants occupy the role of students. In rational epistemologies, students always enter the room as defendants. They must prove to others that they know and that their knowing is valuable and legitimate. Oftentimes they prove this through persuasive arguments or by providing factual evidence. While this is not inherently wrong, what becomes inequitable is that the burden of proof typically falls either on marginalized bodies or marginalized modes of knowing. To undo feeling like and playing the role of "defendant," one has to embrace a new way of being in that space. The teacher is the judge who holds authority to determine whether a knower has met the standards of legitimization. If not, they may be sentenced to more rigorous forms of proving themselves as legitimate before the academic courtroom. The learners' colleagues often serve as the jury, judging whether the knower is presenting accurate information or false information, whether the knower is secure in their own articulation of the evidence, whether the knower should be given a chance to reenter the learning community. This form of epistemological valuation not only exposes one before the "judge" but also before the "jury" of other learners. To reenter a learning community after such strict hazing requires additional internal resources that offer hope in one's own value in spite of the gaze of others. One becomes visible in that space as one who is unsure or uncertain. In this space strict competition predominates; this emboldens colleagues within the space to occupy the role of "prosecutor." Prosecutors feel as if they have to prove the defendant wrong so that they can become visible to the class or those in the courtroom as knowers. They find some sort of satisfaction in devaluing the knowledge of others in order to receive epistemological valuation in front of their colleagues.

For Black women, for example, who are confined by elitist standards, the rush toward legitimization does not merely take the form of epistemological valuation; it takes the form of validating one's very humanity. In the words of bell hooks, "There is always the need to assert and defend the humanity of Black people, including their ability and capacity to reason logically, think coherently, and write lucidly."[7] For if knowledge is not separate from but connected to the knower, then what one knows does have implications for who one is (or how one views who one is), thus making a rejection of one's knowledge feel very much like a rejection of one's personhood. To undo the role of prosecutor, one must reassess the purpose of knowledge. Is knowledge important to prove one's ontological value, or is knowledge important to ensure that the world is a hospitable place for all learners despite their multiple ways of seeing and knowing the world?

Future Trajectories: Other Possibilities for Research

This research leads to broader questions about teaching and learning in theological education and other noncarceral settings. For example, as educators, should identity formation, resilience, and connection be major objectives within our class? In what ways is creating sites for stu-

---

7. bell hooks and Cornel West, *Breaking Bread: Insurgent Black Intellectual Life* (Boston: South End Press, 1991), 137.

dents to appear, become, and connect critical for how educators prepare students to be citizens in the world? For ministry contexts, how does restorative hope as a way of being in the world help our students sustain practices of care for themselves and others? Are there assumptions inherent in noncarceral settings that make it difficult to sustain practices of authenticity, resilience, and connection?

Another rich area of exploration in these contexts is at the intersection of generativity, productivity, and hope. Engaging in a comprehensive study on generativity was beyond the scope of this book. However, the insights emerging from the data create a sense that Erikson and Snarey's theories might be confirmed in a prison setting, where generativity itself is always facing confinement in some shape or form. Furthermore, new ways to conceive of societal generativity must also be considered. To explore the ways in which generativity persists in the prison is itself a study of resilience and one I would like to explore in greater depth in the future.

Theology with art has emerged as an area of great interest in recent years, and indeed art holds great value in carceral spaces. Like restorative hope, art seems to have spiritual meaning and convey spiritual insights. Mining the rich insights that emerge from art in prison settings is an under-researched area that may suggest resources for pastoral care and pedagogy.

Beyond Research: Social Change in the World

In a carceral state, the carceral continuum not only describes where women are situated in relationship to incarceration; it also points to the ways in which even settings outside the criminal justice system support the same penal strategies of isolation, inauthenticity, and rigidness. The question of social change forces one to ask, How can theological educators expand our sphere of influence? How can the learning environment become broad enough that it includes not just a few prisons here or there but the whole justice system, not just a few universities here or there but the whole education system? We find hope in the moments in which social change happens on a micro level, but these hopes always build within us an expectation for more. As Peter McLaren reminds us, "Spaces of hope do appear. But rarely by historical accident. . . . these spaces need to be strategically seized.

Spaces of hope offer encouragement to the forces of justice but they are not sufficient in themselves. Spaces—often private—must be made public. They must be expanded from spaces into spheres—from personal, individual spaces and private epistemologies into public spheres of hope and struggle and collective identities."[8]

Such a broadening of hope-filled spaces resists institutional stagnation, and asks, What spaces of hope might be possible in our world today? The work of hope is an ever-expanding endeavor that becomes more comprehensive as humanity becomes more connected. To create spaces of hope that really disrupt a pipeline to prison forces us to pay close attention to what is happening to emergent generations. Are we, as a society, creating spaces for emergent generations to be authentic, connected, and resilient? Addressing mass incarceration is an ethical and religious responsibility for people of faith. Further, people of faith have resources to offer communities experiencing confinement and dealing with hopelessness. Some of these people of faith are incarcerated and formerly incarcerated women who can offer wisdom and insights that help us understand the many challenges that make it difficult for incarcerated women to hope. This research, then, challenges us to undertake authentic engagement and participation in our world to help bring about this change.

Being Hope: The Church as a Generative Agent of Social Change

In bringing this chapter and book to a close, I want to name that this research has direct implications for concrete practices that faith communities can undertake. I want to explore the concept of generativity in relation to the church's potential to be a generative agent of social change. The concept of generativity versus stagnation has typically been applied to individuals. I propose that the concept of generativity also applies to institutions. Institutional generativity refers to the production and creativity of ideas, policies, and practices that promote the survival, growth, and formation of people, products, and ideas. The survival of these ideas, policies, practices, and people is what enables

8. Peter McLaren, *Life in Schools: An Introduction to Critical Pedagogy in the Foundations of Education*, 4th ed. (Boston: Allyn and Bacon, 2003), 264.

the institution itself to survive. Institutional stagnation, on the other hand, represents the sheer self-absorption that blinds institutions to human concerns and interests. Prisons, universities, and centers of faith can either demonstrate institutional generativity or institutional stagnation. For the purposes of this book, it was important to explore the institutional generativity and institutional stagnation described by women interviewed.

The desire for women on the carceral continuum to express generative hope toward others holds much value; but the need to have a generative other care for them holds just as much value. Viewing institutional care through the lens of generativity helps recognize that not only are women on the carceral continuum dependent on the support and care of institutions (i.e., faith communities) but also that the survival of faith communities depends on the support and care they receive from women on the carceral continuum. The import of communal care that emerged from the faith community, in particular, persisted as a theme throughout the interviews. Oftentimes, women communicated that faith communities should occupy the role of generative other throughout their time on the carceral continuum. Churches who express generative hope toward women on the carceral continuum recognize that women, even those who have been incarcerated, are part of their family. Thus, institutional generativity represents a felt responsibility by the church to care for and ensure the survival and growth of returning citizens. Women who experienced care from the faith community described how it helped relieve the pressure of the collateral consequences of returning to society. Those churches which were most generative viewed women as sisters and daughters who needed to be fully reintegrated into the community. This type of institutional generativity demonstrates a care that encourages women to resist human confinement and feel comfortable being their authentic selves in the community.

However, most of the faith communities that the women themselves described seemed to be stagnant; they did not express genuine care for God's children. According to the interviews, churches had become so self-absorbed in their own ideas and productions that they failed to become generative others to those in prison and those who had been released. The absence of congregations spoke loudly. One woman described the church as *"very su[perficial]. They never dealt with the very inside of a person. They never really showed up.*"[9] Churches' failure to be generative in responding to women on the carceral continuum may even result in what Erikson defines as *rejectivity* or an unwillingness to demonstrate generative concern for specific types of people or groups; this ultimately leads to *pseudospeciation*, which refers to distorted beliefs and behaviors about groups whom one deems to be different from one's own.[10] These perceptual and behavioral distortions result in fear, distancing, and apathy toward providing care. In other words, rather than opening up possibilities that would inspire hope, the silence and indifference of faith communities becomes a threat to hope.

Women who actually still hope in the mission of the church—that the church will become what it should be and act like it should act in regard to mass incarceration—provide helpful advice for faith communities to consider when engaging women on the carceral continuum. These suggestions are not mine, but wisdom shared throughout the interviews:[11]

1. *Make your presence known in the community.* Many women pointed to the myriad visibilities of church. Churches may be hypervisible but ineffective. Buildings show up on every corner with little fruit of their presence in the surrounding community. Churches may also appear in the community in ways that distort rather than promote the message of Christ. Or churches may remain invisible: they are missing in action when those affected by incarceration need them the most. To combat these false visibilities and be critically visible, women suggest churches make their presence known within the community instead of remaining within the four walls of the church. As Nona clearly articulates, "*Show up. Church needs to be everywhere. The church needs to be everywhere but church.*"[12]

2. *Be aware of those in your congregation.* Those within faith communities represent returning citizens as well as the mothers, daughters,

9. Toya, interview with the author, September 15, 2014.

10. Erik H. Erikson and Joan M. Erikson, *The Life Cycle Completed*, extended ed. (New York: W. W. Norton, 1997), 68-69.

11. These solutions primarily focused on the second half of the carceral continuum—that is, during incarceration through release. Nevertheless, there are also clear ways that faith communities can intercept the typical progress of people on the carceral continuum and prevent women and girls from riding the track to incarceration. Future research will explore these interconnections.

12. Nona, interview with the author, January 30, 2015.

brothers, and grandparents of those who are currently incarcerated. Practices of awareness and presence then include listening to the narratives of those who are deeply affected by incarceration. By listening to them and responding to their needs, churches can begin to display institutional generativity. In particular, members in the congregation who share these experiences can be invited to offer support to others in their congregation. Sherry suggests:

> *I feel that they should listen to their community. . . . More than likely someone in their church has had some experience with prison either by a family member or actually themselves, so what they can do, by far that would be my first immediate thing is to have them to connect with their community and their congregation, ask questions. . . . So I would say being conscientious of your community, of their community. When I say community now, I'm talking about their members in their church. That's their community. That's what I'm speaking of so we'll have clarity right there.*[13]

3. Get to know people on the carceral continuum. The narratives of those who have been incarcerated hold great importance for congregations becoming aware of who the people in their congregations really are. But formerly incarcerated women are calling people of faith to do more than merely knowing *about* women who have been incarcerated; they are calling people of faith *to know them*—to invest time and energy into really building relationships with them before, during, and after incarceration. Says Sherry, "*I do think that in order for society to really get it right, that they have to do more of what you're doing. They have to talk to people who's been through it.*"[14]

4. Become aware of the criminal justice system. Becoming aware of how the criminal justice system works enables one to work within the system. As Eden shares: "*During incarceration they can gain knowledge of the prison system with what the prison system actually offers by way of reentry and join together and create a prison ministry in that church, learn the language of the Department of Corrections, because you have to go through them before you can get to those prisons and sit down and draw up a meaningful program to assist.*"[15]

13. Sherry, interview with the author, January 3, 2015.
14. Sherry, interview with the author, January 3, 2015.
15. Eden, interview with the author, April 17, 2014.

5. *Serve as a bridge between the prison and society.* Two of the greatest challenges that jeopardize women's hope are the needs for housing and employment upon their release. Churches, however, can play a mediating role in securing housing and employment by being in touch with women before they are released in order to connect them with housing and employment opportunities. Churches could work intentionally with prisons to help direct their efforts. For example, Eden writes:

> *The prison system should have a list of the persons that has . . . been on the road to reentry. They've put forth the effort to redeem themselves or to make themselves redeemable, and these are the people that should be evaluated by and referred to the church prison ministries. Say, for instance, if you were in prison and you didn't have any skills, and you've put forth your effort to whatever skill that was available, you've applied yourself and you have actually done that, because you wouldn't settle for anything less, you know that was what you needed to have a job out here. . . . And when you get to prison ministry, they would need to help you find a job and reacclimate in that field that you've worked in or in a similar field, but . . . you need a job so that you can be accountable and take care of yourself.*[16]

6. *Do something.* Simply put, hope generates actions. Restorative hope fights against the tendency to remain stagnant by looking for the myriad ways in which the church can care for women along the carceral continuum. As Nona indicates, "*Stop preaching and hire somebody. Stop preaching and let somebody stay with you. Stop preaching and find somebody somewhere to stay. Stop preaching and donate some clothes you can't fit. . . . Stop—Be a resource.*"[17]

Generative praxis for churches includes practices of presence, awareness, and bridge-building that will enable women along the carceral continuum to reintegrate into society effectively. Overall, women had great suggestions about ways that the church as an institution, some of which they themselves now engage, can combat stagnation and engage in generative praxis.

---

16. Eden, interview with the author, April 17, 2014.
17. Nona, interview with the author, January 30, 2015.

Conclusion

I have made bold claims about what restorative hope pedagogy seeks to create—namely authenticity, connection, and resilience. I have shown examples of concrete pedagogical practices that teachers can employ in diverse settings. While a pedagogy of restorative hope is grounded in my work in the prison, it has implications for outside the prison and should be put in conversation with other contexts. Restorative hope is not a rigid concept but an emerging construct that can prompt us to reexamine our role as educators. As a starting point, this book has explained the experience and challenges of finding hope along the carceral continuum and has given examples of how to do so. At the same time, this research has only scratched the surface of the possible pedagogical approaches to restoring hope in carceral and noncarceral settings. It has presented some compelling insights about hope, which I trust have stimulated in you, the reader, further inquiry into the connections between pedagogy, populations in confinement, and hope.

BIBLIOGRAPHY

Alemagno, Sonia A. "Women in Jail: Is Substance Abuse Treatment Enough?" *American Journal of Public Health* 91, no. 5 (2001): 798–800.

Alexander, Bryant Keith. *Performing Black Masculinity: Race, Culture, and Queer Identity*. Crossroads in Qualitative Inquiry. Lanham, MD: AltaMira Press, 2006.

Allen, Suzanne, Chris Flaherty, and Gretchen Ely. "Throwaway Moms: Maternal Incarceration and the Criminalization of Female Poverty." *Journal of Women and Social Work* 25, no. 2 (2012): 160–72.

Alves, Rubem A. *A Theology of Human Hope*. Washington, DC: Corpus Books, 1969.

Arnold, Regina A. "Processes of Victimization and Criminalization of Black Women." *Social Justice* 17, no. 3 (1990): 153–66.

Ayres, Jennifer R. *Good Food: Grounded Practical Theology*. Waco, TX: Baylor University Press, 2013.

Baker-Fletcher, Karen. *Dancing with God: The Trinity from a Womanist Perspective*. St. Louis: Chalice, 2006.

Baxter Magolda, Marcia B. *Making Their Own Way: Narratives for Transforming Higher Education to Promote Self-Development*. Sterling, VA: Stylus, 2001.

Baxter Magolda, Marcia B., Elizabeth G. Creamer, and Peggy S. Meszaros, eds. *Development and Assessment of Self-Authorship: Exploring the Concept across Cultures*. Sterling, VA: Stylus, 2010. Kindle.

Belenky, Mary Field, Blythe McVicker Clinchy, Nancy Rule Goldberger, and Jill Mattuck Tarule. *Women's Ways of Knowing: The Development of Self, Voice, and Mind*. 10th anniversary ed. New York: Basic Books, 1997.

Belknap, Joanne. *The Invisible Woman: Gender, Crime, and Justice*. Wadsworth Contemporary Issues in Crime and Justice Series. 2nd ed. Belmont, CA: Wadsworth, 2001.

Bell, Catherine M. *Ritual: Perspectives and Dimensions*. New York: Oxford University Press, 1997.

Binswanger, Ingrid A. "Chronic Medical Diseases among Jail and Prison Inmates." Society of Correctional Physicians. https://www.lb7.uscourts.gov/documents/15-11023.pdf.

Binswanger Ingrid A., Patrick M. Krueger, and John F. Steiner. "Prevalence of Chronic Medical Conditions among Jail and Prison Inmates in the USA Compared with the General Population." *Journal of Epidemiology and Community Health* 63, no. 11 (2009): 912–19.

Bonnano, George A. "Loss, Trauma and Human Resilience: Have We Underestimated the Human Capacity to Thrive after Extremely Aversive Events?" *American Psychologist* 59, no. 1 (2004): 20–28.

Bouchet, Stacey M. *Children and Families with Incarcerated Parents: Exploring Development in the Field for Opportunities for Growth*. Baltimore, MD: Annie E. Casey Foundation, 2008.

Browne, Angela, Brenda Miller, and Eugene Maguin. "Prevalence and Severity of Lifetime Physical and Sexual Victimization among Incarcerated Women." *International Journal of Law and Psychiatry* 22, nos. 3–4 (1999): 301–22.

Brueggemann, Walter. *Texts under Negotiation: The Bible and Postmodern Imagination*. Minneapolis: Fortress, 1993.

Buckaloo, Bobby J., Kevin S. Krug, and Koury B. Nelson. "Exercise and the Low-Security Inmate." *Prison Journal* 89, no. 3 (2009): 328–43.

Büscher, Monika B., and John Urry. "Mobile Methods and the Empirical." *European Journal of Social Theory* 12, no. 1 (2009): 99–116.

Caletrío, Javier. *Mobilities Paradigm*. Forum Vies Mobiles. September 2, 2016. http://en.forumviesmobiles.org/marks/mobilities-paradigm -3293. Accessed October 11, 2017, at https://www.researchgate .net/publication/308388524_Mobilities_Paradigm.

Carson, E. Ann. *Prisoners in 2019*. Bureau of Justice Statistics. Washington, DC: US Department of Justice, October 2020.

Carson, E. Ann, and Daniela Golinelli. *Prisoners in 2012: Trends in Admissions and Releases, 1991–2012*. Bureau of Justice Statistics. Washington, DC: US Department of Justice, 2013.

Cashin, Andrew, Emily Potter, and Tony Butler. "The Relationship between Exercise and Hopelessness in Prison." *Journal of Psychiatric and Mental Health Nursing* 15, no. 1 (2008): 66–71.

Cawthorne, Alexandra. *The Straight Facts on Women in Poverty*. Washington, DC: Center for American Progress, 2008.

Cecere, David. "Inmates Suffer from Chronic Illness, Poor Access to Health Care." *Harvard Gazette*, January 15, 2009. http://news.harvard.edu/gazette/story/2009/01/inmates-suffer-from-chronic-illness-poor-access-to-health-care/.

Center for Substance Abuse Treatment. *Substance Abuse Treatment for Adults in the Criminal Justice System*. Treatment Improvement Protocol (TIP) Series. Rockville, MD: Substance Abuse and Mental Health Services Administration, 2005, 30–41.

Centers for Disease Control and Prevention. *HIV/AIDS Surveillance Report, 2011*. Rev. ed. Atlanta: US Department of Health and Human Services, 2007. http://www.cdc.gov/hiv/topics/surveillance/resources/reports/.

———. "Women, Injection Drug Use, and the Criminal Justice System." The Body: The HIV/AIDS Resource. August 1, 2001. http://www.thebody.com/cdc/women_idu.html.

Chesney-Lind, Meda, and Lisa Pasko. *The Female Offender: Girls, Women, and Crime*. 3rd ed. Thousand Oaks, CA: SAGE, 2012.

Children's Defense Fund. *A Portrait of Inequality: Black Children in America*. Washington, DC: Children's Defense Fund, 2011.

Church, George J. "The View from Behind Bars." *Time*, November 8, 1990.

Clarke, Jennifer G., Megan R. Hebert, Cynthia Rosengard, Jennifer S. Rose, Kristen M. DaSilva, and Michael D. Stein. "Reproductive Health Care and Family Planning Needs among Incarcerated Women." *American Journal of Public Health* 96, no. 5 (2006): 834–39.

Coleman, Monica A. *Making a Way out of No Way: A Womanist Theology*. Innovations. Minneapolis: Fortress, 2008.

Collins, Patricia Hill. *Black Feminist Thought: Knowledge, Consciousness, and the Politics of Empowerment*. Perspectives on Gender. New York: Routledge, 1991.

Committee on Health Care for Underserved Women. "Reproductive Health Care for Incarcerated Women and Adolescent Females." In *Committee Opinion No. 535*. *Obstetrics and Gynecology* 120, no. 2, pt. 1 (2012): 425–29.

Cone, James H. *A Black Theology of Liberation*. 2nd ed. Maryknoll, NY: Orbis, 1986.

———. *The Cross and the Lynching Tree*. Maryknoll, NY: Orbis, 2013.

———. *God of the Oppressed*. Rev. ed. Maryknoll, NY: Orbis, 1997.

Conquergood, Dwight. "Performing as a Moral Act: Ethical Dimensions of the Ethnography of Performance." *Literature in Performance* 5, no. 2 (1985): 1–13.

Copeland, Shawn M. *Enfleshing Freedom: Body, Race, and Being*. Minneapolis: Fortress, 2010.

"The Cost of a Nation of Incarceration." *CBS News*, April 23, 2012. https://www.cbsnews.com/news/the-cost-of-a-nation-of-incarceration.

Council of State Governments. *What Works in Reentry Clearinghouse*. National Reentry Resource Center: Justice Center, updated 2013. http://whatworks.csgjusticecenter.org/focus_areas/housing.

Crawford, A. Elaine Brown. *Hope in the Holler: A Womanist Theology*. Louisville: Westminster John Knox, 2002.

Cresswell, Tim. "Friction." In *The Routledge Handbook of Mobilities*, edited by Peter Adey, David Bissell, Kevin Hannam, Peter Merriman, and Mimi Sheller, 107–15. New York: Routledge, 2014.

——. *On the Move: Mobility in the Modern Western World*. New York: Routledge, 2006.

——. *Place: An Introduction*. 2nd ed. Malden, MA: Wiley Blackwell, 2015.

Creswell, John W. *Qualitative Inquiry and Research Design: Choosing among Five Traditions*. Thousand Oaks, CA: SAGE, 1998.

Cunningham, Alison, and Linda Baker. *Invisible Victims: The Children of Women in Prison*. London, ON: Centre for Children and Families in the Justice System, December 2004.

——. *Waiting for Mommy: Giving a Voice to the Hidden Victims of Imprisonment*. London, ON: Centre for Children and Families in the Justice System, 2003.

Darlington, Yvonne, and Robert Bland. "Strategies for Encouraging and Maintaining Hope among People Living with Serious Mental Illness." *Australian Social Work* 52, no. 3 (1999): 17–23.

De Groot, Anne S. "Alarming Statistics about Incarcerated Women." *Positively Aware: The Journal of Test Positive Aware Network* (July–August 2001): 19–21.

DeHart, Dana D. "Pathways to Prison: Impact of Victimization in the Lives of Incarcerated Women." Columbia, SC: Center for Child and Family Studies, 2004.

DelGaudio, Sybil. "The Mammy in Hollywood Film: I'd Walk a Million Miles—for One of Her Smiles." *Jump Cut: A Review of Contemporary Media* 28 (1983): 23–25.

Denzin, Norman K., and Yvonna S. Lincoln. *Handbook of Qualitative Research*. 2nd ed. Thousand Oaks, CA: SAGE, 2000.

Desmond, Matthew. *Poor Black Women Are Evicted at Alarming Rates, Setting Off a Chain of Hardship*. Chicago: MacArthur Foundation, 2014.

DeVeaux, Mika'il. "The Trauma of the Incarceration Experience." *Harvard Civil Rights–Civil Liberties Law Review* 48, no. 1 (2013): 257–77.

Dillen, Annemie. "The Resiliency of Children and Spirituality: A Practical Theological Reflection." *International Journal of Children's Spirituality* 17, no. 1 (2012): 61–75.

Ellison, Gregory C. *Cut Dead but Still Alive: Caring for African American Young Men in Today's Culture.* Nashville: Abingdon, 2013.

Erikson, Erik H., and Joan M. Erikson. *The Life Cycle Completed.* Extended ed. New York: W. W. Norton, 1997.

Fallot, Roger D., and Maxine Harris. *Creating Cultures of Trauma-Informed Care (CCTIC): A Self-Assessment and Planning Protocol.* Washington, DC: Community Connections, April 2009.

Farmer, Sarah. "Criminality of Black Youth in Inner-City Schools: 'Moral Panic,' Moral Imagination, and Moral Formation." *Race, Ethnicity, and Education* 13, no. 3 (2010): 367–81.

Farrall, Stephen, Ben Hunter, Gilly Sharpe, and Adam Calverley. *Criminal Careers in Transition: The Social Context of Desistance from Crime.* Clarendon Studies in Criminology. Oxford: Oxford University Press, 2014.

Ferraro, Kathleen J., and Angela M. Moe. "Mothering, Crime, and Incarceration." *Journal of Contemporary Ethnography* 32, no. 1 (2003): 9–40.

Fine, Michelle. *Off White: Readings on Race, Power, and Society.* New York: Routledge, 1997.

———. "Working the Hyphens: Reinventing Self and Other in Qualitative Research." *Handbook of Qualitative Research*, edited by Norman K. Denzin and Yvonna S. Lincoln, 70–82. Thousand Oaks, CA: SAGE, 1994.

Fine, Michelle, and Maria Elena Torre. "Intimate Details: Participatory Action Research in Prison." *Action Research* 4, no. 5 (2006): 253–69.

Fine, Michelle, Maria Elena Torre, Kathy Boudin, Iris Bowen, Judith Clark, Donna Hylton, Migdalia Martinez et al. "Changing Minds: The Impact of College in a Maximum-Security Prison, the Prison Environment, Reincarceration Rates and Post-Release Outcomes." New York: The New York State Department of Correctional Services, 2001.

Fisher, Maisha T. *Writing in Rhythm: Spoken Word Poetry in Urban Classrooms.* Language and Literacy Series. New York: Teachers College Press, 2007.

Floyd-Thomas, Stacey M., ed. *Deeper Shades of Purple: Womanism in Religion and Society.* Religion, Race, and Ethnicity. New York: New York University Press, 2006.

Fontaine, Nargis. "From Mammy to Madea, and Examination of the Behaviors of Tyler Perry's Madea Character in Relation to the Mammy, Jezebel, and Sapphire Stereotypes." Master's thesis, Georgia State University, 2011.

Foster, Charles R., and Grant S. Shockley. *Working with Black Youth: Opportunities for Christian Ministry*. Nashville: Abingdon, 1989.

Foster, Charles R., Fred Smith, and Grant S. Shockley. *Black Religious Experience: Conversations on Double Consciousness and the Work of Grant Shockley*. Nashville: Abingdon, 2003.

Foucault, Michel. *Discipline and Punish: The Birth of the Prison*. New York: Pantheon Books, 1977.

Francis, Leah Gunning. *Ferguson and Faith: Sparking Leadership and Awakening Community*. St. Louis, Chalice, 2015.

Frankl, Viktor E. *Man's Search for Meaning*. Boston: Beacon, 2006.

Freire, Paulo. *Pedagogy of the Oppressed*. Translated by Myra Bergman Ramos. 30th anniversary ed. New York: Continuum, 2000.

Freire, Paulo, and Ana Maria Araújo Freire. *Pedagogy of Hope: Reliving Pedagogy of the Oppressed*. New York: Continuum, 1994.

Fulkerson, Mary McClintock. *Places of Redemption: Theology for a Worldly Church*. New York: Oxford University Press, 2007.

Fullilove, Mindy Thompson, E. Anne Lown, and Robert E. Fullilove. "Crack 'Hos and Skeezers: Traumatic Experiences of Women Crack Users." *Journal of Sex Research* 29, no. 2 (1992): 275–87.

Gacek, James. "'Doing Time' Differently: Imaginative Mobilities to/from Inmates' Inner/Outer Spaces." In *Carceral Mobilities: Interrogating Movement in Incarceration*, edited by Jennifer Turner and Kimberley Peters, 73–84. New York: Routledge, 2017.

Gardner, Howard. *Intelligence Reframed: Multiple Intelligences for the 21st Century*. New York: Basic Books, 1999.

———. *Multiple Intelligences: New Horizons*. Rev. ed. New York: Basic Books, 2006.

Garfinkel, Harold. "Conditions of Successful Degradation Ceremonies." *American Journal of Sociology* 61, no. 5 (1956): 420–24.

Garland, David. *Punishment and Modern Society: A Study in Social Theory*. Studies in Crime and Justice. Chicago: University of Chicago Press, 1990.

Giguere, Rachelle, and Lauren Dundes. "Help Wanted: A Survey of Employer Concerns about Hiring Ex-Convicts." *Criminal Justice Policy Review* 13, no. 4 (2002): 396–408.

Gilyard, Keith. *True to the Language Game: African American Discourse, Cultural Politics, and Pedagogy*. New York: Routledge, 2011.

Godderis, Rebecca. "Dining In: The Symbolic Power of Food in Prison." *Howard Journal of Criminal Justice* 45, no. 3 (2006): 255–67.

God's Deliverers, Inc. "[Eden] and Her Life." YouTube video, 39.00, March 25, 2013. URL omitted.

Goffman, Erving. *Stigma: Notes on the Management of Spoiled Identity*. Spectrum Book. Englewood Cliffs, NJ: Prentice-Hall, 1963.

Golden, Renny. *War on the Family: Mothers in Prison and the Families They Leave Behind*. New York: Routledge, 2005.

Goode, W. Wilson, Charles E. Lewis, and Harold Dean Trulear. *Ministry with Prisoners & Families: The Way Forward*. Valley Forge, PA: Judson Press, 2011.

Graham, Elaine L. "Is Practical Theology a Form of 'Action Research'?" *International Journal of Practical Theology* 17, no. 1 (August 2013): 148–78.

Graham, Elaine L., Heather Walton, and Frances Ward. *Theological Reflection: Methods*. London: SCM, 2005.

Grant, Jacquelyn. "Theological Framework." In *Working with Black Youth: Opportunities for Christian Ministry*, edited by Charles R. Foster and Grant S. Shockley, 55–76. Nashville: Abingdon, 1989.

——. *White Women's Christ and Black Women's Jesus: Feminist Christology and Womanist Response*. American Academy of Religion, Academy Series. Atlanta: Scholars Press, 1989.

Green, Keisha. "Doing Double Dutch Methodology: Playing with the Role of Participant Observer." In *Humanizing Research: Decolonizing Qualitative Inquiry with Youth and Communities*, edited by Django Paris and Maisha T. Winn, 147–60. Thousand Oaks, CA: SAGE, 2014.

Greene, Maxine. *Releasing the Imagination: Essays on Education, the Arts, and Social Change*. Jossey-Bass Education Series. San Francisco: Jossey-Bass, 1995.

Guenther, Lisa. *Solitary Confinement: Social Death and Its Afterlives*. Minneapolis: University of Minnesota Press, 2013.

Guerra, Maria. *Fact Sheet: The State of African American Women in the United States*. Washington, DC: Center for American Progress, 2013.

Gutiérrez, Gustavo. *A Theology of Liberation: History, Politics, and Salvation*. Translated by Caridad Inda and John Eagleson. Rev. ed. Maryknoll, NY: Orbis, 1988.

Haney, Craig. "Psychological Impact of Incarceration: Implications for Post-Prison Adjustment." Paper written for the conference "From Prison to Home: The Effect of Incarceration and Reentry on Children, Families and Communities," 1–19. University of California, Santa Cruz, December 2001.

———. "Mental Health Issues in Long-Term Solitary and 'Supermax' Confinement." *Crime & Delinquency* 49, no. 1 (2003): 124–56.

Harawa, Nina, and Adaora Adimora. "Incarceration, African Americans, and HIV: Advancing a Research Agenda." *Journal of the National Medical Association* 100, no. 1 (2008): 57–62.

Harlow, Caroline W. *Education and Correctional Populations*. Bureau of Justice Statistics. Washington, DC: US Department of Justice, 2003.

Harner, Holly M., Patricia M. Hentz, and Maria Carmela Evangelista. "Grief Interrupted: The Experience of Loss among Incarcerated Women." *Qualitative Health Research* 21, no. 4 (2011): 454–64.

Harner, Holly M., and Suzanne Riley. "The Impact of Incarceration on Women's Mental Health: Responses from Women in a Maximum-Security Prison." *Qualitative Health Research* 23, no. 1 (2013): 26–42.

Harris, Norman. "Afrocentrism: Concept and Method." *Western Journal of Black Studies* 16, no. 3 (1992): 154–59.

Harris-Perry, Melissa. "Changing the Way We See Single Moms." MSNBC, video, January 12, 2014. http://www.msnbc.com/melissa-harris-perry/watch/changing-the-way-we-see-single-moms-114731587919.

Hawthorne, William B., David P. Folsom, David H. Sommerfeld, Nicole M. Lanouette, Marshall Lewis, Gregory A. Aarons, Richard M. Conklin, Ellen Solorzano, Laurie A. Lindamer, and Dilip V. Jeste. "Incarceration among Adults Who Are in the Public Mental Health System: Rates, Risk Factors, and Short-Term Outcomes." *Psychiatric Services* 63, no. 1 (2012): 26–32. doi:10.1176/appi.ps.201000505.

Haymes, Stephen Nathan. *Race, Culture, and the City: A Pedagogy for Black Urban Struggle*. Teacher Empowerment and School Reform. Albany: State University of New York Press, 1995.

Hess, Carol Lakey. *Caretakers of Our Common House: Women's Development in Communities of Faith*. Nashville: Abingdon, 1997.

Hill, Kenneth H. *Religious Education in the African American Tradition: A Comprehensive Introduction*. St. Louis: Chalice, 2007.

HIV Education Prison Project. "Infectious Diseases in Corrections Report (IDCR)." *HEPP News* 3, no. 4 (2000). http://digitalcommons.uri.edu/idcr/14.

Holton, M. Jan. *Building the Resilient Community: Lessons from the Lost Boys of Sudan*. Eugene, OR: Cascade Books, 2011.

hooks, bell, and Cornel West. *Breaking Bread: Insurgent Black Intellectual Life.* Boston: South End Press, 1991.

Hughes, Timothy, and Doris James Wilson. *Reentry Trends in the United States: Inmates Returning to the Community After Serving Time in Prison.* Washington, DC: US Department of Justice, 2004.

James, Doris J., and Lauren E. Glaze. *Mental Health Problems of Prison and Jail Inmates.* Bureau of Justice Statistics. Washington, DC: US Department of Justice, 2006.

Jewekes, Yvonne. "Men Behind Bars: 'Doing' Masculinity as an Adaptation to Imprisonment." *Men and Masculinities* 8, no. 1 (2005): 44–63.

Jewell, K. Sue. *From Mammy to Miss America and Beyond: Cultural Images and the Shaping of U.S. Social Policy.* New York: Routledge, 1993.

Jones, Major J. *Black Awareness: A Theology of Hope.* Nashville: Abingdon, 1971.

Kegan, Robert. *The Evolving Self: Problem and Process in Human Development.* Cambridge, MA: Harvard University Press, 1982.

———. *In Over Our Heads: The Mental Demands of Modern Life.* Cambridge, MA: Harvard University Press, 1994.

Korb, Alex, and Daniel J. Siegel. *The Upward Spiral: Using Neuroscience to Reverse the Course of Depression, One Small Change at a Time.* Oakland, CA: New Harbinger Publications, 2015.

Korstanje, Maximiliano. "Examining the Norse Mythology and the Archetype of Odin: The Inception of Grand-Tour." *Tourism: An International Interdisciplinary Journal* 60, no. 4 (2012): 369–84.

Leonard, Jayne. "What Are the Effects of Solitary Confinement on Health?" *Medical News Today,* August 6, 2020. https://www.medicalnews today.com/articles/solitary-confinement-effects.

Leonardo, Zues. *Critical Pedagogy and Race.* Malden, MA: Blackwell, 2005.

Li, David K. "Family of Kalief Browder, Young Man Who Killed Himself After Jail, Gets $3.3M from New York." *US News,* January 24, 2019. https://www.nbcnews.com/news/us-news/family-kalief-browder -young-man-who-killed-himself-after-jail-n962466.

Link, Bruce G., and Jo C. Phelan. "Conceptualizing Stigma." *Annual Review of Sociology* 27 (2001): 363–85.

Loftis, Chris. "Mental Flexibility." In *Encyclopedia of Clinical Neuropsychology,* edited by Jeffrey Kreutzer, John DeLuca, and Bruce Caplan, 1572. New York: Springer, 2010.

Logan, James Samuel. *Good Punishment? Christian Moral Practice and U.S. Imprisonment.* Grand Rapids: Eerdmans, 2008.

Loyd, Jenna M., Matt Mitchelson, and Andrew Burridge. *Beyond Walls and*

Cages: Prisons, Borders, and Global Crisis. Athens: University of Georgia Press, 2012.

Lynch, William F. *Images of Hope: Imagination as Healer of the Hopeless*. Baltimore: Helicon, 1965.

MacNaughton, Glenda, and Karina Davis. *"Race" and Early Childhood Education: An International Approach to Identity, Politics, and Pedagogy*. Critical Cultural Studies of Childhood. New York: Palgrave Macmillan, 2009.

Maruna, Shadd. *Making Good: How Ex-Convicts Reform and Rebuild Their Lives*. Washington, DC: American Psychological Association, 2001.

——. "Reentry as a Rite of Passage." *Punishment & Society* 13, no. 1 (2011): 3–27.

Maruna, Shadd, and Russell Immarigeon. *After Crime and Punishment: Pathways to Offender Reintegration*. Portland, OR: Willan, 2004.

Maruna, Shadd, Louise Wilson, and Kathryn Curran. "Why God Is Often Found Behind Bars: Prison Conversions and the Crisis of Self-Narrative." *Research in Human Development* 3, nos. 2–3 (2006): 161–84.

Maruschak, Laura M. *HIV in Prisons, 2020—Statistical Tables*. Bureau of Justice Statistics. Washington, DC: US Department of Justice, 2022.

Maruschak, Laura M., Jennifer Bronson, and Mariel Alper. *Parents in Prison and Their Minor Children: Survey of Prison Inmates, 2016*. Bureau of Justice Statistics. Washington, DC: US Department of Justice, 2021.

Maslow, Abraham H. *The Farther Reaches of Human Nature*. New York: Viking, 1971.

——. "A Theory of Human Motivation." *Psychological Review* 50, no. 4 (1943): 370–96.

McAdams, Dan P. *The Stories We Live By: Personal Myths and the Making of the Self*. New York: William Morrow, 1993.

McAdams, Dan P., Ruthellen Josselson, and Amia Lieblich, eds. *Identity and Story: Creating Self in Narrative*. The Narrative Study of Lives. Washington, DC: American Psychological Association, 2006.

McBride, Jennifer. *Radical Discipleship: A Liturgical Politics of the Gospel*. Minneapolis: Fortress, 2017.

——. *You Shall Not Condemn: A Story of Faith and Advocacy on Death Row*. Eugene, OR: Cascade Books, 2022.

McDaniels-Wilson, Cathy, and Joanne Belknap. "The Extensive Sexual Violation and Sexual Abuse Histories of Incarcerated Women." *Violence Against Women* 14, no. 10 (2008): 1090–1127.

McLaren, Peter. *Life in Schools: An Introduction to Critical Pedagogy in the Foundations of Education.* 4th ed. Boston: Allyn and Bacon, 2003.

Meiners, Erica. *Right to Be Hostile: Schools, Prisons, and the Making of Public Enemies.* New York: Routledge, 2007.

Meiners, Erica, and Maisha T. Winn. *Education and Incarceration.* New York: Routledge, 2011.

Meyerson, Jessica, Christa Otteson, and Krysten Lynn Ryba. *Childhood Disrupted: Understanding the Features and Effects of Maternal Incarceration.* St. Paul: Wilder Research, 2010.

Miller, Valerie, Lisa VeneKlasen, Molly Reilly, and Cindy Clark. *Concepts for Revisioning Power for Justice, Equality and Peace.* Making Change Happen: Power, no. 3. Washington, DC: Just Associates, 2006. https://justassociates.org/wp-content/uploads/2020/08/mch3_2011_final_0.pdf.

Mincke, Christophe, and Anne Lemonne. "Prison and (Im)Mobility: What about Foucault?" *Mobilities* 9, no. 4 (2014): 528–49.

Moe, Angela M., and Kathleen J. Ferraro. "Criminalized Mothers: The Value and Devaluation of Parenthood from Behind Bars." *Sociology Faculty Publications* Paper 7 (2006): 5–10.

Moguldom Media Group. "Moguldom Studios Releases Compelling Documentary." Moguldom Media, http://moguldomstudios.com/post-type-press-archive/moguldom-studios-releases-compelling-documentary-72.

Moltmann, Jürgen. *Experiences of God.* Philadelphia: Fortress, 1980.

———. *The Future of Hope: Theology as Eschatology.* New York: Herder and Herder, 1970.

———. *Theology of Hope: On the Ground and the Implications of a Christian Eschatology.* London: SCM, 1967.

Moore, Mary Elizabeth. *Teaching as a Sacramental Act.* Cleveland: Pilgrim, 2004.

———. *Teaching from the Heart: Theology and Educational Method.* Minneapolis: Fortress, 1991.

National Partnership for Women and Families. *America's Women and the Wage Gap.* Washington, DC: National Partnership for Women and Families, September 2014.

Nielsen, Mette Bladt, and Kurt Aagaard. "Free Space in the Processes of Action Research." *Action Research* 11, no. 3 (2013): 369–85.

O'Collins, Gerald. *Man and His New Hopes.* New York: Herder and Herder, 1969.

Olive, Victoria C. "Sexual Assault Against Women of Color." *Journal of Student Research* 1 (2012): 1–9.

Owen, Quinn. "Former Female Inmates Speak about Widespread Sexual Abuse by Prison Staff." ABC, December 13, 2022. https://abcnews .go.com/Politics/senate-report-documents-widespread-sexual-abuse -female-inmates/story?id=95157791.

Palmer, Parker J. *To Know as We Are Known: A Spirituality of Education*. San Francisco: Harper & Row, 1983.

Parenti, Christian. *Lockdown America: Police and Prisons in the Age of Crisis*. New York: Verso, 1999.

Paris, Django, and Maisha T. Winn. *Humanizing Research: Decolonizing Qualitative Inquiry with Youth and Communities*. Thousand Oaks, CA: SAGE, 2014.

Parker, Evelyn L. *The Sacred Selves of Adolescent Girls: Hard Stories of Race, Class, and Gender*. Cleveland: Pilgrim Press, 2006.

———. *Trouble Don't Last Always: Emancipatory Hope among African American Adolescents*. Cleveland: Pilgrim, 2003.

Parrotta, Kylie L., and Gretchen H. Thompson. "Sociology of the Prison Classroom: Marginalized Identities and Sociological Imaginations Behind Bars." *Teaching Sociology* 39, no. 2 (2011): 165–78.

Patterson, Orlando. *Slavery and Social Death: A Comparative Study*. Cambridge, MA: Harvard University Press, 1982.

Patton, Michael Quinn. *Qualitative Research & Evaluation Methods*. 3rd ed. Thousand Oaks, CA: SAGE, 2002.

Peters, Kimberley, and Jennifer Turner. "Carceral Mobilities: A Manifesto for Mobilities, an Agenda for Carceral Studies." In *Carceral Mobilities: Interrogating Movement in Incarceration*, edited by Jennifer Turner and Kimberley Peters, 1–13. New York: Routledge, 2017.

Peters, Rebecca Todd. *Solidarity Ethics: Transformation in a Globalized World*. Minneapolis: Fortress, 2014.

Pew Center on the States. *One in 100: Behind Bars in America 2008*. Public Safety Performance Project. Washington, DC: Pew Charitable Trusts, February 2008. https://www.pewtrusts.org/en/research -and-analysis/reports/2008/02/28/one-in-100-behind-bars-in -america-2008.

Poehlmann, Julie. "New Study Shows Children of Incarcerated Mothers Experience Multiple Challenges." *Family Matters: A Family Impact Seminar Newsletter for Wisconsin Policymakers* 3, no. 2 (2003): 1–2.

Pratt-Clarke, Menah A. E. *Critical Race, Feminism, and Education: A Social*

Justice Model. Postcolonial Studies in Education. New York: Palgrave Macmillan, 2010.

Rambo, Shelly. *Spirit and Trauma: A Theology of Remaining.* Louisville: Westminster John Knox, 2010.

Richie, Beth. *Arrested Justice: Black Women, Violence, and America's Prison Nation.* New York: New York University Press, 2012.

———. *Compelled to Crime: The Gender Entrapment of Battered Black Women.* New York: Routledge, 1996.

Ross, Rosetta E. *Witnessing and Testifying: Black Women, Religion, and Civil Rights.* Minneapolis: Fortress, 2003.

Russell, Letty M., J. Shannon-Clarkson, and Kate M. Ott. *Just Hospitality: God's Welcome in a World of Difference.* Louisville: Westminster John Knox, 2009.

Saldaña, Johnny. *The Coding Manual for Qualitative Researchers.* Thousand Oaks, CA: SAGE, 2009.

Schlosser, Eric. "The Prison-Industrial Complex." *Atlantic*, December 1, 1988. https://www.theatlantic.com/magazine/archive/1998/12/the-prison -industrial-complex/304669/.

Schnittker, Jason. "The Psychological Dimensions and the Social Consequences of Incarceration." *ANNALS of the American Academy of Political and Social Science* 651, no. 1 (2014): 122–38.

Scott, Robert. "Using Critical Pedagogy to Connect Prison Education and Prison Abolitionism." *Saint Louis University Public Law Review* 33, no. 2 (2014): 401–15.

Segundo, Juan Luis. *Liberation of Theology.* Maryknoll, NY: Orbis, 1976.

The Sentencing Project. *Incarcerated Women and Girls.* Washington, DC: Sentencing Project, 2021. https://www.sentencingproject.org/fact-sheet /incarcerated-women-and-girls/.

Sheller, Mimi, and John Urry. "The New Mobilities Paradigm." *Environment and Planning A: Economy and Space* 38, no. 2 (2006): 207–26.

Shenton, Andrew K. "Strategies for Ensuring Trustworthiness in Qualitative Research Projects." *Education for Information* 22 (2004): 63–75.

Shor, Ira. *Empowering Education: Critical Teaching for Social Change.* Chicago: University of Chicago Press, 1992.

Shriver, Maria, and the Center for American Progress. "Powerful and Powerless." In *The Shriver Report: A Woman's Nation Pushes Back from the Brink,* edited by Olivia Morgan and Karen Skelton, 11–43. New York: Palgrave Macmillan, 2014.

Sison, Antonio D. *World Cinema, Theology, and the Human: Humanity in Deep Focus.* New York: Routledge, 2012.

Smoyer, Amy B. "Good and Healthy: Foodways and Construction of Identity in a Women's Prison." *Howard Journal of Criminal Justice* 53, no. 5 (2014): 525–41.

———. "Making Fatty Girl Cakes: Food and Resistance in a Women's Prison." *Prison Journal* 96, no. 2 (2016): 191–209.

Smyth, Julie. "Dual Punishment: Incarcerated Mothers and Their Children." *Columbia Social Work Review* 3 (2012): 33–45.

Snyder, T. Richard. *The Protestant Ethic and the Spirit of Punishment.* Grand Rapids: Eerdmans, 2001.

Steinberg, Robin. "Re-Entry for Dignity and a 'Productive' Life." Lecture, Shepherd Higher Education Consortium on Poverty Symposium, Virginia Military Institute, Lexington, VA, July 31, 2017.

Stern, Kaia. *Voices from American Prisons: Faith, Education, and Healing.* New York: Taylor & Francis, 2014.

Stevenson, Bryan. *Just Mercy: A Story of Justice and Redemption.* New York: Spiegel & Grau, 2014.

Strommen, Merton P., and Richard A. Hardel. *Passing on the Faith: A Radical New Model for Youth and Family Ministry.* Winona, MN: St. Mary's Press, Christian Brothers Publications, 2000.

Substance Abuse and Mental Health Services Administration. *Half of Women on Probation or Parole Experience Mental Illness.* Rockville, MD: Center for Behavioral Health Statistics and Quality, 2012.

Taylor, Barbara Brown. *Learning to Walk in the Dark.* Norwich: Canterbury Press, 2014.

Tillich, Paul. *The Courage to Be.* The Terry Lectures. New Haven: Yale University Press, 1952.

Titus, Craig Steven. *Resilience and the Virtue of Fortitude: Aquinas in Dialogue with the Psychosocial Sciences.* Washington, DC: Catholic University of America Press, 2006.

Torres, Myriam N., and Loui V. Reyes. *Research as Praxis: Democratizing Education Epistemologies.* New York: Peter Lang, 2011.

Torrey, E. Fuller, Aaron D. Kennard, Donald F. Eslinger, Harry Richard Lamb, and James Pavle. *More Mentally Ill Persons Are in Jails and Prisons Than Hospitals: A Survey of the States.* Arlington, VA: Treatment Advocacy Center, May 2010.

Torrey, E. Fuller, Mary T. Zdanowicz, Aaron D. Kennard, Harry Richard Lamb, Donald F. Eslinger, Michael C. Biasotti, and Doris A. Fuller.

The Treatment of Persons with Mental Illness in Prisons and Jails: A State Survey. Arlington, VA: Treatment Advocacy Center, April 2014.

Townes, Emilie M. *Embracing the Spirit: Womanist Perspectives on Hope, Salvation, and Transformation.* The Bishop Henry Mcneal Turner/Sojourner Truth Series in Black Religion. Maryknoll, NY: Orbis, 1997.

———. *Womanist Justice, Womanist Hope.* American Academy of Religion, Academy Series. Atlanta: Scholars Press, 1993.

Tree, Sara Rain. *Solitary Confinement and Prison Safety: Solitary Watch Fact Sheet #4.* Washington, DC: Solitary Watch, 2023.

Turner, Victor Witter. *Dramas, Fields, and Metaphors: Symbolic Action in Human Society.* Ithaca, NY: Cornell University Press, 1975.

Ugelvik, Thomas. "The Hidden Food: Mealtime Resistance and Identity Work in a Norwegian Prison." *Punishment & Society* 13, no. 1 (2011): 47–63.

Urry, John. "Social Networks, Mobile Lives and Social Inequalities." *Journal of Transport Geography* 21, no. 1 (2012): 24–30.

US Census Bureau. *Current Population Survey, Annual Social and Economic Supplement: Table PINC-05: Work Experience in 2013—People 15 Years Old and Over by Total Money Earnings in 2013, Age, Race, Hispanic Origin, and Sex.* July 7, 2014. Retrieved July 7, 2015. http://www.census.gov/hhes/www.cpstables/032014/perinc/pinc05_000.htm.

Valentine, Gill, and Beth Longstaff. "Doing Porridge: Food and Social Relations in a Male Prison." *Journal of Material Culture* 3, no. 2 (1998): 131–52.

Volf, Miroslav. *Exclusion and Embrace: A Theological Exploration of Identity, Otherness, and Reconciliation.* Nashville: Abingdon, 1996.

Wacquant, Loïc. *Prisons of Poverty.* Minneapolis: University of Minnesota Press, 2009.

———. *Punishing the Poor: The Neoliberal Government of Social Insecurity.* Durham: Duke University Press, 2009.

Walker, Alice. *In Search of Our Mothers' Gardens: Womanist Prose.* San Diego: Harcourt Brace Jovanovich, 1983.

Walsh, Froma. *Strengthening Family Resilience.* 2nd ed. New York: Guilford Press, 2006.

Ward, James, Di Bailey, and Sian Boyd. "Participatory Action Research in the Development and Delivery of Self-Harm Awareness Sessions in Prison: Involving Service Users in Staff Development." *Prison Service Journal* 202 (2012): 20–25.

Warren, John T. *Performing Purity: Whiteness, Pedagogy, and the Reconstitution of Power*. Critical Intercultural Communication Studies. New York: Peter Lang, 2003.

Weis, Lois, and Michelle Fine. *Construction Sites: Excavating Race, Class, and Gender among Urban Youth*. Teaching for Social Justice Series. New York: Teachers College Press, 2000.

———. *Working Method: Research and Social Justice*. New York: Routledge, 2004.

West, Carolyn M., and Kalimah Johnson. "Sexual Violence in the Lives of African American Women." Harrisburg, PA: VAWnet, a project of the National Resource Center on Domestic Violence, March 2013.

Westfield, Nancy Lynne. *Dear Sisters: A Womanist Practice of Hospitality*. Cleveland: Pilgrim, 2001.

———. "'Mama Why. . .?' A Womanist Epistemology of Hope." In *Deeper Shades of Purple: Womanism in Religion and Society*, edited by Stacey M. Floyd-Thomas, 128–39. New York: New York University Press, 2006.

Westfield, Nancy Lynne, and Arthur L. Pressley. "Teaching Black: God-Talk with Black Thinkers." In *Being Black, Teaching Black: Politics and Pedagogy in Religious Studies*, edited by Nancy Lynne Westfield, 137–62. Nashville: Abingdon, 2008.

White, David F. *Practicing Discernment with Youth: A Transformative Youth Ministry Approach*. Youth Ministry Alternatives. Cleveland: Pilgrim Press, 2005.

Williams, Delores S. *Sisters in the Wilderness: The Challenge of Womanist God-Talk*. Maryknoll, NY: Orbis, 1993.

Winn, Maisha T. *Girl Time: Literacy, Justice, and the School-to-Prison Pipeline*. Teaching for Social Justice Series. New York: Teachers College Press, 2011.

Yarbrough, Marilyn, with Crystal Bennett. "Cassandra and the 'Sistahs': The Peculiar Treatment of African American Women in the Myth of Women as Liars." *Journal of Gender, Race & Justice* 3, no. 2 (Spring, 2000): 625–58.

Young, Josiah U. *Dogged Strength within the Veil: Africana Spirituality and the Mysterious Love of God*. Harrisburg, PA: Trinity Press International, 2003.

Young, Vernetta D., and Rebecca Reviere. *Women Behind Bars: Gender and Race in US Prisons*. Boulder, CO: Lynne Rienner, 2006.

Zlotnick, Caron. *Treatment of Incarcerated Women with Substance Abuse and Posttraumatic Stress Disorder*. Rockville, MD: National Criminal Justice Reference Service, July 2002. https://www.ojp.gov/pdffiles1/nij/grants/195165.pdf.

INDEX

Alexander, Bryant Keith, 150n
Alves, Rubem A., 12
American College of Obstetricians and Gynecologists, 15
art: and creative resilience, 54-61; and embodied resilience, 64-65; food preparation and meal-sharing as, 54-59, 128; future possibilities for research in carceral settings, 174; making and sharing art in the prison classroom, 141-42, 156, 157, 162-64; physical adornments (hair and toenails), 64-65; physical exercise as, 65; re-creating/redecorating carceral spaces, 59-61
Ayres, Jennifer R., 58

Baker-Fletcher, Karen, 12
Baxter Magolda, Marcia B., 138-39
Black church, 39
Black Feminist Thought: Knowledge, Consciousness, and the Politics of Empowerment (Collins), 28
Black liberation theologians, 12
Black women: and the "art of cunning," 55-56; "dogged strength" in resisting negative self-images, 64n; employment barriers, 22; and epistemological valuation, 173; "gender entrapment" and trauma, 33-34; and the "holler," 68-69; housing challenges in poor neighborhoods, 21, 49; maternal incarceration and Black maternal stigma, 27-29; and mental illness, 32; physical health disparities,

15; poverty's impact, 21, 22, 23, 28-29, 33-34, 49; and resilience, 55-56, 64n, 68-69, 70, 71; self-contemplation, 144; self-fragmentation and impact of racism, 144; sexual violence and "Cassandra curse" stereotype, 34-35; social challenges and crises of hope, 21, 22, 23, 24, 49; stigmas and negative stereotypes, 18-19, 27-29, 34-35; and "structural dislocation," 24; substance abuse stigmas, 18-19; and womanist theology and pedagogy, 151-52
bodies: as epistemological resource in womanist pedagogy, 151-52; the loss of bodily dignity in prison, 109-11; physical and psychological stress, 110; physical exercise in prison, 65-67, 128; physical health in prison, 15-20; prison uniforms and color-coding, 24-25, 109; strip searches, 63, 109-11, 117. *See also* embodied resilience; physical health
Browder, Kalief, 80
Brueggemann, Walter, 62
Büscher, Monika B., 60

carceral continuum, 5-7; crises of hope and, 14-42; definition, 5, 6, 43n, 174; descriptive understanding of carceral place/space, 5-6; hope and, 1-13; and identity construction, 7, 105-29; phenomenological understanding of carceral place/space, 6; social constructionist understanding of carceral place/space, 6-7

7-8, 10-13, 167; and immobility, 2-4, 8,
10-11, 47-48, 54, 88, 98; place-making
and, 60-61
Moltmann, Jürgen, 12, 93
Myeshia (pseudonym), 1n, 45-49, 51,
52-54, 72, 73-74, 76, 128, 166

natal alienation, 87
National Partnership for Women and
Families, 22
"Never Would Have Made It" (song), 72
Nona (pseudonym), 1n, 63, 81-83,
110-11, 117, 126, 159, 177, 179

parole, 5, 49, 97
pathway-to-crime theorists, 23
Patterson, Orlando, 24, 87
Peters, Kimberley, 6
phenomenological understanding of
carceral place/space, 7
physical exercise, 65-67, 128
physical health, 15-20; benefits of
physical exercise, 65-67, 128; and
Black women's health disparities, 15;
chronic diseases, 15-16, 66; infectious
diseases, 16; physical and sexual
victimization, 19-20, 32; reproductive
health, 16-17; substance abuse/addic-
tion, 17-19, 30
police brutality, xi
postpartum depression, 17
poverty, 22-23; and Black maternal
stigma, 28-29; and caregivers of
children of incarcerated parents, 27;
feminization of, 23; and housing, 21,
49; impact on Black women, 21, 22, 23,
28-29, 33-34, 49; Latina women, 23; as
pathway to the carceral continuum,
23, 24; and single motherhood, 22-23;
and social constructionist view of
incarceration, 6-7
practical theology, xi, xiv, xv, 11
Pratt-Clarke, Menah A. E., 150n
pregnancies among incarcerated
women, 16-17, 26. See also maternal
incarceration

prisonization, 107. See also identity
construction
probation, 5, 97
proximity and institutional connection, 99-102
psychological and emotional challenges, 31-37; Black women, 32, 33-35,
36; emotional trauma, 33-36; grieving, mourning, and transition processes, 36-37; histories of abuse and
victimization, 33-35; incarceration
as trauma, 35-36; mental health and
mental illness, 31-33; solitary confinement, 3, 32, 79-80; stigma of incarceration for the recently released
person, 33, 35-36; strip searches, 63,
109-11, 117; violence witnessed/expe-
rienced in prison, 35

Rambo, Shelly, 167
recidivism, 5, 20-21, 43, 50
"redemption script," 169-70
reentry to society. See returning
citizens
relationships. See meaningful
relationships
remaining, theology of, 167
reproductive health, 16-17, 26
resilience, 43-77, 146-59, 166-67; Black
women and, 55-56, 64n, 68-69, 70, 71;
building in the theological classroom,
146-59; creative resilience, 54-62;
critical knowing as a tool for, 145-52;
dogged resilience, 44-54, 166; embodied resilience, 63-70, 146; Frankl
on hope in the midst of suffering, 75,
76; God and hope in prison, 70, 71-73,
157-58; as response to human suffering, 53-54, 74-75, 76-77; and returning
citizens, 45-54, 166; rooted in hope,
73-77, 146; and "testifyin'," 67-70;
three facets, 73-74
restorative hope pedagogy, 137-52, 159,
161-64, 165-80; critical knowing as a
tool for resilience, 145-52; implications for education in noncarceral

Williams, Delores S., 11–12, 55–56, 70, 72–73
Winn, Maisha T., ix
womanist pedagogy, 11–12, 58, 150–52; body/embodiment as epistemological resource, 151–52; epistemology of hope, 151–52

women of color. *See* Black women; Latina women
wrong-until-proven-right cultures, 170, 171–73

Young, Josiah U., 64n
Yvette (pseudonym), 1n, 48–49, 51, 74